FIRST EDITION

Andy Chard

Published by Platform 5 Publishing Ltd,
52 Broadfield Road, Sheffield, S8 0XJ, England.

Printed in England by The Lavenham Press, Lavenham, Suffolk.

ISBN 978 1 909431 28 7

Front Cover Top: Swanage Railway: Recently outshopped Battle of Britain 4-6-2 34081 "92 Squadron" climbs the bank at Leeson Wood, working the 14.20 from Swanage on 1st April 2017 during the "Strictly Bulleid" gala. **Eike Sekine**

Front Cover Bottom: East Lancashire Railway: Under the oversight of Holcombe Tower near Ramsbottom, which was built in memory of locally born Robert Peel, Class 55 No. 55022 approaches the site of the East Lancashire Railway's newest station at Burrs Country Park, during a diesel event on 22 September 2012 which saw five Class 55 Deltics working on the railway. **Paul Gerrard**

Back Cover: Bluebell Railway: The Bluebell Railway was one of the first standard gauge preserved railways in the world and it is now home to a fine collection of heritage locomotives and rolling stock. On 9 October 2014 SECR P Class 0-6-0T No. 178 awaits departure from the railway's southern terminus, Sheffield Park. **Ian Beardsley**

Above: Great Central Railway: The Great Central Railway is currently the only double-track heritage line in Britain and recreates the experience of what it was like to travel on the main line rail network in the past. During the "Goods Galore" event on 12 May 2018 BR Standard Class 7MT 70013 "Oliver Cromwell" is seen making a spirited departure from Loughborough with the 14.00 Loughborough Central–Leicester North. **Ian Beardsley**

Contents

Preface

Since the mid-1980s when I started taking an interest in Britain's railways, I noticed that certain types of trains and railway infrastructure were being phased out by British Rail. In the generation prior to that, Britain's heritage railways had played an invaluable role in saving and preserving railway lines, period architecture and rolling stock. There were far fewer of these small, independent railways then and some of their rolling stock and practices could still be seen on the national rail network. In the generation since, the railways have moved into the privatisation era and seen record numbers of passengers; large scale modernisation has been necessary. Retirement of rolling stock has escalated and Network Rail now carry out massive infrastructure upgrades every year. These changes are eradicating older trains, Victorian architecture and semaphore signalling from entire regions, as the recent development of Reading station or the North Wales Coast resignalling projects have, for example, brought about. In the 21st Century there is now a considerable difference between what the public experience when they travel from A to B by train and a journey on a heritage railway. The role of these living and moving museums has grown in importance. They not only preserve heritage trains, Victorian architecture and practices such as exchanging tokens, but provide the opportunity to travel through some beautiful landscapes in comfort, on what at one point was new technology.

There are now more than 100 sites operating heritage trains and substantially more when narrow gauge railways and tramways are included. This book lists all the heritage railways and museums within Great Britain and the Channel Islands, where trains carry passengers on a standard gauge railway (4 foot 8½ inches). It introduces some fascinating corners of Great Britain, with quintessential rural branch lines and sites which bring Britain's industrial or military history to life, including Northampton Ironstone Railway, Tanfield and Chatham Dockyard. Others don't fit into any obvious category and are better seen than described; Appleby Froddingham, Bressingham and Fawley Hill, for example. It is also a guide for rail enthusiasts, with comprehensive stock lists for the locomotives and multiple units at each site, plus mileage figures and details of the railway-related attractions. There is a diverse geographical spread, with routes which traverse the Scottish Highlands (Strathspey, Keith & Dufftown), the rugged North of England (Wensleydale, Eden Valley, Stainmore, Lakeside and Haverthwaite), rural Wales (Llangollen and others), urban areas (Bristol Harbour, Ribble and Epping Ongar) and dramatic coastal views (North Norfolk, Dartmouth and West Somerset). Each site has its own merit and I hope that readers will be inspired to explore and support many of railways listed in this book.

Andy Chard
Manchester, 2019

Maps used in this book

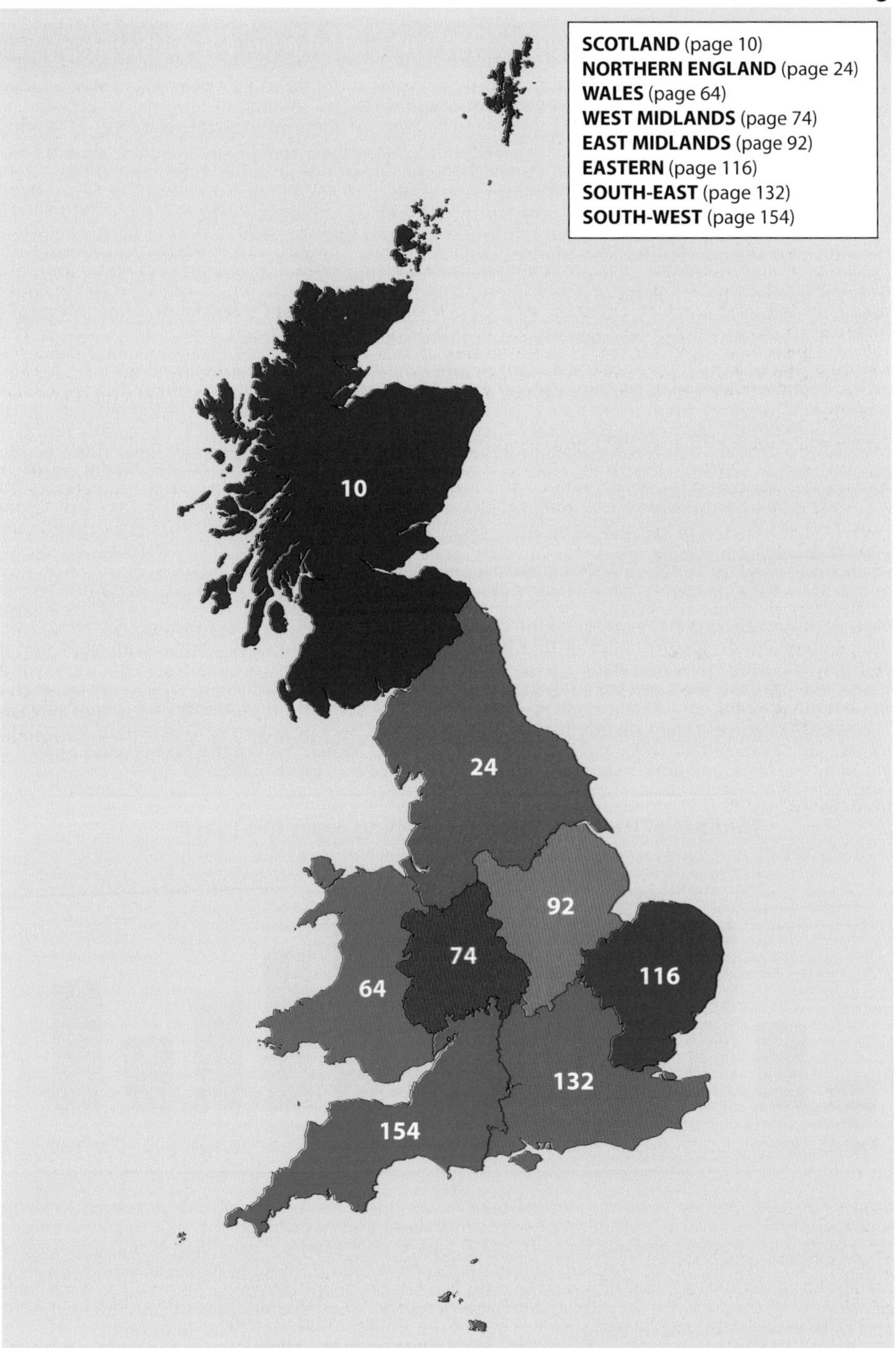

SCOTLAND (page 10)
NORTHERN ENGLAND (page 24)
WALES (page 64)
WEST MIDLANDS (page 74)
EAST MIDLANDS (page 92)
EASTERN (page 116)
SOUTH-EAST (page 132)
SOUTH-WEST (page 154)
10
24
92
74
116
64
132
154

An Introduction to Britain's Heritage Railway Movement

Two monumental changes took place on Britain's railways during the 1950s and 1960s, which drove and accelerated the creation of the heritage railway movement; the mass withdrawal of steam locomotives and the closure of thousands of miles of railway lines. Many people were roused to form railway preservation groups. Some worked to save routes, such as the pioneers of the Keighley and Worth Valley Railway, which reopened in 1968, only a few years after it was closed by British Rail. Other groups wanted to save steam locomotives from being scrapped and find a new home to operate these, with an increased urgency once British Rail banned steam locomotives from working on the main line in 1968. The two aims of saving railways and saving locomotives married well and were the objectives of many early heritage railways. Whilst the speed with which BR closed lines, lifted track, demolished stations and sold land for development has been well rued over the years, if BR had not acted so fast, the early preservationists may not have been galvanised to act so quickly either and some of today's well-established heritage railways may not otherwise be with us today.

The heritage railway movement has been growing and evolving since its beginning. As well as steam locomotives which remain popular with enthusiasts and the public alike, diversification and innovation have opened up new opportunities. Followers of diesel locomotives, industrial shunters and multiple units have established bases and now have regular fixtures at a number of railways. Some sites have no steam locomotives and at others railways have been newly constructed at locations with no railway history, neither of which undermine their viability. Some groups have restored coaching stock, steam or diesel locomotives to main line standards and hire these to commercial and charter operators, generating invaluable income to plough back into the heritage railway. In some cases, the members' expertise has been utilised to create specialist subsidiaries or businesses, such as South Devon Railway Engineering at its namesake home, or the Scottish Railway Preservation Society at the Bo'ness & Kinneil Railway, which operate main line charter trains and hire its coaching stock to other operators.

New heritage railways have opened almost every year since 1960 and as the chart below shows, the opening dates for the sites in this book are spread fairly evenly across well over half a century. It usually takes many years from the formation of a preservation group to the time when trains are first operated and the individual listings summarise the journey of each group, many of which have chapters that are yet to be written. The section on proposed heritage railways showcases some of the more advanced projects, where they are nearing the point of operating trains. There are plenty of further prospective heritage routes, where the preservation groups are at an earlier stage and these may enter the scope of this book in future.

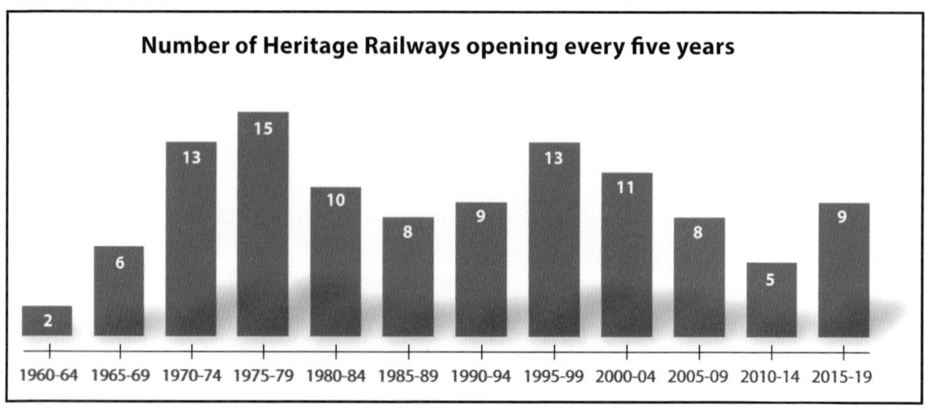

Every heritage railway is comprised of people, as much as it is of infrastructure and rolling stock. Committed and tenacious pioneers fundraised and negotiated the purchase of railway trackbeds, locomotives and carriages from BR and its successors. The rolling stock, depots and station buildings had to be restored and in many cases rebuilt, before any trains could run. The backbone of what has been achieved to date is a legion of volunteers, who now form the vast majority of the workforce on today's heritage railways. New volunteers are continually sought and railways are likely to be delighted to hear from readers that may be able to help!

Each site is reliant on visitors and every pound spent on tickets, in gift shops and buffets helps the railways to cover their large operating costs. Many restoration projects or railway extensions are on hold until sufficient funds have been raised, such as restoring the rope-hauled system at Bowes Railway, or reuniting the two halves of the Great Central Railway. For smaller sites it can be a financial challenge to keep operating each year, at the Bideford Railway for example, at the time of writing in early 2019 volunteers are working to return the only locomotive to service in time for the running season. All the railways need as much publicity and support as possible, whether it is the Llanelli & Mynydd Mawr Railway which only opened in late 2017, one of the pioneers dating back to the 1960s, or those in the final chapter of this book which are on the brink of adding to the story of Britain's heritage railways.

Layout of Information

The heritage railway listings have been split into nine regions. The first eight regions are arranged in geographical order from north to south and the final section lists heritage railways which are nearing the point of operating passenger trains. Within each region, the railways are in alphabetical order and each listing follows the same format.

1. Introduction and History

The history of each site is summarised, including key dates and landmarks from the time the railway was created, through its evolution to heritage status today. Many sites make the journey of ascension, decline and restoration; however, some have taken a different route or become a heritage railway after an entirely different history. The focus on how the site came to be heritage railway briefly gives credit to many years of hard work and persistence by its founders. As heritage railways are a fluid and increasingly growing movement, future extension plans have been researched and are included. Some are long-term aspirations and for others, railway track has been laid as this book has been written and printed. Of the 109 railways listed, 59 are either working towards or in the process of extending the length of their operational railway.

2. Contact Details

Contact details follow the same format and if necessary the railway's website can be consulted for the latest timetable information, locomotive rosters or special event details.

3. Transport Links

Where there is a main line rail connection, this is stated. Otherwise the nearest main line railway station and its distance from the site is given, as it may be possible to walk or travel by taxi. Car parking facilities are listed for all sites, with postcodes for satnav systems and where there is no charge for parking, this is mentioned. Where a railway can be reached by another mode of transport, details of this are given. For example, a number of railway lines share their route with cycle paths or walkways and some of these have cycle hire facilities adjacent to stations. Others can be reached by boat, including the Battlefield Line (by canal) or Swanage, Lakeside & Haverthwaite and Dartmouth Railways which all have connecting waterborne services.

4. Opening Times

The dates and times on which the railway operates are summarised. These vary greatly across sites, with some opening more than 360 days each year, through to those which open on a select few dates. The majority of railways have a set pattern of running dates and times; however, these can be subject to change.

5. Line Mileage and Journey Time

The line mileage figures provide information on the length of each railway and the distance between stations. Mileages are given to the nearest quarter of a mile, in line with the format of national rail network timetables. Where the operational section is short (generally less than one mile) or there is only one station or boarding point, mileage figures are not shown in list format. The journey times are the minimum time needed to make a round trip and can vary depending on the starting point. Further time should be allowed where journeys are broken to explore the attractions and facilities along the route.

6. Stock List

All standard or broad gauge main line locomotives, industrial locomotives and multiple units based at each site are listed. These lists do not include vehicles which are not standard or broad gauge, London Underground, coaches and other items of rolling stock such as wagons. Steam locomotives are shown first, followed by diesel and electric locomotives and then multiple units. The lists are arranged in approximate increasing size order, within each type. See 6.1 for details of types. Stock lists show vehicles based at the railway in 2019, some of which may not be present on a given date, such as when a locomotive visits another heritage railway, is on short-term hire to a main line operator or at another site for repairs. Further technical information and details of the names and former numbers carried by main line locomotives and multiple units can be found in Platform 5 Publishing's 'Preserved Locomotives of British Railways' and 'Diesel and Electric Loco Register'.

6.1 Rolling Stock Type

The vast majority of rolling stock listed is comprised of steam locomotives, diesel locomotives and multiple units, with a small number of more unusual vehicles. Each item listed falls into one of the following categories.

Steam: Steam locomotives, with all main line and industrial examples at each railway listed.
Diesel: Locomotives with diesel engines. All main line, shunting and industrial examples are given.
Electric: Locomotives powered by electricity, supplied by AC overhead, DC overhead or DC third rail systems.
Electro-Diesel: Locomotives with diesel engines, which are also capable of drawing electric power.
Battery: Battery-powered locomotives.
Gas Turbine: Locomotives powered by gas turbines.
Petrol: Locomotive powered by a petrol engine (only one is listed).
Steam Railcar: Steam powered single car (only one is listed).
DMU: Diesel Multiple Units; single or multiple carriages powered by self-contained diesel engines.
DEMU: Electric Multiple Units fitted with a diesel engine, enabling power from either source.
EMU: Electric Multiple Units; self-contained carriages powered by overhead or third rail electric power supplies.
Battery EMU: Battery-powered multiple units.

6.2 Number

This lists the number carried, or in some cases the name, by which the vehicle can be identified. Industrial locomotives which have not been given a number or name are listed by their works number, which was allocated by the locomotive builder. Where a locomotive's name is visible and the identifying number is not, for clarity both the name and number are given. Where the number is a low and commonly held value, such as a one or two digit number, the works number is also shown in brackets if this is known. In some cases a second previously carried number has been added in brackets, where this may be helpful in identifying or distinguishing the vehicle from another. The number currently carried is listed, irrespective of whether that was the most recently carried number in main line service, which in some cases means that locomotives of the same class are listed with very different numbers. For example, steam locomotive 21C123 at Bluebell Railway (BR number 34023) carries its SR number, whereas classmate 34059 at the same location carries its BR number (its previous SR number was 21C159). For multiple units, individual vehicle numbers are given, as the partners to which they are attached can be changed.

6.3 Builder

The builder that constructed the locomotive or multiple unit is shown. These are a combination of commercial locomotive builders, railway companies including British Rail/Railways and modern organisations that have constructed replica or new-build locomotives. Some of the locomotive builders have been abbreviated and a complete list of the builders and their full names is given in Appendix I.

6.4 Details

For all steam locomotives and smaller diesel locomotives with driving wheels connected by coupling rods, the Whyte notation is used. The three numbers separated by dashes consist of the leading (non-driving) wheels, followed by the number of driving wheels and then the number of trailing (non-driving) wheels. Most steam locomotives have one of the following suffixes: T – side tank, PT – pannier tank, ST – saddle tank, WT – well tank, CT – crane tank, F – fireless, VBT – vertical boiler tank, VBGT – vertical boiler geared tank. For example, 2-4-0ST would be a saddle tank locomotive with 2 leading wheels, 4 driving wheels and no trailing wheels. For locomotives where driving wheels are connected by means other than coupling rods, w is used to indicate powered axles. For example, 4w indicates a four-wheeled bogie with all four wheels powered. For some main line diesel and electric locomotives, the number of driven axles is represented by a letter (A = 1, B = 2, C = 3), followed by a number which states the number of non-powered axles. When the letter o is used, this indicates that each axle is individually powered. The majority of multiple units and the remaining diesel and electric locomotives are listed by their TOPS class. This is a classification system introduced by British Railways in 1968 which classified locomotives by a two digit class number and multiple units by a three digit class number.

7. Attractions

This lists attractions at the site, particularly those which are railway related, such as museums, restored signal boxes and miniature railways, as well as any other facilities or services which may be of interest. Some of the more well known attractions in the surrounding area are also given, including nearby heritage railways, to give ideas for combined visits.

8. Special Events during 2019

Heritage railways hold a rich variety of events every year, including beer festivals, live music, transport themed events, family activities and Santa Specials. Many of these attract thousands of visitors and can be a good opportunity to explore something new, inspire children, or avoid a busier period, depending on one's priorities! Information on the special events has been provided by the railways and is given in good faith.

9. Appendices

Appendix I gives the abbreviations used and the full names of all locomotive and multiple unit builders in the individual railway listings.

Appendix II lists the general abbreviations used in this book.

Appendix III lists all the heritage railways in alphabetical order, with their region and the page number on which they can be found. This acts as a useful index to find the entry for each railway in this book.

Updates and Contact Details

Every effort has been made to ensure the information given in correct, with each of the railways and a large variety of reference sources having been consulted. The content has been updated to February 2019 and the author would be pleased to hear from any reader with information about any inaccuracies or suggestions for enhancements to future editions. Please send any comments to the publisher's address on the title page of this book, or by email to: updates@platform5.com. The author and publisher cannot take responsibility for any errors, changes or cancellations that may take place.

▲ **Bo'ness & Kinneil Railway:** A pair of 0-6-0ST steam locomotives, 68007 and 19, power away from Kinneil Halt with the 1330 from Bo'ness on Sunday 4 December 2016, having built up a good head of steam for the climb to Birkhill. The leading loco has been painted black to resemble a BR Class J94 but is actually former NCB No. 7, acquired from Comrie Colliery in West Fife. **Ian Lothian**

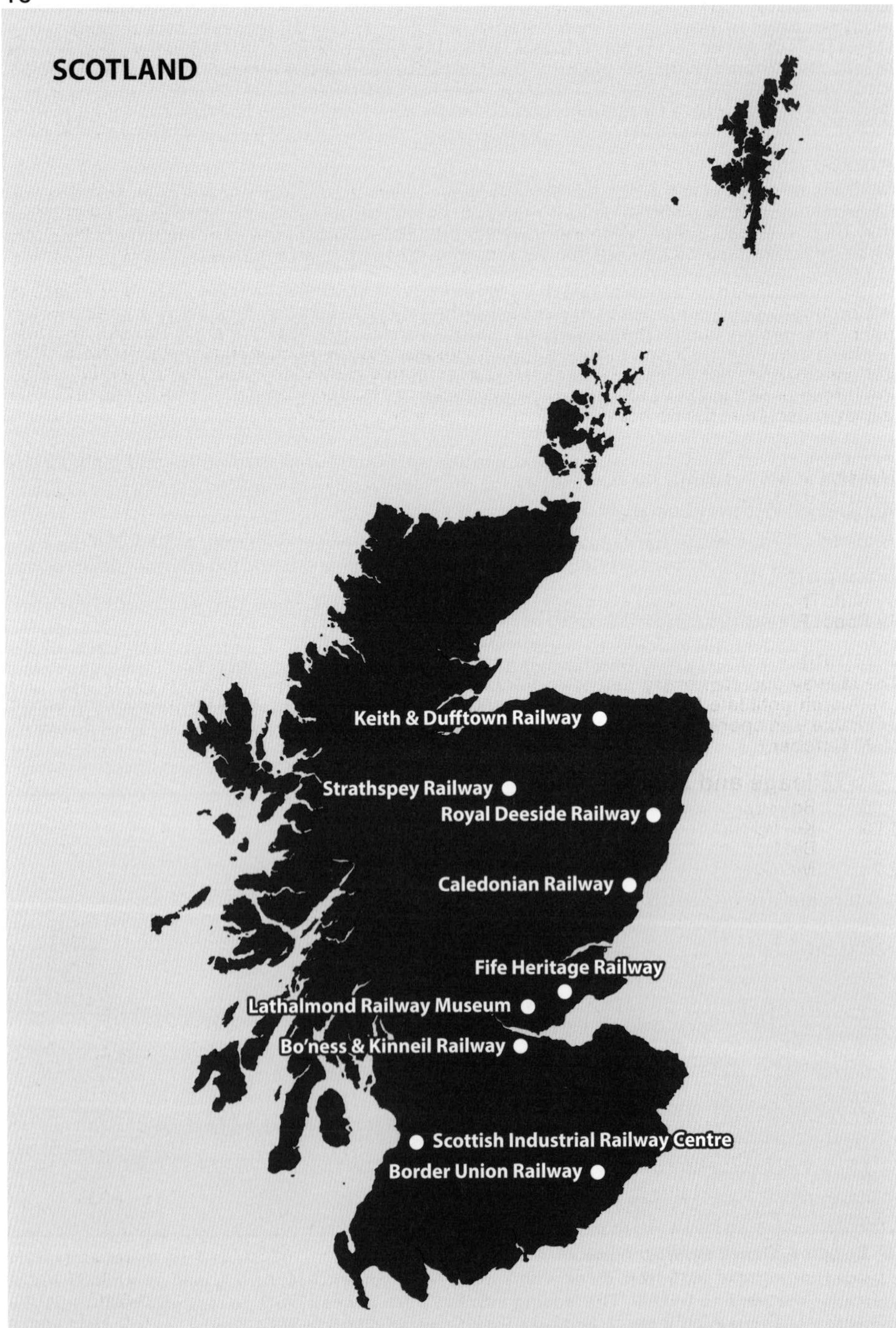
SCOTLAND
Keith & Dufftown Railway
Strathspey Railway
Royal Deeside Railway
Caledonian Railway
Fife Heritage Railway
Lathalmond Railway Museum
Bo'ness & Kinneil Railway
Scottish Industrial Railway Centre
Border Union Railway

Region 1 – Scotland

Bo'ness & Kinneil Railway

Introduction and History

The branch line from Manuel to Bo'ness Harbour on the Firth of Forth opened in 1848 and was initially only used for carrying minerals and other freight. Passenger services did not commence until 1856 and were withdrawn a century later in 1956, when Bo'ness station was closed. The branch line continued to be used for carrying freight; however, the station was demolished and its original site is now a car park. The Scottish Railway Preservation Society (SRPS) formed in 1961 and started a collection of steam locomotives, which was initially housed at a base in Falkirk, until 1979 when the society acquired the Bo'ness site. The first trains in preservation ran in 1981 after a new station was constructed at Bo'ness on the site of former sidings, near to where the original station stood. All the buildings at Bo'ness have been brought from other stations or railway sites. The running line was extended to Kinneil Halt in 1987, Birkhill in 1989 and it reached Manuel in 2010, although the station at Manuel was not opened until 2013. The railway museum at the Bo'ness site opened in 1995 and was extended in 2002.

Contact Details

Website: www.bkrailway.co.uk
Tel: 01506 822298
Email: enquiries.railway@srps.org.uk
Address: Bo'ness & Kinneil Railway, Bo'ness Station, Union Street, Bo'ness, EH51 9AQ.

Transport Links

By Rail: The nearest railway station is Linlithgow, which is four miles away.
By Road: Free car parking is available at Bo'ness (EH51 9AQ).

Opening Times

The railway operates every Saturday, Sunday and Tuesday and selected other weekdays from late March until late October. Trains operate approximately 10.45–16.30 depending on which timetable is in operation. The museum at Bo'ness is open 11.00–16.30 every day from 23 March to 27 October.

Line Mileage and Journey Time

0.00	Bo'ness
1.00	Kinneil Halt
3.50	Birkhill
4.75	Manuel

A return journey takes about one hour.

Stock List

Type	*Number*	*Builder*	*Details*
Steam	9561	Sentinel	4wVBT
Steam	9627	Sentinel	4wVBT
Steam	9631	Sentinel	4wVBT
Steam	6 (2127)	Andrew Barclay	0-4-0CT
Steam	3 (2046)	Andrew Barclay	0-4-0ST
Steam	3 (1937)	Andrew Barclay	0-4-0ST
Steam	4 (2043)	Andrew Barclay	0-4-0ST
Steam	3640	Hawthorn Leslie	0-4-0ST
Steam	13 (2203)	Neilson Reid	0-4-0ST
Steam	68095	North British	0-4-0ST
Steam	CITY OF ABERDEEN (912)	Black Hawthorn	0-4-0ST
Steam	419	Caledonian Railway	0-4-4T
Steam	65243	Neilson & Co	0-6-0
Steam	LORD ASHFIELD (1989)	Andrew Barclay	0-6-0F
Steam	3 LADY VICTORIA	Andrew Barclay	0-6-0ST
Steam	68007	Bagnall	0-6-0ST
Steam	17 (2880)	Hunslet	0-6-0ST

Steam	19 (3818)	Hunslet	0-6-0ST
Steam	5 (3837)	Hunslet	0-6-0ST
Steam	20 (2068)	Andrew Barclay	0-6-0T
Steam	24 (2335)	Andrew Barclay	0-6-0T
Steam	1 (5710)	Neilson & Co	0-6-0T
Steam	61994	LNER	2-6-0
Steam	80105	British Railways	2-6-4T
Steam	45170	North British	2-8-0
Steam	49 (62277)	North British	4-4-0
Steam	246 (62712)	LNER	4-4-0
Diesel	4210140	Fowler	0-4-0
Diesel	D2767	North British	0-4-0
Diesel	Tiger (27415)	North British	0-4-0
Diesel	1 (421439)	Ruston & Hornsby	0-4-0
Diesel	262998	Ruston & Hornsby	0-4-0
Diesel	3 (423658)	Ruston & Hornsby	0-4-0
Diesel	321733	Ruston & Hornsby	0-4-0
Diesel	7 (275883)	Ruston & Hornsby	0-4-0
Diesel	P6687	Ruston & Hornsby	0-4-0
Diesel	802 (457299)	Ruston & Hornsby	0-4-0
Diesel	1 (343)	Andrew Barclay	0-6-0
Diesel	D3558	British Railways	Class 08
Diesel	20020	English Electric	Class 20
Diesel	25235	British Railways	Class 25
Diesel	26024	BRCW	Class 26
Diesel	27001	BRCW	Class 27
Diesel	27005	BRCW	Class 27
Diesel	37067/37703	English Electric	Class 37
Diesel	37214	English Electric	Class 37
Diesel	37261	English Electric	Class 37
Diesel	47643	British Railways	Class 47
Electric	1131	Fairfield Shipbuilding & Engine Co.	0-4-0
Electric	84001	North British	Class 84
DMU	51017, 51043, 59404 & 79443	British Railways	Class 126
EMU	61503, 75597 & 75632	Pressed Steel	Class 303

Attractions

The Museum of Scottish Railways at Bo'ness is Scotland's second largest railway museum. There is also a Brass Rubbing Trail, an 'O' gauge model railway and a picnic area at Bo'ness. Steam and diesel footplate experiences are available on the railway. Other attractions in the area include the Kinneil Estate and Museum, Kinneil Nature Reserve, Bo'ness Motor Museum, the Linlithgow Museum, Linlithgow Palace and the city of Edinburgh.

Special Events During 2019

19–22 April: Easter Egg Specials.
11–12 May: Day Out with Thomas 10.30–15.30.
16 June: Father's Day Event.
21 June: Evening Fish & Chip Steam Train.
27–28 July: Day Out with Thomas 10.30–15.30.
3 August: 1950s Event.
7–8 September: Day Out With Thomas 10.30–15.30.
1 November: Fish & Chip Steam Train.
2–3 November: Steam Gala.
30 November–22 December: Santa Specials.
28 December: Winter Diesel Gala.
30–31 December: Hogmanay "Black Bun" Special Trains.

▲ **Bo'ness & Kinneil Railway:** After running round its train at Birkhill on 30 May 2015, Class 26 No. 26038 is ready to return to Bo'ness, terminus of the Bo'ness & Kinneil Railway. Work is currently under way to erect a second platform here, using a footbridge salvaged from West Calder station, which was replaced during recent electrification of the Glasgow to Edinburgh via Shotts route.
Paul Gerrard

▼ **Caledonian Railway:** The Calendonian Railway is home to a number of locomotives with a Scottish history, including Class 27 No. D5370 which is seen between Brechin and Bridge of Dun on 15 August 2015, during one of the railway's regular diesel Saturdays. **Paul Gerrard**

Border Union Railway

Introduction and History
The Border Union Railway, which was marketed as the Waverley Route, ran from Edinburgh to Carlisle via Hawick. It opened in 1862, providing an alternative route from Scotland to England across tough terrain, which required many curves and steep gradients. It was earmarked for closure in Dr Beeching's 1963 report and, despite fierce opposition, it was closed in 1969. Between 2012 and 2015, the northern section of the railway was relaid between Edinburgh and Tweedbank and now forms the well-used Borders Railway. In 2002 the Waverley Route Heritage Association obtained a lease for a section of trackbed south of Whitrope Tunnel and its base at Whitrope Heritage Centre is on this. The centre formally opened in 2012 and has a short section of running track. The railway hopes to extend south by a further two miles in the near future, taking it to Riccarton Junction.

Contact Details
Website: wrha.org.uk
Telephone: 07366 260584
Email: info@wrha.org.uk
Address: Border Union Railway, Whitrope, Hawick, Roxburghshire, TD9 9TY.

Transport Links
By Rail: The site is in a remote location and the nearest stations are Tweedbank (29 miles) and Carlisle (34 miles).
By Road: Car parking is available at Whitrope Heritage Centre (TD9 9TY), which is on the B6399, immediately south of Whitrope Tunnel.

Opening Times
Railway operating days are from 10.00 to 16.00 on the first Saturday and Sunday of each month from May until October, with trains running at 40-minute intervals. There will also be two bank holiday weekend galas, see special events below. Train services are operated by the railbus, although the Fowler shunter will run on alternate running days if it is repaired in time for the 2019 season.

Line Mileage and Journey Time
0.00	Whitrope Tunnel
0.25	Whitrope Halt
0.50	Golden Bridge

A return jouney takes about 30 minutes.

Stock List
Type	*Number*	*Builder*	*Details*
Diesel	411319	Ruston & Hornsby	0-4-0
Diesel	4240015	Fowler	0-6-0
Diesel	D5340	BRCW	Class 26
DMU	RB004	BREL/Leyland	Prototype Railbus
EMU	69316	BREL	Class 422

Attractions
The Class 141 prototype railbus is used for carrying passengers and during the 2019 running season, it is hoped that the John Fowler & Co. shunter will be used to haul passengers in a newly restored brake van. There is an exhibition showing the history and operations of the railway, which includes a signalling experience and various artefacts. The buffet coach provides refreshments and contains further railway exhibits. Other attractions in the region include Hermitage Castle to the south, the village of Newcastleton with a Stane from the Seven Stanes Walk and a nearby golf course. To the north, Hawick is the home of cashmere, with textile outlets, a whisky distillery and the annual common riding.

Special Events During 2019
21–21 April: Spring Gala to open the 2019 season.
24–25 August: Gala Event.

Caledonian Railway

Introduction and History
The railway between Brechin and Bridge of Dun opened in 1848 and later became part of the original Caledonian Railway. The line closed to passenger services in 1952 but continued to be used for freight traffic for almost 30 years until this ended in 1981. Two groups formed in 1979, the Caledonian Railway (Brechin) and the Brechin Railway Preservation Society, to preserve the line. The first locomotive arrived in 1979; however, it wasn't until 1993 when a Light Railway Order was obtained, that passenger services could start to run between Brechin and Bridge of Dun. Initially there were aspirations to extend the railway a further three and a half miles from Bridge of Dun to Dubton where the trackbed has been built upon, but this is no longer being pursued.

Contact Details
Website: www.caledonianrailway.com
Tel: 01356 622992
Email: enquiries@caledonianrailway.com
Address: Caledonian Railway, The Station, Park Road, Brechin, DD9 7AF.

Transport Links
By Rail: The nearest railway station is Montrose, which is eight miles away.
By Road: Free car parking is available at both Brechin (DD9 7AF) and Bridge of Dun (DD10 9LH).

Opening Times
The railway is open most Saturdays and Sundays from June to September, with selected other running dates (see special events).

Line Mileage and Journey Time
0.00 Brechin
4.00 Bridge of Dun

A return journey takes about one hour.

Stock List

Type	*Number*	*Builder*	*Details*
Steam	1863	Andrew Barclay	0-4-0ST
Steam	1376 Patricia	Peckett	0-4-0ST
Steam	6 (2749)	Bagnall	0-6-0ST
Steam	16 (2759)	Bagnall	0-6-0ST
Steam	2879	Hunslet	0-6-0ST
Steam	2153	Peckett	0-6-0ST
Steam	MENELAUS	Peckett	0-6-0ST
Steam	2107	Andrew Barclay	0-6-0T
Steam	46464	British Railways	2-6-0
Diesel	3747	Hibberd	0-4-0
Diesel	421700	Ruston & Hornsby	0-4-0
Diesel	458957	Ruston & Hornsby	0-4-0
Diesel	211 ROLLS	Yorkshire Engine Co.	0-4-0
Diesel	212 ROYCE	Yorkshire Engine Co.	0-4-0
Diesel	D3059	British Railways	Class 08
Diesel	12052	British Railways	Class 11
Diesel	12093	British Railways	Class 11
Diesel	25072	British Railways	Class 25
Diesel	25083	British Railways	Class 25
Diesel	26035	BRCW	Class 26
Diesel	D5301	BRCW	Class 26
Diesel	D5314	BRCW	Class 26
Diesel	D5353	BRCW	Class 27
Diesel	D5370	BRCW	Class 27
Diesel	37097	English Electric	Class 37

Attractions
The railway has a large collection of steam and diesel locomotives comparative to its size; the original railway station and railway yard can be seen at Brechin. Nearby attractions include Brechin Castle and Gardens (June & July only), Lunan Bay, Montrose Basin Nature Reserve and the coastal town of Montrose.

Special Events During 2019
20–21 April: Easter Eggspress.
25 May & 7 September: Take the Sloe Train.
Steam Sundays: 2, 9, 16, 23 & 30 June, 7, 21 & 28 July, 4 & 11 August, 1 & 8 September.
Diesel Saturdays: 15, 22, 29 June, 6, 20 & 27 July, 3, 10 & 31 August, 7 September.
15 & 22 June: Whisky Whistler.
13–14 July & 24–25 August: Day Out With Thomas.
20 July & 10 August: Frying Scotsman.
3 August: Murder on the Brechin Express.
17–18 August: Diesel Weekend.
8, 14–15 & 21–22 December: Santa Specials.

Fife Heritage Railway

Introduction and History
The Lochty Private Railway ran on a former mineral railway in Fife from 1967 until it closed in 1992. The Kingdom of Fife Railway Preservation Society then formed in 1992 to find a new home for the remaining railway stock, which was initially moved to the closed railway site at Methil Power Station. In 2001 the society acquired the nearby former marshalling yard at Kirkland, near Leven, and in 2003 after laying track and landscaping the site, the rolling stock was moved there. It opened to the public in 2008; the first steam train ran in 2016 and the railway now has half a mile of track, an engine shed and a number of sidings. Future plans include building a display shed and the railway hopes to gain access to the disused Leven branch. This runs adjacent to the site and would increase the line length to two miles, running to Cameron Bridge.

Contact Details
Website: www.fifeheritagerailway.co.uk
Email: Written enquiries can be made via the website.
Address: Fife Heritage Railway, Kirkland Sidings, Leven, Fife, KY8 4RB.

Transport Links
By Rail: The nearest railway station is Markinch, which is six miles from the railway.
By Road: Parking is available (KY8 4RB).

Opening Times
Open days are on the last Sunday of the month from April to October, when trains give passenger rides on the site, see special events below. Visitors are also welcome on Saturdays and Tuesdays to view the various projects under way.

Line Mileage and Journey Time
The railway currently runs for half a mile and the journey time is relatively short.

Stock List

Type	*Number*	*Builder*	*Details*
Steam	10 FORTH	Andrew Barclay	0-4-0ST
Steam	17	Andrew Barclay	0-4-0ST
Diesel	4	Ruston & Hornsby	0-4-0
Diesel	400 RIVER EDEN	North British	0-4-0
Diesel	1	Ruston & Hornsby	0-4-0
Diesel	2 The Garvie Flyer	Ruston & Hornsby	0-4-0
Diesel	7	Ruston & Hornsby	0-4-0
Diesel	10	North British	0-6-0

Attractions

Other nearby attractions include Methil Heritage Centre, Leven Beach and Riverside Park in Glenrothes. The Lathalmond Railway Museum is 23 miles away (see page 19) and the Bo'ness & Kinneil Railway (see page 11) is 35 miles away.

Special Events During 2019

The 2019 Sunday running dates will include these themed days:

28 April: Easter Bunny.
26 May: Diesel Gala.
30 June: Leven Car Rally.
28 July: Teddy Bears' Picnic.
25 August: Summer/Penny Fayre.
29 September: Steam Gala.
27 October: Halloween.
7–8 December: Santa Specials.

Keith & Dufftown Railway

Introduction and History

The three railway lines which converge at Keith were constructed in stages. The route from Aberdeen reached Keith in 1856 and the line from Inverness in 1858, creating a through route. The branch from Keith to Dufftown opened in 1862 and was extended from Dufftown to Nethy Bridge in 1863. It had rail connections at many of the distilleries along the route, allowing whisky to be transported by rail. Through passenger services from Keith to Aviemore via Dufftown ceased in 1965, followed by freight in 1968. Whisky trains ran from Aberlour to Keith until 1971 and from Dufftown until 1985. Occasional charter services continued to run to Dufftown, until the last of these ran in 1991. The Keith and Dufftown Railway acquired the line in 1998 and the first trains in preservation ran in 2000. The railway is no longer connected to the national network, as a short section of track in Keith has been lifted; however, it is hoped that this can be reinstated in the future.

Contact Details

Website: www.keith-dufftown-railway.co.uk
Tel: 01542 882123
Email: info@keith-dufftown-railway.co.uk
Address: Keith Town Station, Keith, Banffshire, AB55 5BR.

Transport Links

By Rail: The nearest station is Keith, which is less than one mile from Keith Town station.
By Road: Free parking is available at Dufftown (AB55 4BA) and Keith Town station (AB55 5BR).

Opening Times

During 2019 trains operate every Saturday and Sunday from 6 April to 29 September, plus Fridays 19 April, 3 May and all Fridays 31 May to 27 September. Trains will also run on Monday 22 April and Thursday 2 May.

Line Mileage and Journey Time

0.00	Dufftown
4.50	Drummuir
10.25	Keith Town

A return journey takes about 1 hour 40 minutes from Dufftown (longer if starting from Keith).

Stock List

Type	*Number*	*Builder*	*Details*
Diesel	The Wee Mac	Clayton	0-4-0
Diesel	415	Andrew Barclay	0-4-0
Diesel	Spirit O Fife	English Electric	0-6-0
DMU	50628, 51568, 52053, 56224 & 56491	British Railways	Class 108
DMU	55500 & 55501	BREL/Leyland	Class 140

Attractions

Keith Town station has a shop, which includes various railway books and model railway items. The railway offers a diesel shunter driving experience, which is unusual among heritage railways, as driving experiences tend to use main line steam or diesel locomotives. At Dufftown visitors can look around the loco shed and heritage centre by arrangement, plus the shop and Sidings Café inside converted carriages. The station is less than one mile from the centre of historic Dufftown, which is known as the whisky capital of the world and has seven working distilleries. Other attractions in the region include the 13th Century Balvenie Castle and the Speyside Way, which is a traffic-free path along much of the railway trackbed to Grantown-on-Spey near the Strathspey Railway (see page 22), which is approximately 33 miles away.

Special Events During 2019

19–22 April: Children's Easter Bunny Challenge.
2–5 May: Spirit of Speyside Whisky Festival.
7 June: Pie & Pint Special, departs Dufftown 19.00.
15–16 June: 1940s Weekend.
2–4 August: Teddy Bears' Weekend.
7 September: Fish & Chip Special, departs Dufftown at 18.00.
Late September: Autumn Speyside Whisky Festival.
25–26 October: Ghost Train, departs Dufftown at 18.00.
7–8, 14–15 & 21–22 December: Santa Specials, depart Dufftown at 11.30 & 14.15 each day.

▲ **Royal Deeside Railway:** Class 03 No. D2134 is seen at Milton of Crathes station on 19 October 2018. The station and buildings at Milton of Crathes have been newly built in an authentic heritage style, as the original Crathes station building is now a private residence. **Tony Christie**

Lathalmond Railway Museum

Introduction and History

This region of Fife was home to a number of railways and narrow gauge tramways built to carry minerals, the first of which opened in 1864. During the Second World War, the Royal Navy built a stores and transit depot on the Lathalmond site, for the nearby Rosyth Dockyard and this facility used the extensive railway network until 1971. The Royal Navy site closed in 1993 and in 1995 part of the grounds were acquired by the Scottish Vintage Bus Museum to house its exhibits. In 1997 the Shed47 Railway Restoration Group was formed, with the aim of re-establishing some of the vast railway network that occupied the site, which the group share with the bus museum.

Contact Details

Website: www.shed47.org
Tel: 07379 914801
Email: mail@shed47.org
Address: Shed47 Railway Restoration Group at SVBM, M90 Commerce Park, Lathalmond, KY12 OSJ.

Transport Links

By Rail: The nearest station is Dunfermline Town, which is three miles away.
By Road: Car parking is available on site (KY12 OSJ).

Opening Times

During 2019 the museum will open every Sunday from 21 April to 27 October inclusive, except 30 June, 13 & 20 October when it is closed. Trains will be running on 21 April, 19 & 26 May, 2, 16 & 23 June, 21 & 28 July, 17–18 & 25 August, 1 & 29 September & 27 October.

Line Mileage and Journey Time

The standard gauge railway line is 400m long and the journey time is relatively short.

Stock List

Type	*Number*	*Builder*	*Details*
Steam	17	Andrew Barclay	0-4-0ST
Steam	29	Andrew Barclay	0-4-0ST
Diesel	250	Hunslet	0-4-0
Diesel	251	Hunslet	0-4-0
Diesel	4	Fowler	0-4-0

Attractions

The site is shared with the Scottish Vintage Bus Museum, which opens simultaneously. The railway museum, station and shop will formally open in April 2019 and the site also houses the 1942-built loco shed, a working weighbridge and a 2-ft gauge railway, which runs for 300m. The Knockhill Racing Circuit is nearby; to the east is the Fife Heritage Railway (see page 16) and to the south is the Forth Bridge, across which is the Bo'ness & Kinniel Railway (see page 11) and the city of Edinburgh.

Special Events During 2019

The vintage bus museum has special events on 19 May, 2 & 16 June, 28 July, 17 & 18 August and 1 September (subject to a charge by the bus museum) and standard and narrow gauge trains will run on these dates from 11.00. Other events may be added during 2019 – please check the website.

Royal Deeside Railway

Introduction and History

When the railway from Aberdeen to Banchory was completed in 1853, Crathes Castle station on the route opened as a private station for the Laird of Crathes. The line was extended to Aboyne in 1859 and to its final terminus Ballater in 1866. In 1863 Crathes Castle became a public railway station, being renamed Crathes and until the route's closure in 1966, it was regularly used by the Royal Family to reach Balmoral Castle. The Royal Deeside Railway Preservation Society formed in 2003 and began restoration of the line in 2003, with a base at Crathes and as the previous station is a private residence, the new Milton of Crathes station was built at a more accessible location. The railway currently runs for one mile and is gradually being extended westwards along the original trackbed. It is hoped that engineering projects will be completed in time to enable trains to run to West Lodge during 2019. The long-term aim is to reach Banchory, which will give the line a running length of over 2 miles.

Contact Details

Website: www.deeside-railway.co.uk
Tel: 01330 844416
Email: opsdir@deeside-railway.co.uk
Address: The Royal Deeside Railway, Milton of Crathes, Banchory, Aberdeenshire, AB31 5QH.

Transport Links

By Rail: The nearest railway stations are Portlethen (14 miles) and Aberdeen (16 miles).
By Road: Parking for the railway is available at the Milton of Crathes art & craft village (AB31 5QH).

Opening Times

Trains depart on the hour 11.00–16.00 every Sunday from 31 March to 20 October and on selected Wednesdays and Saturdays during April, July and August. Services are steam or Class 03 diesel-hauled on alternate dates.

Line Mileage and Journey Time

From Milton of Crathes the railway operates for one mile. A return journey takes about 20 minutes.

Stock List

Type	*Number*	*Builder*	*Details*
Steam	BON ACCORD	Andrew Barclay	0-4-0ST
Steam	6 (2110)	Peckett	0-4-0ST
Steam	SALMON	Andrew Barclay	0-6-0ST
Diesel	D2037	British Railways	Class 03
Diesel	D2094	British Railways	Class 03
Diesel	D2134	British Railways	Class 03
Battery EMU	79998 & 79999	British Railways	Derby Lightweight

Attractions

The railway is situated within the Milton of Crathes complex which includes craft shops, galleries, a children's play area and a restaurant. The railway has a Victorian station, a railway carriage tearoom, a shop and great views of the surrounding hills as it follows the River Dee. Steam driving experiences are available. The region is home to Crathes Castle garden and estate, the city of Aberdeen, Balmoral Castle, Craigievar Castle and Grampian Transport Museum.

Special Events During 2019

23 March: Photographic Charter.
31 March: Mother's Day with Cream Teas.
20 October: End of Season Gala.
30 November, 1, 7–8, 14–15 & 21–24 December: Santa Specials.
30–31 December: Mince Pie Specials.

Scottish Industrial Railway Centre

Introduction and History

The railway between Ayr and Dalmellington opened in 1856, carrying passengers and freight from the iron and coal pits at Dalmellington. Passenger services were withdrawn in 1964 and regular freight traffic continued to use the branch until 1978, when many of the collieries closed. The Ayrshire Railway Preservation Group (ARPG) formed in 1974, with the aim of preserving the area's railway heritage. The group were initially based at the former Minnivey Colliery in Ayrshire from 1980 and in 2002 they moved to the current site at Dunaskin, on the former Dalmellington branch. The centre has a collection of industrial steam and diesel locomotives, many of which were built by Andrew Barclay and Sons at nearby Kilmarnock. There is a short operational railway line.

Contact Details

Website: www.scottishindustrialrailwaycentre.org.uk
Email: info@scottishindustrialrailwaycentre.org.uk
Address: Scottish Industrial Railway Centre, Dunaskin, Dalmellington Road, Waterside, Patna, Ayr, KA6 7JH.

Transport Links

By Rail: The nearest stations to the Dunaskin site are Maybole (11 miles) and Ayr (12 miles).
By Road: Free parking is available at the centre.

Opening Times

The centre opens 11.00–16.30 on selected Sundays from April to September. During these times trains operate and these are usually steam-hauled.

Line Mileage and Journey Time

0.00	Dunaskin
1.75	Minnivey

A return journey takes about half an hour.

Stock List

Type	*Number*	*Builder*	*Details*
Steam	8 (1952)	Andrew Barclay	0-4-0F
Steam	1 (2368)	Andrew Barclay	0-4-0ST
Steam	10 (2244)	Andrew Barclay	0-4-0ST
Steam	16 (1116)	Andrew Barclay	0-4-0ST
Steam	19 (1614)	Andrew Barclay	0-4-0ST
Steam	23 (2260)	Andrew Barclay	0-4-0ST
Steam	25 (2358)	Andrew Barclay	0-6-0ST
Diesel	Lily of the Valley	Fowler	0-4-0
Diesel	Powfoot No. 1	Andrew Barclay	0-4-0
Diesel	AC118 M3571	Andrew Barclay	0-4-0
Diesel	BE116 DY322	Ruston & Hornsby	0-4-0
Diesel	107	Hunslet	0-4-0
Diesel	324 Blinkin Bees	Ruston & Hornsby	0-4-0
Diesel	7	Andrew Barclay	0-4-0
Diesel	417890 Johnnie Walker	Ruston & Hornsby	0-4-0
Diesel	421697	Ruston & Hornsby	0-4-0
Diesel	10012	Sentinel	0-4-0
Diesel	27644	North British	0-4-0

Attractions

Steam trains give brake van rides between Dunaskin and Minnivey on the former industrial railway line. There are a variety of steam and diesel locomotives to see, with standard and narrow gauge exhibits, plus a model railway and photographic archives to explore. Nearby attractions include the Galloway Forest Park, the Scottish Dark Sky Observatory, the village of Straiton and the coast and beaches on the southern Firth of Clyde.

Strathspey Railway

Introduction and History

The railway from Aviemore to Forres, which includes the route of today's Strathspey Railway, opened in 1863. The route from Dufftown to Nethy Bridge also opened in 1863 and was extended south to Boat of Garten in 1866. The Aviemore to Forres via Boat of Garten route was the original Highland Main Line, until the direct route from Aviemore to Inverness was completed in 1898. This led to the line via Boat of Garten becoming a secondary route and passenger services eventually ceased in 1965. Freight services, which mainly consisted of whisky traffic, ended in 1968 when the line was closed. The first preservation group formed in 1971, buying the trackbed from British Rail; their first trains ran from a site north of Aviemore to Boat of Garten in 1978. The railway was extended into the main line station at Aviemore in 1998; in 2002 a further extension north to Broomhill opened and there are long-term plans for the railway to continue north to Grantown-on-Spey.

Contact Details

Website: www.strathspeyrailway.co.uk
Tel: 01479 810725
Email: Written enquiries can be made via the website.
Address: Strathspey Railway, Aviemore Station, Dalfaber Road, Aviemore, PH22 1PY.

Transport Links

By Rail: Main line rail connection at Aviemore; just cross the footbridge to Platform 3.
By Road: Car parking is available at Aviemore (PH22 1PD – main line station postcode), Boat of Garten (PH24 3BH) and Broomhill (PH26 3LX).

Opening Times

The 2019 operating season starts on 30 March, with trains running on Saturdays, Sundays and some weekdays until late October. Santa Specials will also run during weekends in December. Trains usually run between 10.30 and 16.30; however, this may differ during special events.

Line Mileage and Journey Time

0.00	Aviemore
5.25	Boat of Garten
9.25	Broomhill

A return journey takes about 1 hour 40 minutes.

Stock List

Type	*Number*	*Builder*	*Details*
Steam	2 (2020)	Andrew Barclay	0-4-0ST
Steam	828	Caledonian Railway	0-6-0
Steam	9	Robert Stephenson & Hawthorns	0-6-0ST
Steam	WPR17 (2017)	Andrew Barclay	0-6-0T
Steam	46512	British Railways	2-6-0
Steam	45025	Vulcan Foundry	4-6-0
Diesel	517	Andrew Barclay	0-4-0
Diesel	27549	North British	0-4-0
Diesel	265618	Ruston & Hornsby	0-4-0
Diesel	260756	Ruston & Hornsby	0-4-0
Diesel	D2774	North British	D2/10
Diesel	D3605	British Railways	Class 08
Diesel	D5302	BRCW	Class 26
Diesel	D5325	BRCW	Class 26
Diesel	D5394	BRCW	Class 27
Diesel	D5862	Brush Traction	Class 31
DMU	51990, 52008 & 52030	British Railways	Class 107
DMU	56047	British Railways	Class 114
DMU	51367, 51402 & 59511	Pressed Steel	Class 117

Attractions

The railway has a variety of heritage rolling stock and is located in spectacular Scottish highland scenery. There are plans to open a museum at Boat of Garten, although this may not be ready for 2019. Aviemore is in the Monadhliath and Cairngorm mountain region and Boat of Garten has a golf and tennis club. The RSPB observation hide at the Osprey Centre is 1.5 miles from the station. There are many walks and cycle routes in the area, most notably the Speyside Way which follows much of the former railway line and the Keith & Dufftown Railway (see page 17) is at the northern end of this, approximately 33 miles away.

Special Events During 2019

13–14 July: Summer Event.
26–27 October: Halloween Event.
30 November & weekend in December: Santa Express.
27 December–2 January 2020: Mince Pie Specials.

▲ **Strathspey Railway:** The delightful station at Boat of Garden on the Strathspey Railway, complete with well-maintained floral displays, basks in the late-autumn sunshine on 17 October 2018.
Tony Christie

NORTHERN ENGLAND
Aln Valley Railway
North Tyneside Steam Railway
Tanfield Railway
Bowes Railway
Beamish
Weardale Railway
Locomotion
Eden Valley Railway
Stainmore Railway
Wensleydale Railway
North Yorkshire Moors Railway
Lakeside & Haverthwaite Railway
Yorkshire Wolds Railway
Embsay & Bolton Abbey Steam Railway
Derwent Valley Light Railway
National Railway Museum
Poulton & Wyre Railway (proposed)
Keighley & Worth Valley Railway
Middleton Railway
Ribble Steam Railway
East Lancashire Railway
Science & Industry Museum
Elsecar Heritage Railway
Crewe Heritage Centre

Region 2 – Northern England

Aln Valley Railway

Introduction and History
The branch line from Alnmouth to Alnwick opened in 1850 and remained in use for well over a century, until it closed to both passenger and freight traffic in 1968. The Aln Valley Railway was first formed in the 1990s and has built a new station and base at the Lionheart site on the outskirts of Alnwick as the trackbed nearer the town centre has been built upon. The first passenger trains ran on a short stretch of track in 2013 and trains now operate for almost three quarters of a mile to Alndyke Farm Crossing. In 2018 the railway received a £156 000 grant, enabling work to start on extending it by over half a mile to Greenrigg Bridge, where a new halt will be built. This will take the line approximately half way to Alnmouth, which is the railway's long-term aim.

Contact Details
Website: www.alnvalleyrailway.co.uk
Tel: 0300 030 3311
Email: getintouch@alnvalleyrailway.co.uk
Address: Lionheart Railway Station, Lionheart Enterprise Park, Alnwick, NE66 2EZ.

Transport Links
By Rail: Alnmouth Railway Station is four and a half miles by road.
By Road: Ample parking is available at the Lionheart site (NE66 2HT), which is close to the A1 and Alnwick town centre. Parking is free, although a voluntary contribution may be requested at special events.
By Bike: There is a cycle route from the centre of Alnwick to the nearby Lionheart Enterprise Park.

Opening Times
The railway operates every Saturday, Sunday and Bank Holiday from April to September, except 11 & 18 May, plus selected weekdays and weekends in October and December.

Line Mileage and Journey Time
The railway is currently slightly less than three quarters of a mile long and when the extension to Greenrigg Halt is complete, it will increase to one mile and a third. The journey time is relatively short.

Stock List

Type	*Number*	*Builder*	*Details*
Steam	3799 PENICUIK	Hawthorn Leslie	0-4-0ST
Steam	60 (3686)	Hunslet	0-6-0ST
Steam	48 (WD 75015)	Hunslet	0-6-0ST
Steam	9 RICHBORO	Hudswell Clarke	0-6-0T
Diesel	265617	Ruston & Hornsby	0-4-0
Diesel	L2	Ruston & Hornsby	0-4-0
Diesel	615	Andrew Barclay	0-6-0
Diesel	8199	Drewry	0-6-0
Diesel	12088	British Railways	Class 11

Attractions
The Alnwick site has a museum, restored vintage carriages, a café, shop, children's playground and model railway with several layouts. 'Driver for a Tenner' experiences are available with diesel locomotives. Alnwick has a number of attractions including Alnwick Castle. Nearby popular destinations include Holy Island, Dunstanburgh Castle and Craster, home of the kipper.

Special Events during 2019
20–22 April: Easter Steam Weekend, with Easter Bunny Hunt 21–22 April.
26 May: Music Festival.
15–16 June: Classic & Vintage Vehicles Weekend.
6–7 July: 1940s Weekend.

28 July: Summer Fair.
10–11 August: Teddy Bears' Picnic.
31 August–1 September: Model RailEx.
26–27 October: Halloween Ghost Trains.
7, 8, 14, 15, 18, 21 & 22 December: Santa Specials.
27–29 December: Mince Pie Specials.

Beamish: The Living Museum of the North

Introduction and History
Beamish is a 350-acre site, housing a number of interactive displays of industrial life through Georgian, Victorian, Edwardian and 20th Century England. The museum opened on its current site in 1972 and has a variety of original and replica buildings, a working tramway and standard and narrow gauge railway lines. There is a railway station which was relocated from Rowley, County Durham and this was reopened by poet Sir John Betjeman in 1976.

Contact Details
Website: www.beamish.org.uk
Tel: 0191 370 4000
Email: museum@beamish.org.uk
Address: Beamish Museum, Regional Resource Centre, Beamish, County Durham, DH9 0RG.

Transport Links
By Rail: Chester-le-Street is the nearest railway station and is five miles away.
By Road: Ample car parking is available at the museum.

Opening Times
The museum is open 10.00–17.00 (to 16.00 until 6 April) every day during 2019 except 25 & 26 December. Trains operate at weekends, bank holidays and school holidays only.

Line Mileage and Journey Time
The railway from Rowley station is approximately one sixth of a mile and the journey time is relatively short.

Stock List

Type	*Number*	*Builder*	*Details*
Steam	Hetton Lyon	George Stephenson	0-4-0
Steam	"Puffing Billy" (replica)	Alan Keef	0-4-0
Steam	"Steam Elephant" (replica)	Alan Keef	0-6-0
Steam	7006	Robert Stephenson & Hawthorns	0-4-0CT
Steam	1370	Peckett	0-4-0ST
Steam	5 MALLEABLE	South Durham Steel & Iron	0-4-0ST
Steam	18	Stephen Lewin	0-4-0ST
Steam	17	Head Wrightson	0-4-0VBT
Steam	1	Head Wrightson	0-4-0VBGT
Steam	WISSINGTON	Hudswell Clarke	0-6-0ST
Steam	1532 NEWCASTLE	Manning Wardle	0-6-0ST
Steam	2309 HAYDOCK	Robert Stephenson & Co	0-6-0T
Steam	1	Black Hawthorn	2-4-0CT

Attractions
The museum includes an 1820s landscape and wagonway, a 1900s town, a pit village, colliery and 1940s farm. There is a one and a half mile working tramway and an operational railway with an 1850 goods shed, an 1896 signal box, a wrought iron footbridge and a coal drop. There are extensive collections of domestic, rural, industrial and transport related exhibits. A number of experiences are available, including 'Colliery Steam Engine Driver', 'Tram Experience', 'Carriage Driving Experience', 'Steam Roller Experience' and 'Pit Pony Experience'. Nearby heritage railways include Tanfield Railway (three miles, see page 56), Bowes Railway (eight miles, see page 27) Stephenson Railway Museum (16 miles, see page 47). The cities of Newcastle and Sunderland are ten and 14 miles from Beamish respectively.

Special Events during 2019

11–14 April: Great North Steam Fair.
19–22 April: Easter Fun at Beamish.
27–28 April: Horses at Work.
5–6 May: May Day Celebrations.
10–12 May: Georgian Fair and Meccano Exhibition (11-12 May).
15–16 June: Morris Car Rally & Scott Motorcycle Rally.
26–30 June: Old King Coal.
11–14 July: Festival of the 1950s.
29 August–29 September: Great North Festival of Agriculture.
23–31 October: Halloween Events.
16 November–24 December: Christmas at Beamish, with Ice Rink.

Bowes Railway

Introduction and History

The first section of Bowes Railway opened in 1826, making it one of the world's first railways. When completed it was 15 miles long and used for carrying coal from pits in Durham to the River Tyne at Jarrow. Trains were locomotive-hauled at each end of the railway and the six mile middle section was rope-worked, as this included some very steep gradients. Most of the line was closed between 1968 and 1974 and the final three and a half mile section was operated by the National Coal Board. The original part of the railway which dates from 1826 was acquired for preservation in 1976 and it is now the only remaining standard gauge rope-hauled railway in the world.

Contact Details

Website: www.bowesrailway.uk
Email: bowesrailway1826@gmail.com
Address: Bowes Railway, Springwell Road, Gateshead, NE9 7QJ.

Transport Links

By Rail: Heworth Metro station is two and a half miles and Newcastle railway station is four and a half miles away.
By Road: Car parking is available at Bowes Railway (NE9 7QJ).

Opening Times

Bowes Railway is open 10.00–15.00 on Thursdays, Fridays and Saturdays, plus the first Sunday of the month. Guided tours are available on request.

Line Mileage and Journey Time

The section which carries passengers is one mile from Springwell station to the line's end at Wrekenton. A return journey takes about 30 minutes.

Stock List

Type	*Number*	*Builder*	*Details*
Steam	22	Andrew Barclay	0-4-0ST
Steam	WST	Andrew Barclay	0-4-0ST
Diesel	101	Hibberd	0-4-0
Diesel	6263	Hunslet	0-4-0
Diesel	476140	Ruston & Hornsby	0-4-0

Attractions

The standard gauge rope-hauled railway is unique. It is not currently operational, however visitors can enjoy a guided tour of the two haulier houses by booking in advance, or on a special event date. Train rides in brake vans are due to start in 2019, subject to approval from the Office of Rail and Road (ORR) which is expected to be in place during 2019. Trains will be diesel-hauled initially and steam-hauled when locomotive boiler repairs are complete. Nearby transport-themed attractions include the Tanfield Railway (see page 56), Beamish (see page 26) and the North-East Land, Sea & Air Museum. Newcastle, Sunderland and the coast are all only a few miles away.

◀ **Aln Valley Railway:** Drewry 0-6-0 industrial diesel locomotive 8199 (a close relation of the BR Class 04) propels a brakevan into the platform road at Lionheart station with a "Driver for a Tenner" service on 2 August 2018. **Ben Bucki**

▼ **Crewe Heritage Centre:** Bo-Bo electric locomotive 87035 "Robert Burns" stands next to Class 37 No. 37108 at Crewe Heritage Centre on 27 July 2018. Crewe Heritage Centre is also home to the only remaining Class 370 Advanced Passenger Train (APT). **Brad Joyce**

Crewe Heritage Centre

Introduction and History
Crewe Heritage Centre opened in 1987 and is located on the site of the railway yard immediately north of Crewe station, between the Chester line and West Coast Main Line, at the point where they split. The site includes Crewe North Junction signal box, which has been preserved since it was taken out of use, complete with a viewing balcony which is ideal for watching passing trains. A main line rail connection allows visiting steam and diesel locomotives and some of the home-based locomotives to travel to other sites.

Contact Details
Website: www.crewehc.org
Tel: 01270 212130
Email: Written enquiries can be made via the website.
Address: The Crewe Heritage Centre Trust Ltd, Vernon Way, Crewe, Cheshire, CW1 2DB.

Transport Links
By Rail: The Heritage Centre is less than a mile from Crewe railway station.
By Road: Car parking is available on site (CW1 2DB).

Opening Times
The Centre opens 10.00–16.30 (last admission 15.00) on Saturdays, Sundays and Bank Holidays from April to October inclusive.

Line Mileage and Journey Time
There are various standard gauge lines and sidings at the centre, a short stretch of which is sometimes used for giving brake van rides using diesel locomotives 03073 or 47192.

Stock List

Type	*Number*	*Builder*	*Details*
Diesel	10007	Sentinel	0-4-0
Diesel	03073	British Railways	Class 03
Diesel	37108	English Electric	Class 37
Diesel	47192	British Railways	Class 47
Electric	87035	BREL	Class 87
EMU	48103, 48106, 48404, 48602, 48603, 49002, 49006	BREL	Class 370

Attractions
The centre is home to one of the two remaining Advanced Passenger Trains (APT). It also contains three complete signal boxes showing how they were used and the viewing platform which gives direct views of trains travelling through Crewe. There is a selection of locomotives to see and a 7¼ in gauge miniature railway which visitors can ride on. The region is also home to Crewe's Lyceum Theatre, Crewe Hall, Nantwich, Tatton Park and Jodrell Bank.

Special Events during 2019
16 March: Toy & Train Collectors Fair.*
23 March: Best of British Railways Event.*
6–7 April: Diesel Gala.
26–27 April: 3rd Berries, Beans & Beer Festival.*
4–5 May: Creative Crewe Music Event.*
15–16 June: Signalling Gala Weekend.
28–29 September: Wheels of War Weekend & 40s Dance*
5 October: Toy & Train Collectors Fair.*

* Events hosted by the Heritage Centre, organised by third parties.

Derwent Valley Light Railway

Introduction and History

The railway from York Layerthorne to Cliff Common near Selby opened in 1913 as a light railway, with lower speed limits and weight limits from its beginning. Regular passenger services were withdrawn as early as 1926, although passenger specials used the route occasionally. The line continued to carry a variety of local goods, some via the railway connection to the Rowntree factory in York. The railway was one of the few to remain in private ownership both after the 1923 Grouping and the formation of British Railways in 1948. The southern section between Wheldrake and Cliff Common was closed in 1964, after the main line connection near Selby had been lost and levels of traffic were declining. Seasonal passenger steam trains returned to the northern section between 1977 and 1979, but after a further decline in use the remainder of the railway closed in 1981; the track was later lifted. In 1982 the Yorkshire Farming Museum acquired the Murton Park site, which included a section of the railway. In the following years, the Derwent Valley Light Railway Society relaid a section of track and built the new Murton Park station. The first trains in preservation ran in 1992.

Contact Details

Website: www.dvlr.org.uk
Tel: 01904 489966
Email: info@dvlr.org.uk
Address: Derwent Valley Light Railway, c/o Murton Park, Murton Lane, Murton, York, YO19 5UF.

Transport Links

By Rail: The nearest station is York, which is four miles away.
By Road: Free parking is available at Murton Park (YO19 5UF), chargeable only during occasional special events.

Opening Times

Trains operate on Sundays and Bank Holidays from 21 April until late September and during December for Santa Specials, departing Murton Park station between 11.15 and 16.00. Entry to the railway is with a ticket to the Murton Park complex, comprising of the Derwent Valley Light Railway and Yorkshire Museum of Farming.

Line Mileage and Journey Time

The railway operates for three quarters of a mile from Murton Park and the journey time is relatively short.

Stock List

Type	*Number*	*Builder*	*Details*
Diesel	4100005	Fowler	0-4-0
Diesel	4200022	Fowler	0-4-0
Diesel	4100005 CHURCHILL	Fowler	0-4-0
Diesel	3 (441934)	Ruston & Hornsby	0-4-0
Diesel	3 KEN COOKE	Ruston & Hornsby	0-4-0
Diesel	JIM (417892)	Ruston & Hornsby	0-4-0
Diesel	OCTAVIUS ATKINSON (466630)	Ruston & Hornsby	0-4-0
Diesel	327964	Ruston & Hornsby	0-6-0
Diesel	03079	British Railways	Class 03
Diesel	D2245	Robert Stephenson & Hawthorns	Class 04

Attractions

The operational signal box at Murton Park was transferred from Muston, near Filey, and the station building was transferred from Wheldrake and rebuilt at Murton Park. There is a museum and shop at the Murton Park base and diesel 'Driver for a Fiver' experiences are available. The adjacent Yorkshire Museum of Farming has a variety of animals, exhibits, a nature trail and a reconstructed Viking village. The Roman city of York is four miles from Murton Park and has many attractions including the National Railway Museum (see page 45), City Walls, The Shambles and York Minster.

Special Events during 2019

December: Santa Specials.

East Lancashire Railway

Introduction and History

The railway between Heywood and Bury opened in 1841, followed by the line between Clifton Junction, Bury and Rawtenstall, which opened in 1846 and was extended north to Bacup in 1852. The section between Rawtenstall and Bacup closed in 1966, when trains then terminated at Rawtenstall. Passenger services between Heywood and Bury were withdrawn in 1970 and between Bury and Rawtenstall in 1972. Freight trains from Bury to Rawtenstall continued until 1980, when British Rail closed Bolton Street station in Bury and relocated the railway to nearby Bury Interchange. The route from Manchester to Bury used third rail electric multiple units until 1992, when these were superseded by Metrolink trams, which continue to Bury Interchange today. The first preserved trains ran between Bury and Ramsbottom in 1987 when the East Lancashire Railway opened. These were extended to Rawtenstall in 1991 and to Heywood in 2003, after a steeply graded line was built across the Metrolink line to Bury. The railway remains connected the main line network between Heywood and Castleton. This is only used by occasional charter trains, however, the railway plans to extend to a new station at Castleton, which would increase its length by a further one and a half miles.

Contact Details

Website: www.eastlancsrailway.org.uk
Tel: 0333 320 2830 or 0161 764 7790.
Email: enquiries@eastlancsrailway.org.uk
Address: East Lancashire Railway, Bolton Street Station, Bury, Lancashire, BL9 0EY.

Transport Links

By Rail: Bury Interchange (Metrolink) is less than half a mile away from Bolton Street station.
By Road: Parking is available at all stations, however this is subject to charges at Bury (BL9 0EY) and is limited at Ramsbottom (BL0 9AL) and Rawtenstall (BB4 6AG). There is ample free parking at Heywood (OL10 1NH).

▲ **East Lancashire Railway:** The East Lancashire Railway has a strong tradition of using diesel traction and organised an event in 2014 to bring together ten surviving Class 14s to mark the 50th anniversary of the class. 14901 and D9521 pause at Irwell Vale with a Heywood to Rawtenstall service on 27 July 2014. **Paul Gerrard**

Opening Times

Trains operate on Saturdays and Sundays all year round, plus a large number of weekdays from April to September and selected weekdays in winter. Departures are between approximately 09.30 and 16.00 depending on which timetable is operating.

Line Mileage and Journey Time

0.00	Heywood
4.00	Bury Bolton Street
5.25	Burrs Country Park
6.50	Summerseat
8.00	Ramsbottom
10.00	Irwell Vale
12.00	Rawtenstall

A return journey takes up to 2 hours 40 minutes, depending on the starting point.

Stock List

Type	*Number*	*Builder*	*Details*
Steam	1 (1927)	Andrew Barclay	0-4-0ST
Steam	1370	Peckett	0-4-0ST
Steam	52322	Lancashire & Yorkshire	0-6-0
Steam	2890	Hunslet	0-6-0ST
Steam	752	Beyer Peacock	0-6-0ST
Steam	65 (3163)	Hunslet	0-6-0ST
Steam	32 (680)	Hudswell Clarke	0-6-0T
Steam	47298	Hunslet	0-6-0T
Steam	47324	North British	0-6-0T
Steam	13065	LMS	2-6-0
Steam	46428	British Railways	2-6-0
Steam	80080	British Railways	2-6-4T
Steam	80097	British Railways	2-6-4T
Steam	3855	GWR	2-8-0
Steam	7229	GWR	2-8-2T
Steam	45212	Armstrong Whitworth	4-6-0
Steam	45407	Armstrong Whitworth	4-6-0
Steam	44871	LMS	4-6-0
Steam	34092	British Railways	4-6-2
Steam	35009	Southern Railway	4-6-2
Diesel	3438	Hibberd	0-4-0
Diesel	9009	Simplex	0-4-0
Diesel	4002	Hudswell Clarke	0-6-0
Diesel	D2956	Andrew Barclay	Class 01
Diesel	D2062	British Railways	Class 03
Diesel	07013	Ruston & Hornsby	Class 07
Diesel	08164	British Railways	Class 08
Diesel	08479	British Railways	Class 08
Diesel	08944	British Railways	Class 08
Diesel	09024	British Railways	Class 09
Diesel	D9502	British Railways	Class 14
Diesel	D9531	British Railways	Class 14
Diesel	D8233	British Thomson-Houston	Class 15
Diesel	20087	English Electric	Class 20
Diesel	D8110	English Electric	Class 20
Diesel	D5054	British Railways	Class 24
Diesel	D7629	Beyer Peacock	Class 25
Diesel	D5705	Metropolitan Vickers	Class 28
Diesel	6536	BRCW	Class 33
Diesel	33046	BRCW	Class 33
Diesel	33109	BRCW	Class 33
Diesel	D7076	Beyer Peacock	Class 35
Diesel	37109	English Electric	Class 37
Diesel	37679	English Electric	Class 37
Diesel	40135	English Electric	Class 40

Diesel	40145	English Electric	Class 40
Diesel	D832	British Railways	Class 42
Diesel	45108	British Railways	Class 45
Diesel	45135	British Railways	Class 45
Diesel	47765	British Railways	Class 47
Diesel	D1501	Brush Traction	Class 47
Diesel	50015	English Electric	Class 50
Diesel	D1041	British Railways	Class 52
Diesel	56006	Electroputere	Class 56
DMU	50437, 50455, 50494, 50517, 50556 & 59137	BRCW	Class 104
DMU	51485 & 56121	Cravens	Class 105
DMU	51813, 51842 & 59701	BRCW	Class 110
DMU	51339 & 51382	Pressed Steel	Class 117
DMU	56289	Pressed Steel	Class 121
DMU	55001	GRCW	Class 122
DEMU	60130 & 60904	British Railways	Class 207
EMU	70549	British Railways	Class 411
EMU	65451 & 77172	British Railways	Class 504

Attractions

Bury Transport Museum is adjacent to Bolton Street station. The railway offers Real Ale Trail guided tours, with information on the history of the area; platform 2 at Bolton Street is home to The Trackside real ale pub. Photography, steam and diesel driving experiences are available. Attractions in the area include Bury Art Museum, Bury's Fusilier Museum, Helmshore Mills Textile Museum, Irwell Sculpture Trail, Greater Manchester Museum of Transport, The Whitaker Museum & Art Gallery and Ski Rossendale.

Special Events during 2019

8–10 March: Spring Steam Gala.
4–6 July: Summer Diesel Spectacular.
21 September: English Electric Theme Day.
18–20 October: Autumn Steam Gala.
9 November: Scenic Railcar Day.

A variety of dining, wine tasting and murder mystery trains are available through the year.

Eden Valley Railway

Introduction and History

The railway between Clifton near Penrith and Kirkby Stephen via Warcop opened in 1862, forming a through route across the Pennines to Bishop Auckland and Darlington. Closure was proposed in 1959 and following a battle resisting this, passenger traffic ended in 1962, when the Appleby to Clifton section closed. The line south of Warcop closed in 1974 when quarry traffic ended and after Ministry of Defence trains ceased in 1989 the line fell into disuse. The Eden Valley Railway Society formed in 1995 and operated the first trains in preservation during 2003. The railway has gradually extended north from its Warcop base and aims to extend a further three miles to Appleby, giving a northern terminus close to Appleby's main line station.

Contact Details

Website: www.evr-cumbria.org.uk
Tel: 017683 42309
Email: enquiries@evr-cumbria.org.uk
Address: Eden Valley Railway, Warcop Station, Warcop, Appleby, Cumbria, CA16 6PR.

Transport Links

By Rail: Appleby is the nearest railway station and is six miles from the Warcop site.
By Road: Car parking is available at Warcop (CA16 6PR), which is the only site with public access.

Opening Times

Trains operate each Sunday and Bank Holidays from April to October inclusive and some additional dates during July and August.

Line Mileage and Journey Time

0.00 Warcop
2.25 Operational line end

A return journey takes less than one hour.

Stock List

Type	*Number*	*Builder*	*Details*
Diesel	2181	Drewry	0-4-0
Diesel	21	Fowler	0-4-0
Diesel	ND3815 (2389)	Hunslet	0-4-0
Diesel	130c	Thomas Hill	0-4-0
Diesel	8343	Robert Stephenson & Hawthorns	0-6-0
Diesel	37042	English Electric	Class 37
Diesel	47799	British Railways	Class 47
DEMU	60108, 60658 & 60808	British Railways	Class 205
EMU	61798, 61799, 70229 & 70354	British Railways	Class 411
EMU	61804, 61805, 70539 & 70607	British Railways	Class 411
EMU	68003, 68005 & 68010	British Railways	Class 419

Attractions

'Driver for a Fiver' experiences on diesel shunter number 21 are available on Sundays during the operating season (subject to staff availability, so please check before travelling for this). The second-hand book shop has a large stock of railway books, tickets and many non-railway books. There are two model railways of different gauges ('N' and 'O') and a small museum in the signal box. Hot drinks and light snacks are also available. The Stainmore Railway at Kirkby Stephen is eight miles away (see page 54), making a combined visit possible on a day that both sites are open. The railway is located between the Yorkshire Dales National Park, the Lake District and the North Pennines (an Area of Outstanding Natural Beauty), giving many opportunities to explore the landscape of northern England.

▲ **Embsay & Bolton Abbey Steam Railway:** Superbly restored North Eastern Railway petrol-electric autocar 3170 – built in 1904 at York Works and now recognised as the world's first passenger carrying rail vehicle with an internal combustion engine – is seen at Bolton Abbey, the western terminus of the Embsay & Bolton Abbey Steam Railway, following its relaunch on 19 October 2018. **Ian Beardsley**

Elsecar Heritage Railway

Introduction and History

The railway is on a branch line which left the Barnsley to Mexborough route at Elsecar Junction. It opened in 1850 and carried iron and coal from a number of local mines and ironworks. It was not a passenger route, however Earl Fitzwilliam ran private trains from his own station at Elsecar, which is now part of the Heritage Centre. The Elsecar site was known as Elsecar Goods Station and this closed in the early 1970s. The northern section of the branch survived until Cortonwood Colliery closed in 1984 and the track was lifted shortly afterwards. In 1994 Barnsley Council opened the Elsecar Heritage Centre to showcase the area's industrial heritage. The railway was part of this and after the track had been relaid and a platform built, the first trains ran in 1996. Responsibility for the railway passed to Elsecar Heritage Railway in 2006. The railway is in the process of extending by a further half mile to Cortonwood and track for this section has recently been laid.

Contact Details

Website: www.elsecarrailway.co.uk
Tel: 01226 746746
Email: enquiries@elsecarrailway.co.uk
Address: Elsecar Heritage Railway, Wath Road, Elsecar, Barnsley, S74 8HJ.

Transport Links

By Rail: The nearest station is Elsecar which is about half a mile away.
By Road: Free parking is available (S74 8HJ).
By Bike: On the Trans-Pennine Trail.

Opening Times

The railway operates 10.00–16.00 on every Sunday in 2019 and on selected other dates. Elsecar Heritage Centre opens 10.00–16.00 Monday to Sunday (11.00 on first Monday of the month).

Line Mileage and Journey Time

0.00	Elsecar Rockingham
1.00	Hemmingfield
1.50	Cortonwood (not yet operational)

A return journey takes about half an hour.

Stock List

Type	*Number*	*Builder*	*Details*
Steam	7	Sentinel	4wVBT
Steam	10	Sentinel	4wVBT
Steam	9599	Sentinel	4wVBT
Steam	BIRKENHEAD	Robert Stephenson & Hawthorns	0-4-0ST
Steam	EARL FITZWILLIAM	Avonside	0-6-0ST
Steam	15	Hunslet	0-6-0ST
Steam	2150	Peckett	0-6-0ST
Diesel	ELIZABETH	Sentinel	0-4-0
Diesel	Louise (6950)	Hunslet	0-6-0
Diesel	2895	Yorkshire Engine Co.	0-6-0

Attractions

The railway is based within Elsecar Heritage Centre, which has various exhibits from the area's industrial history, including the Elsecar New Colliery and the Newcomen Beam Engine which dates from 1795. Driving experiences are available using both steam and diesel locomotives over the line's steep gradients. Peckett 2150 "Mardy Monster" which is the most powerful industrial locomotives built in the UK, is due to return to steam in 2019. The Trans-Pennine Trail follows the route of the line and runs between the railway and the Elsecar Canal. Other attractions in the area include Locke Park, RSPB Old Moor and Worsbrough Mill & Country Park.

Embsay & Bolton Abbey Steam Railway

Introduction and History

The railway between Skipton and Ilkley opened in 1888 and after declining use, it was closed by British Railways in 1965. The first preservation group formed in 1968, initially hoping to preserve the line from Skipton to Grassington, which deviated from the route to Bolton Abbey and Ilkley at Embsay Junction. The majority of the Grassington line survived and continues to be used today by freight trains to Rylstone; the group instead acquired Embsay station in the early 1970s. The first section of the railway opened to the public in 1981 and this was extended to Holywell Halt in 1987 and to the current terminus, Bolton Abbey in 1997. There are long-term aims to extend the railway further east to Addingham and for the line to reconnect to Embsay Junction, enabling the return of through trains from Bolton Abbey to Skipton.

Contact Details

Website: www.embsayboltonabbeyrailway.org.uk
Tel: 01756 710614
Email: enquiries@embsayboltonabbeyrailway.org.uk
Address: Bolton Abbey Station, Skipton, North Yorkshire, BD23 6AF.

Transport Links

By Rail: The nearest station is Skipton, which is two miles from Embsay.
By Road: There is ample parking at Bolton Abbey (BD23 6AF) and Embsay (BD23 6QX) stations.
By Vintage Bus: From Skipton Town Hall car park (near the castle) on selected dates. Refer to the website for details.

Opening Times

The railway operates on most Saturdays, Sundays and Bank Holidays through the year, plus Tuesdays from April to October and every day in August. Train departures are between 10.30 and 16.00 or 17.00.

Line Mileage and Journey Time

0.00	Embsay
1.25	Holywell Halt
3.50	Bolton Abbey

A return journey takes about one hour.

Stock List

Type	Number	Builder	Details
Steam	7164 (7232)	Sentinel	4wVBGT
Steam	22 (2320)	Andrew Barclay	0-4-0ST
Steam	YORK No.1 (2474)	Yorkshire Engine Co.	0-4-0ST
Steam	1450	Hudswell Clarke	0-6-0ST
Steam	1821	Hudswell Clarke	0-6-0ST
Steam	HARRY (1776)	Hudswell Clarke	0-6-0ST
Steam	ILLINGWORTH	Hudswell Clarke	0-6-0ST
Steam	SLOUGH ESTATES No. 5	Hudswell Clarke	0-6-0ST
Steam	1440	Hunslet	0-6-0ST
Steam	2414	Hunslet	0-6-0ST
Steam	3785	Hunslet	0-6-0ST
Steam	3788	Hunslet	0-6-0ST
Steam	7 BEATRICE	Hunslet	0-6-0ST
Steam	8 (3776)	Hunslet	0-6-0ST
Steam	PRIMROSE No.2	Hunslet	0-6-0ST
Steam	S134 WHELDALE	Hunslet	0-6-0ST
Steam	WD194 (3794)	Hunslet	0-6-0ST
Steam	7086	Robert Stephenson & Hawthorns	0-6-0ST
Steam	5643	GWR	0-6-2T
Diesel	1 (440)	Andrew Barclay	0-4-0
Diesel	The Bug/Clockwork Orange	Baguley	0-4-0
Diesel	4200003	Fowler	0-4-0
Diesel	H.W. ROBINSON (4100003)	Fowler	0-4-0

Diesel	887	Ruston & Hornsby	0-4-0
Diesel	36	Hudswell Clarke	0-6-0
Diesel	D2203	Vulcan Foundry	Class 04
Diesel	08054	British Railways	Class 08
Diesel	08773	British Railways	Class 08
Diesel	38	British Railways	Class 14
Diesel	31119	Brush Traction	Class 31
Diesel	D5600	Brush Traction	Class 31
Diesel	37294	English Electric	Class 37
Diesel	D1524	Brush Traction	Class 47
DMU	3170	NER	Autocar

Attractions

Bolton Abbey station is home to the Hambleton Valley Miniature Railway, a signal box display which can be accessed when staff are present, and a wetland area. Embsay station has a gift shop, bookshop and picnic area. The site of Bolton Abbey, the priory and River Wharfe are about one and a half miles from Bolton Abbey station. The market town of Skipton is nearby, where Skipton Castle, canal boat trips and Craven Museum and Gallery can be found. The Keighley & Worth Valley Railway (see below) is relatively close and the area is on the edge of the Yorkshire Dales National Park.

Special Events during 2019

31 March: Mother's Day Specials.
16 June: Father's Day Event.
22–23 June: Vintage Vehicle Weekend.
26–27 October: Halloween Specials.
December: Santa Specials.

Keighley & Worth Valley Railway

Introduction and History

The branch line from Keighley to Oxenhope, which follows the route of the River Worth, opened in 1867. Passenger services ceased in 1961, followed by freight in 1962. Shortly after this, a group of local people and rail enthusiasts formed a preservation society and purchased the line from British Railways. The railway reopened to passengers in 1968, making it one of the pioneers of railway preservation. The 1970 film 'The Railway Children' was filmed on the railway, with Oakworth station being used as a film set. The film greatly raised the profile and popularity of the railway, which at the time was one of a very small number of operational heritage railway lines. The K&WVR remains connected to the main line at Keighley, where the station is shared with its main line counterpart. Occasional main line charter trains travel through to Oxenhope, such as when the railway celebrated it 50th anniversary in 2018.

Contact Details

Website: www.kwvr.co.uk
Tel: 01535 645214
Email: admin@kwvr.co.uk
Address: Keighley & Worth Valley Railway, The Railway Station, Haworth, West Yorkshire, BD22 8NJ.

Transport Links

By Rail: Main line connection at Keighley; just walk over the footbridge. A through ticket can be booked for a supplement, which includes a K&WVR Day Rover ticket and entrance to the railway's museums.
By Road: Parking is available at all stations except Damems, which it is not recommended to drive to, as the access road is unmade. All car parks are free, except Haworth (BD22 8NJ) which is pay and display. Keighley station car park (BD21 4HP) can be very busy Monday–Saturday as it is shared with the main line station. Ingrow West (BD21 5AX) has a large free car park.

Opening Times

Trains operate on Saturdays, Sundays and selected weekdays throughout the year and daily June–August and during school holidays.

Line Mileage and Journey Time

0.00	Keighley
1.25	Ingrow West
2.00	Damems
2.25	Oakworth
3.50	Haworth
4.75	Oxenhope

A return journey takes about 1 hour 15 minutes.

Stock List

Type	*Number*	*Builder*	*Details*
Steam	LORD MAYOR	Hudswell Clarke	0-4-0ST
Steam	51218	Lancashire & Yorkshire	0-4-0ST
Steam	957	Beyer Peacock	0-6-0
Steam	43924	Midland Railway	0-6-0
Steam	5775	GWR	0-6-0PT
Steam	118	Hudswell Clarke	0-6-0ST
Steam	1704	Hudswell Clarke	0-6-0ST
Steam	31	Hudswell Clarke	0-6-0T
Steam	47279	Vulcan Foundry	0-6-0T
Steam	1054	LNWR	0-6-2T
Steam	85	Neilson Reid	0-6-2T
Steam	78022	British Railways	2-6-0
Steam	41241	British Railways	2-6-2T
Steam	80002	British Railways	2-6-4T
Steam	90733	Vulcan Foundry	2-8-0
Steam	48431	GWR	2-8-0
Steam	5820	Lima Locomotive Co.	2-8-0
Steam	75078	British Railways	4-6-0
Steam	45596	North British	4-6-0
Diesel	431763	Ruston & Hornsby	0-4-0
Diesel	23 MERLIN	Hudswell Clarke	0-6-0
Diesel	D2511	Hudswell Clarke	0-6-0
Diesel	32 HUSKISSON	Hunslet	0-6-0
Diesel	D0226 VULCAN	English Electric	Experimental 0-6-0
Diesel	08266	British Railways	Class 08
Diesel	08993	British Railways	Class 08
Diesel	20031	English Electric	Class 20
Diesel	25059	British Railways	Class 25
Diesel	37075	English Electric	Class 37
DMU	51189 & 51803	Metropolitan Cammell	Class 101
DMU	50928 & 51565	British Railways	Class 108
DMU	79962 & 79964	Waggon und Maschinenbau	Railbus

Attractions

Items of railway interest along the route include the Museum of Rail Travel and the Loco Maintenance & Restoration Centre at Ingrow, the Railway Exhibition Shed at Oxenhope and a well-stocked railway bookshop at Haworth. There is a connecting bus to Haworth old village and Bronte Parsonage from Haworth station. Other nearby attractions include Saltaire, Bingley Five Rise Locks, the city of Bradford and the Embsay & Bolton Abbey Steam Railway (see page 36).

Special Events during 2019

8–10 March: Spring Steam Gala.
Selected Sundays in March and April & May: Sparkle & Steam.
27 April, 11 May, 29 June, 13 July, 31 August & 5 October: Haworth Haddock.
3–6 May: Diesel & Mixed Traffic Gala.
December: Santa & Mince Pie Specials.

▲ **Keighley & Worth Valley Railway:** Following the closure of Keighley station in 1962, a preservation group had acquired and reopened the line by 1968, preserving the station's architecture and features. These frame Class 20 No. 20031 as it prepares to leave with the 1530 to Oxenhope on 13 June 2015. The loco continues to earn its keep today, almost 60 years since it entered service in January 1960. **Andy Chard**

▼ **Locomotion, Shildon:** The National Railway Museum's outpost at Shildon is home to a varied collection of rolling stock and other smaller objects from the national collection, including a number of well-known exhibits such as the experimental gas turbine Advanced Passenger Train. On 26 September 2018 LMS Class 5MT 4-6-0 No. 5000, the prototype DELTIC and unrebuilt Battle of Britain Class 4-6-2 No. 34051 "Winston Churchill" are found inside the main display building at the museum. **Ian Beardsley**

Lakeside & Haverthwaite Railway

Introduction and History

The eight-mile branch from Ulverston to Lakeside on the banks of Lake Windermere opened in 1869. Initially it predominantly carried freight, including iron ore, sulphur and coal to power the steam vessels. In the 20th Century freight use declined and the railway was increasingly used by holidaymakers travelling to the Lake District. During the 1930s and 1940s passenger services were suspended for a number of long periods. The railway permanently closed to passengers in 1965 and the final freight and enthusiast special trains ran in 1967. In the same year a group of enthusiasts formed The Lakeside Railway Society and began negotiations with British Rail to acquire the line. The trackbed was purchased in 1970; however, improvements to the A590 meant that the southern section could not be saved and this was lifted in 1971. The heritage railway reopened in 1973 and today operates for the majority of the year, with trains continuing to connect with lake cruises on Lake Windermere, as they first did in 1869.

Contact Details

Website: www.lakesiderailway.co.uk
Tel: 015395 31594
Email: Written enquiries can be made from the website.
Address: Haverthwaite Railway Station, Near Ulverston, Cumbria, LA12 8AL.

Transport Links

By Rail: Ulverston and Cark railway stations are both six miles from Haverthwaite.
By Road: Car parking is available at Haverthwaite station (LA12 8AL).
By Boat: Windermere Lake Cruises operate every day except Christmas Day. Please check the timetable for connection times with trains before travelling.

Opening Times

Trains operate every day from 30 March to 31 October and on selected weekends during December. Departures are between 10.00 and 17.00 on most days, although timetables vary.

▲ **Lakeside & Haverthwaite Railway:** LMS Class 4MT 2-6-4T 42073, in lined BR black livery and hauling a short rake of 'blood and custard' coaching stock, climbs through the woods at Great Hagg, near Newby Bridge on 19 November 2017. **Robert Falconer**

Line Mileage and Journey Time

0.00 Haverthwaite
2.00 Newby Bridge
3.00 Lakeside

A return journey takes at least half an hour.

Stock List

Type	*Number*	*Builder*	*Details*
Steam	2333 DAVID	Andrew Barclay	0-4-0ST
Steam	2682	Bagnall	0-6-0ST
Steam	2996 VICTOR	Bagnall	0-6-0ST
Steam	3698 REPULSE	Hunslet	0-6-0ST
Steam	1245	Andrew Barclay	0-6-0T
Steam	46441	British Railways	2-6-0
Steam	42073	British Railways	2-6-4T
Steam	42085	British Railways	2-6-4T
Diesel	7120	LMS	0-6-0
Diesel	D2072	British Railways	Class 03
Diesel	D2117	British Railways	Class 03
Diesel	20214	English Electric	Class 20
DMU	52071 & 52077	BRCW	Class 110

Attractions

Visitors can look around the engine shed in Haverthwaite and see a selection of steam and diesel locomotives. The station has a picnic area, woodland adventure playground, gift shop and tea room. The Lakeland Motor Museum is a short walk from Haverthwaite station. At Lakeside, the station is adjacent to the Lakes Aquarium and the pier on Lake Windermere, where cruises to Bowness and Ambleside leave. On the opposite shore of Lake Windermere is Fell Foot National Trust Park, with views of Windermere and the fells. The railway is within the Lake District National Park, which has many other attractions and spectacular natural scenery.

Special Events during 2019

19–22 April: Easter Egg Weekend.
Fridays in April, May, September & October: Local Pensioner Days.
21–25 October: Witches & Wizards Week.
30 Nov, 1, 7–8 & 14–15 December: Santa Specials.

Locomotion, Shildon

Introduction and History

The railway from Stockton and Darlington arrived at Shildon in 1825, when the line opened to carry coal from the area's collieries. When "Locomotion" No. 1 departed from Stockton in October 1825, this was the world's first steam-hauled passenger train. The railway initially also carried passengers in horse-drawn coaches; however, these had been replaced by locomotive-hauled trains by 1833. Locomotion is a railway museum with a short demonstration railway, which operates on part of the original Stockton and Darlington Railway. The museum opened in 2004 as a satellite site of the National Railway Museum in York and is adjacent to Shildon station, which is served by regular trains on the Darlington–Bishop Auckland line.

Contact Details

Website: www.locomotion.org.uk
Tel: 01904 685780
Email: info@locomotion.org.uk
Address: Locomotion, Dale Road Industrial Estate, Dale Road, Shildon, DL4 2RE.

Transport Links

By Rail: The nearest station is Shildon, which is a three-minute walk from the museum.
By Road: There is plenty of free parking at the site (DL4 2RE).

Opening Times

The Museum is open 10.00–17.00 (16.00 from November) every day in 2019 except 24–26 December. Steam train rides operate on selected dates through the year.

Line Mileage and Journey Time

The demonstration line is just over a quarter of a mile long and the journey time is relatively short.

Stock List

Type	*Number*	*Builder*	*Details*
Steam	LOCOMOTION (Replica)	Locomotion Enterprises	0-4-0
Steam	SANS PAREIL	Timothy Hackworth	0-4-0
Steam	SANS PAREIL (Replica)	BREL	0-4-0
Steam	IMPERIAL No.1	Andrew Barclay	0-4-0F
Steam	JUNO	Hunslet	0-6-0ST
Steam	44 CONWAY	Kitson	0-6-0ST
Steam	77 (7412)	Robert Stephenson & Hawthorns	0-6-0ST
Steam	65033	NER	0-6-0
Steam	49395	LNWR	0-8-0
Steam	790	LNWR	2-4-0
Steam	4771	LNER	2-6-2
Steam	1621	NER	4-4-0
Steam	251	GNR	4-4-2
Steam	5000	LMS	4-6-0
Steam	34051	Southern Railway	4-6-2
Steam	390	Sharp Stewart	4-8-0
Diesel	D2090	British Railways	Class 03
Diesel	08064	British Railways	Class 08
Diesel	08911	British Railways	Class 08
Diesel	DELTIC	English Electric	Co-Co
Electric	755	Siemens	Bo
Electric	1 (26500)	Brush Traction	Bo-Bo
Electric	E5001	British Railways	Class 71
Gas Turbine	PC1, PC2, TC1 & TC2	BREL	APT-E
EMU	65217 & 65417	Metropolitan Cammell	Class 306
EMU	65617	BRCW	Class 306
EMU	11179	Southern Railway	4 Cor
EMU	10656 & 12123	Southern Railway	2 Bil
EMU	61275 & 75395	British Railways	Class 414

Attractions

The museum houses a number of exhibits from the National Collection, including the prototype gas turbine Advanced Passenger Train and the prototype DELTIC locomotive. Some exhibits periodically move to and from the National Railway Museum's main site in York and other heritage railway sites. Guided tours of selected railway vehicles take place daily. The museum shop has a large number of railway related books, gifts and model railway items. The Weardale Railway (see page 59) is four miles from Locomotion and the Wensleydale Railway (see page 60) is 26 miles away. Other attractions in the area include National Trust Moulton Hall, Darlington and the city of Durham.

Special Events during 2019

27–31 March: GL5 Rally demonstrating 5 inch gauge steam.
4–6 May: Festival of Steam.
11–22 May: Men's Voices: Stepping out of the Box.
26–27 May: Meccano Magic.
1–2 June: Shildon Model Railway Club Exhibition.
11 August: Classic Bus Rally.
21–22 September: Shildon Gala with guest locomotives.
5–6 October: Shildon Model Railway Club Exhibition.
16–17 November: Lego Event.

Middleton Railway

Introduction and History

The Middleton Railway operates from a site to the south of Leeds city centre with a rich industrial railway history and boasts a number of firsts. It was initially a horse-drawn wagonway used to carry coal on wooden tracks and in 1759 became the first railway to be authorised by an Act of Parliament. It has operated trains every year since, making it the oldest continuously operating railway in the world. It was the site where Matthew Murray's "Salamanca" became the first commercially-operated steam locomotive in 1812, and in June 1960 it became the first standard gauge preserved railway, two months before the Bluebell Railway began operating. It remains connected to the national network at Leeds Midland Road, on the route between Leeds and Woodlesford. There are plans to extend the railway further south into Middleton Park and funds are currently being raised for a new shed, which will be necessary to house carriages for the extension project.

Contact Details

Website: www.middletonrailway.org.uk
Tel: 0845 680 1758
Email: info@middletonrailway.org.uk
Address: The Middleton Railway, The Station, Moor Road, Hunslet, Leeds, LS10 2JQ.

Transport Links

By Rail: The nearest railway station is Leeds, which is under two miles away.
By Road: Free car parking is available at Moor Road station (LS10 2JQ).

Opening Times

Trains operate on Saturdays and Sundays from April to December and on some Wednesdays during school holidays, between 11.00 and 16.00 on most days.

Line Mileage and Journey Time

0.00 Moor Road
1.00 Middleton Park

A return journey takes about 25 minutes.

Stock List

Type	Number	Builder	Details
Steam	68153	Sentinel	4wT
Steam	6	Hawthorn Leslie	0-4-0ST
Steam	HENRY DE LACY II	Hudswell Clarke	0-4-0ST
Steam	Mirvale	Hudswell Clarke	0-4-0ST
Steam	SLOUGH ESTATES No. 3	Hudswell Clarke	0-4-0ST
Steam	No. 11	Hunslet	0-4-0ST
Steam	2103	Peckett	0-4-0ST
Steam	1684	Hunslet	0-4-0T
Steam	1310	NER	0-4-0T
Steam	385	Hartmann	0-4-0WT
Steam	BROOKES No. 1	Hunslet	0-6-0ST
Steam	MATTHEW MURRAY	Manning Wardle	0-6-0ST
Steam	SIR BERKELEY	Manning Wardle	0-6-0ST
Steam	M.S.C No. 67	Hudswell Clarke	0-6-0T
Steam	1540	Hunslet	2-6-2T
Diesel	CARROLL	Hudswell Clarke	0-4-0
Diesel	MARY	Hudswell Clarke	0-4-0
Diesel	D2999	Beyer Peacock	0-4-0
Diesel	3900002	Fowler	0-4-0
Diesel	HARRY	Fowler	0-4-0
Diesel	1786	Hunslet	0-4-0
Diesel	6981	Hunslet	0-4-0
Diesel	AUSTINS No. 1	Peckett	0-4-0
Diesel	7051	Hunslet	0-6-0
Diesel	MD&HB 45	Hudswell Clarke	0-6-0
DMU	RDB998901	Drewry	Railcar

▲ **Middleton Railway:** The Middleton Railway held a 'Last Coals to Leeds' themed gala over the last weekend of September 2018. Hudswell Clarke No. 45, formerly of the Mersey Docks and Harbour Board, operated alongside various steam locomotives and is seen arriving at Park Halt station in the afternoon of 29 September 2018. **Ben Bucki**

▼ **National Railway Museum, York:** Great Northern Railway Stirling design Class A2 4-2-2 No. 1, dating from 1870, is on display on the turntable at the National Railway Museum, York on 7 June 2018. LMS Class 4MT No. 2500 and 3 Sub EMU vehicle 8143 can be seen behind. **Robert Pritchard**

Attractions
The Engine House and museum have many historical and hands-on exhibits from the railway's long history and there is a shop, small café and conference facility at the Moor Road site. Middleton Park is accessible from its namesake station on the railway, with its ancient woodland, grassland, boating lake and visitor centre to explore. Nearby attractions in Leeds include the Royal Armouries, the Tetley and Leeds City Museum.

Special Events during 2019
6–7 April: Opening Weekend.
13 April: Community Day.
20–22 April: Easter Event.
4–6 May: Bluebell Walks, Teddy Bears Adventure & Charity Weekend.
15–16 June: Father's Day Weekend Footplate Experience.
22–23 June: Mixed Traffic Weekend.
6–7 July: Steam Punk Market.
13–14 July: Model Railway.
18 August: Bus Rally.
7–8 September: Heritage Open Days.
21–22 September: Anything Goes Event.
21–22 October: Sci-Fi Weekend.

National Railway Museum, York

Introduction and History
The National Railway Museum is adjacent to York railway station and the East Coast Main Line. It opened in 1975 on the site of the former York North depot and was the amalgamation of two previous railway museums which both closed in 1973; British Railways' Transport Museum in Clapham and York Railway Museum which was established by the London and North Eastern Railway in 1928. The Museum holds the National Collection of historically important locomotives and rolling stock and a vast collection of railway artefacts. Much of the rolling stock and many artefacts are on display, although some are at the museum's sister site at Shildon (see page 41) or on loan to other museums or heritage railways.

Contact Details
Website: www.railwaymuseum.org.uk
Tel: 03330 161010
Email: info@railwaymuseum.org.uk
Address: National Railway Museum, Leeman Road, York, YO26 4XJ.

Transport Links
By Rail: The museum is less than half a mile from York railway station.
By Road: The museum car park costs £10 per day.

Opening Times
During 2019 the museum opens 10.00–18.00 (17.00 from November) every day except 24–26 December. Steam train rides are due to operate every Saturday, Sunday and Bank Holiday until 22 December 2019 and on selected other dates during school holidays.

Line Mileage and Journey Time
Steam trains travel on a quarter-mile demonstration line in the South Yard and a return journey takes about 15 minutes.

Stock List

Type	*Number*	*Builder*	*Details*
Steam	ROCKET (replica)	Robert Stephenson & Co	0-2-2
Steam	ROCKET (replica)	Locomotion Enterprises	0-2-2
Steam	BAUXITE No. 2	Black Hawthorn	0-4-0
Steam	3 "Coppernob"	Bury Curtis & Kennedy	0-4-0
Steam	Agenoria	Foster Rastrick	0-4-0
Steam	AGECROFT No. 1	Robert Stephenson & Hawthorns	0-4-0ST
Steam	214 GLADSTONE	LBSCR	0-4-2

Steam	245	LSWR	0-4-4T
Steam	1275	Dübs & Company	0-6-0
Steam	C1 (33001)	Southern Railway	0-6-0
Steam	1247	Sharp Stewart	0-6-0ST
Steam	82 BOXHILL	LBSCR	0-6-0T
Steam	92220	British Railways	2-10-0
Steam	66	Kitson	2-2-4T
Steam	1008	Lancashire & Yorkshire	2-4-2T
Steam	13000	LMS	2-6-0
Steam	2500	LMS	2-6-4T
Steam	1	GNR	4-2-2
Steam	673	Midland Railway	4-2-2
Steam	737	SECR	4-4-0
Steam	990	GNR	4-4-2
Steam	4003	GWR	4-6-0
Steam	6229	LMS	4-6-2
Steam	4468	LNER	4-6-2
Steam	60007	LNER	4-6-2
Steam	60103	LNER	4-6-2
Steam	35029	Southern Railway	4-6-2
Steam	KF7	Vulcan Foundry	4-8-4
Diesel	7050	English Electric	0-4-0
Diesel	D2860	Yorkshire Engine Co.	Class 02
Diesel	09017	British Railways	Class 09
Diesel	D8000	English Electric	Class 20
Diesel	31018	Brush Traction	Class 31
Diesel	D6700	English Electric	Class 37
Diesel	D200	English Electric	Class 40
Diesel	47798	British Railways	Class 47
Diesel	D1023	British Railways	Class 52
Diesel	D9002	English Electric	Class 55
Electric	26020	British Railways	Class 76
Electric	87001	BREL	Class 87
Battery	1	North Staffordshire Railway	2-A
DMU	4	Park Royal	Railcar
DMU	51562 & 51922	British Railways	Class 108
EMU	8143	Southern Railway	3 Sub
EMU	28249	Metropolitan Cammell	LNWR
EMU	3308	GEC-Alsthom	Class 373
EMU	22-141	Hitachi	O Series

Attractions

The large site has a varied collection of exhibits including "Mallard", the world's fastest steam locomotive, Queen Victoria's royal train carriages, examples of the Japanese Bullet Train, Eurostar and important diesel locomotives. A large number of locomotive nameplates are mounted on the wall of the Great Hall. Hands-on activities and regular talks include signalling demonstrations, how a steam engine works and daily turntable demonstrations. The site has a miniature railway, steam train rides and a viewing balcony adjacent to the East Coast Main Line. York city centre is within walking distance, where York Minster, The Shambles, City Walls and many other attractions can be found. The Derwent Valley Light Railway (see page 30) is four miles away.

Special Events during 2019

Until 28 April: Testing Exhibition.

North Tyneside Steam Railway and Stephenson Railway Museum

Introduction and History
The museum and railway are located on former rail wagonways in an area rich in industrial and railway history. After coal trains ceased, the site of the museum and current railway were used as a testing centre by the Tyne and Wear Metro in the 1970s before it started operating. In the early 1980s North Tyneside Council then acquired the test sheds and a partnership was made with Tyne & Wear Museums to create a facility with a steam-hauled passenger railway. A single track line was relaid from the museum to Percy Main, being completed in 1989 and the first passenger trains ran in 1991. Today the museum showcases the railway pioneers George Stephenson and his son Robert.

Contact Details
Website: www.stephensonrailwaymuseum.org.uk and www.ntsra.org.uk
Tel: 0191 200 7146
Email: info@stephensonrailwaymuseum.org.uk
Address: Stephenson Railway Museum, Middle Engine Lane, North Shields, Tyne & Wear, NE29 8DX.

Transport Links
By Rail: The museum is two miles from Percy Main on the Tyne and Wear Metro, Yellow Route.
By Road: There is free parking at the museum (NE29 8DX).

Opening Times
The museum is open 11.00–16.00 every Saturday, Sunday and Bank Holiday between 6 April and 3 November, plus the following dates during school holidays: 18–22 February, 8–22 April, 27–31 May, 22 July–30 August and 28 October–1 November. Railway operating days are on Sundays and Bank Holidays, with trains leaving at 11.30, 12.30, 14.00 and 15.00. Trains may run on other dates during school holidays and the museum can be telephoned on the day to find out which locomotive is working.

Line Mileage and Journey Time
0.00 Middle Engine Lane
1.75 Percy Main

A return journey takes around half an hour.

Stock List

Type	*Number*	*Builder*	*Details*
Steam	Billy	George Stephenson	0-4-0
Steam	401 SIR THOMAS BURT	Bagnall	0-6-0ST
Steam	5 JACKIE MILBURN	Peckett	0-6-0ST
Steam	5	Kitson	0-6-0T
Steam	1 TED GARRET JP MP	Robert Stephenson & Hawthorns	0-6-0T
Diesel	10	Consett	0-6-0
Diesel	D2078	British Railways	Class 03
Diesel	08915	British Railways	Class 08
Electric	E4	Siemans Harton	Electric E4
Electric	3267	Metropolitan Cammell	Motor Parcel Van

Attractions
The Museum has a range of exhibits including George Stephenson's 1816 locomotive "Billy", which is the world's third oldest surviving steam locomotive and a forerunner to the famous "Rocket". There are interactive exhibitions explaining how trains work and the impact coal and electricity has had on railways and people's lives. Steam or diesel locomotives carry passengers in vintage carriages on the museum's own railway line. Heritage railways in the area include the Bowes Railway (ten miles, see page 27), the Tanfield Railway (12 miles, see page 56) and Beamish museum (17 miles, see page 26). The city of Newcastle upon Tyne, Whitley Bay and the coast are all near to the location of the museum.

Special Events during 2019
27 April, 29 June & 28 September: Drive a Diesel Locomotive.

North Yorkshire Moors Railway

Introduction and History

The railway from Whitby to Grosmont opened in 1835 and was extended south to Pickering in 1836. It was extended further south from Pickering to Rillington in 1845, where it joined the present day York–Scarborough line. The route between Grosmont and Levisham was realigned in 1865, when the present station at Goathland opened. Passenger services between Whitby and Malton via Pickering ceased in 1965 and freight services ended in 1966. The North Yorkshire Moors Railway (NYMR) began in 1967 when a group of local people formed the North Yorkshire Moors Railway Preservation Society, with the aim of reopening the line. After a number of open days, the railway between Grosmont and Pickering reopened in 1973. Since 2007 the NYMR has operated trains on Network Rail's Esk Valley route to Whitby, with less frequent services continuing to Battersby too. This required the NYMR to become a registered Train Operating Company and gives the railway more than 40 miles of railway over which it can operate trains.

Contact Details

Website: www.nymr.co.uk
Tel: 01751 472508
Email: info@nymr.co.uk
Address: North Yorkshire Moors Railway, 12 Park Street, Pickering, North Yorkshire, YO18 7AJ.

Transport Links

By Rail: The NYMR connects with main line services at Grosmont and Whitby.
By Road: There are car parks at Pickering (YO18 7AJ), Levisham (YO18 7NN), Goathland (YO22 5NF), Grosmont (YO22 5QE) and Whitby (YO21 1YN). Charges apply at each of these.

Opening Times

Trains operate every day from late March to early November, between approximately 09.30 and 18.30 or 19.30, depending on which timetable is in use.

Line Mileage and Journey Time

0.00	Whitby	0.00	Grosmont
6.25	Grosmont	3.25	Glaisdale
9.75	Goathland	17.75	Battersby (Grosmont to Battersby during special events only)
15.00	Newtondale Halt		
18.25	Levisham		
24.25	Pickering		

A return journey from Whitby to Pickering (or vice versa) takes about four hours, or two hours 40 minutes between Grosmont and Pickering.

Stock List

Type	*Number*	*Builder*	*Details*
Steam	"Lucie " (1625)	Cockerill	0-4-0VBT
Steam	2702	Bagnall	0-4-0ST
Steam	3180	Hunslet	0-6-0ST
Steam	65894	LNER	0-6-0
Steam	29 (4263)	Robert Stephenson & Hawthorns	0-6-2T
Steam	5 (3377)	Robert Stephenson & Hawthorns	0-6-2T
Steam	63395	NER	0-8-0
Steam	76079	British Railways	2-6-0
Steam	62005	North British	2-6-0
Steam	80135	British Railways	2-6-4T
Steam	80136	British Railways	2-6-4T
Steam	2253	Baldwin Locomotive Works	2-8-0
Steam	3672	North British	2-10-0
Steam	92134	British Railways	2-10-0
Steam	926	Southern Railway	4-4-0
Steam	45428	Armstrong Whitworth	4-6-0
Steam	75029	British Railways	4-6-0
Steam	44806	LMS	4-6-0
Steam	61264	North British	4-6-0

▲ **North Yorkshire Moors Railway:** BR Standard Class 4MT 2-6-4T 80136 is the centre of attention as it departs from Grosmont with the 1102 shuttle to Goathland on 30 September 2016. **Peter Foster**

▼ **North Yorkshire Moors Railway:** The North Eastern Locomotive Preservation Group celebrated its 50th anniversary by creating amazing railway scenes of the past including this photo charter over the North Yorkshire Moors Railway on 31 October 2016. LNER Class K1 2-6-0 62005 emerges from the eerie Halloween mist near Newtondale. **Robert Falconer**

Steam	825	Southern Railway	4-6-0
Steam	30830	Southern Railway	4-6-0
Steam	34101	British Railways	4-6-2
Diesel	12139	English Electric	0-6-0
Diesel	D2207	Vulcan Foundry	Class 04
Diesel	08495	British Railways	Class 08
Diesel	08556	British Railways	Class 08
Diesel	08850	British Railways	Class 08
Diesel	D5032	British Railways	Class 24
Diesel	D5061	British Railways	Class 24
Diesel	D7628	Beyer Peacock	Class 25
Diesel	26038	BRCW	Class 26
Diesel	37264	English Electric	Class 37
DMU	50160, 50164, 50204, 51511 & 59539	Metropolitan Cammell	Class 101

Attractions

The railway offers digital photography workshops, steam and diesel driving experiences and engine shed tours which last two hours. The tours are available on selected dates, cost £10 (£5 children) and need to be booked in advance. There are a number of tea rooms along the route, a railway bookshop at Pickering and a 1950s railway memorabilia shop at Grosmont. Between Whitby, Pickering and the North Yorkshire Moors National Park through which the line travels, there are a large number of attractions, natural features and scenery to explore.

Special Events during 2019

30 March–7 April: LNER Class A4 60009 "Union of South Africa" will work passenger trains.
4–6 May: Behind the Scenes.
13–14 July: '60s Fest.
27–29 September: Annual Steam Gala.
11–13 October: Railway in Wartime.
26–31 October: Halloween Trains.
30 November and 1, 7–8, 14–15 & 21–22 December: Santa Specials.

Ribble Steam Railway

Introduction and History

The branch, which leaves the West Coast Main Line immediately south of Preston station and continues to Preston Docks, opened in 1882. It remains in use today, with regular oil tank trains using the route to reach the site of the Ribble Steam Railway, where they are shunted to the nearby bitumen works. When Southport Railway Museum closed in 1999, many of the exhibits were transferred to the Preston site. The Ribble Steam Railway has been operating heritage passenger trains on a stretch of the industrial railway since 2005.

Contact Details

Website: www.ribblesteam.org.uk
Tel: 01772 728800
Email: enquiries@ribblesteam.co.uk
Address: Ribble Steam Railway, Chain Caul Road, Preston, Lancashire, PR2 2PD.

Transport Links

By Rail: The nearest railway station is Preston, which is two and a half miles away.
By Road: Free car parking is available (PR2 2PD).

Opening Times

The railway operates 10.30–17.00 each Saturday and Sunday from April to September, with hourly departures until 16.00. Trains are usually steam-hauled, except on diesel gala days.

Line Mileage and Journey Time

0.00 Museum station
1.50 Line end / Network Rail boundary

A return journey takes about 20 minutes.

Stock List

Type	*Number*	*Builder*	*Details*
Steam	9373	Sentinel	4wVBT
Steam	8024	Sentinel	4wVBT
Steam	Heysham No. 2 (1950)	Andrew Barclay	0-4-0F
Steam	Glenfield 1	Andrew Barclay	0-4-0CT
Steam	17	Sharp Stewart	0-4-0ST
Steam	19	Lancashire & Yorkshire	0-4-0ST
Steam	1865	Andrew Barclay	0-4-0ST
Steam	BRITISH GYPSUM No. 4	Andrew Barclay	0-4-0ST
Steam	EFFICIENT	Andrew Barclay	0-4-0ST
Steam	JN DERBYSHIRE	Andrew Barclay	0-4-0ST
Steam	JOHN HOWE	Andrew Barclay	0-4-0ST
Steam	272	Grant Richie	0-4-0ST
Steam	1439	LNWR	0-4-0ST
Steam	1935 HORNET	Peckett	0-4-0ST
Steam	737 DAPHNE	Peckett	0-4-0ST
Steam	1999	Peckett	0-4-0ST
Steam	1925 CALIBAN	Peckett	0-4-0ST
Steam	2003 JOHN BLENKINSOP	Peckett	0-4-0ST
Steam	7485 AGECROFT No. 2	Robert Stephenson & Hawthorns	0-4-0ST
Steam	THE KING (48)	Borrows	0-4-0WT
Steam	WINDLE (53)	Borrows	0-4-0WT
Steam	20	Sharp Stewart	0-4-0
Steam	NIDDRIE 7	Andrew Barclay	0-6-0ST
Steam	1883	Avonside	0-6-0ST
Steam	1568	Avonside	0-6-0ST
Steam	MDHB 26	Avonside	0-6-0ST
Steam	COURAGEOUS	Bagnall	0-6-0ST
Steam	21 (3931)	Hawthorn Leslie	0-6-0ST
Steam	3696 RESPITE	Hunslet	0-6-0ST
Steam	3793 SHROPSHIRE	Hunslet	0-6-0ST
Steam	CUMBRIA	Hunslet	0-6-0ST
Steam	GLASSHOUGHTON No. 4	Hunslet	0-6-0ST
Steam	WALKDEN	Hunslet	0-6-0ST
Steam	1954	Hunslet	0-6-0ST
Steam	1636 FONMON	Peckett	0-6-0ST
Steam	3155 WALKDEN	Hunslet	0-6-0ST
Steam	30072	Vulcan Iron Works	0-6-0T
Steam	5643	GWR	0-6-2T
Steam	4979	GWR	4-6-0
Diesel	1031	Hudswell Clarke	0-4-0
Diesel	D628 MIGHTY ATOM	Hudswell Clarke	0-4-0
Diesel	D629 SPARKY	Hudswell Clarke	0-4-0
Diesel	21999 FLUFF	Fowler	0-4-0
Diesel	4160001 PERSIL	Fowler	0-4-0
Diesel	27653 BICC	North British	0-4-0
Diesel	10226 ENERGY	Sentinel	0-4-0
Diesel	10282 ENTERPRISE	Sentinel	0-4-0
Diesel	10283 PROGRESS	Sentinel	0-4-0
Diesel	STANLOW No. 4	Thomas Hill	0-4-0
Diesel	D2870	Yorkshire Engine Co.	0-4-0
Diesel	663	English Electric	0-6-0
Diesel	671	English Electric	0-6-0
Diesel	03189	British Railways	Class 03
Diesel	D2148	British Railways	Class 03
Diesel	D2595	Hunslet	Class 05
Diesel	D9539	British Railways	Class 14
Petrol	965 HOTTO	Howard	Petrol Loco
Battery	EE788	English Electric	Battery Loco
Battery	2000	Greenwood & Batley	Battery Loco
DMU	79960	Waggon und Maschinenbau	Railbus

▲ **Ribble Steam Railway:** The Ribble Steam Railway usually has a diesel gala at the beginning and end of each year's passenger running season. During the diesel gala on 5 March 2016 Class 05, D2595, is ready to depart with a shuttle to the Strand Road Network Rail boundary. The line sees traffic all year round as the adjacent Total bitumen plant is supplied by rail. **Andy Chard**

▼ **Science and Industry Museum, Manchester:** EM2 electric loco 1505 "Ariadne" is seen in the Science & Industry Museum in Manchester on 25 October 2014. This loco spent many years in service with Nederlandse Spoorwegen (Netherlands Railways) and still carries its Dutch livery. **Robert Pritchard**

Attractions
The railway has the largest collection of industrial locomotives in the country and the ticket price includes unlimited travel for the day and access to exhibits in the museum and workshop. The line follows an interesting route, passing Preston Marina and across a swing bridge. There is also a café, miniature railway and children's playground at the site. Preston town centre is close and the Ribble Estuary National Nature Reserve, Fylde coast and Lytham St Annes are all nearby.

Special Events during 2019
23–24 March: Diesel Gala.
31 March: Mother's Day Cream Tea.
19–22 April: Easter Weekend/Model Tram Group (FE).
27–28 April: Steam Gala.
4–6 May: Bank Holiday Friendly Engines (FE).
25–27 May: Bank Holiday Teddy Bear Event (FE).
15–16 June: Classic Cars and Afternoon Tea.
20 July: Crazy Trains (FE).
3–4 August: Tramways Event.
24–26 August: Friendly Engines.
28–29 September: Steam Gala.
5–6 October: Diesel Gala.
26–27 October: Spooky Trains.
Various dates in December: Santa Specials.

(FE) Family Event

Science and Industry Museum, Manchester

Introduction and History
When it opened in 1830, the Liverpool and Manchester Railway was the first railway in the world to operate steam-hauled trains between two cities. Liverpool Road station in Manchester was the eastern terminus and is now the oldest surviving passenger railway station in the world. It closed in 1975, was purchased by the local council in 1978 and renovated in order to become the new home of the Science and Industry Museum. This opened in 1983 and now has a large variety of exhibits, including locomotives, industrial machines and aeroplanes. The site was connected to the main line rail network until 2016, when the Orsdall Chord was constructed. This new railway line severed the museum's rail connection in order to create a rail link between Manchester's Piccadilly, Oxford Road and Victoria stations and reduced the length of the museum's railway line considerably.

Contact Details
Website: www.scienceandindustrymuseum.org.uk
Tel: 0161 832 2244
Email: contact@scienceandindustrymuseum.org.uk
Address: Science and Industry Museum, Liverpool Road, Manchester, M3 4FP.

Transport Links
By Rail: Deansgate (main line) and Deansgate-Castlefield (Metrolink) stations are less than a quarter of a mile away.
By Road: The museum is in the city centre and has no car park; chargeable parking is available nearby.

Opening Times
The museum opens 10.00–17.00 every day, except 24–26 December and 1 January. It hopes to operate trains carrying passengers during 2019 and this is subject to completion of works on the site. Please check whether or when trains are operating before travelling.

Line Mileage and Journey Time
The operational railway and journey time are both relatively short.

Stock List

Type	Number	Builder	Details
Steam	ROCKET	Robert Stephenson & Co.	0-2-2
Steam	NOVELTY (replica)	Science Museum	0-2-2WT
Steam	PLANET (replica)	Friends of MOSI	2-2-0
Electric	1505	British Railways	Class 77

Attractions
In addition to the locomotives and railway exhibits, the museum has displays on various aspects of the region's scientific and industrial heritage, including textiles, computing, other modes of transport and a collection of aircraft. There are a variety of attractions in Manchester city centre including Manchester Art Gallery, People's History Museum, the National Football Museum and a number of theatres and shopping outlets.

Special Events during 2019
Until 28 April: Electricity – The Spark of Life Exhibition.
Until 8 September: Stephenson's Rocket Returns.
Saturdays & Sundays at 12.30 & 13.30: Loco-Motion, Family Show.

Stainmore Railway

Introduction and History
The railway between Barnard Castle and Tebay via Kirkby Stephen East opened in 1861, with the northern spur to Clifton and Penrith via Appleby opening in 1862 (see Eden Valley Railway, page 33). Passenger services were withdrawn on the Kirkby Stephen East–Tebay route in 1952, although summer Saturday holiday trains continued to use it until 1961. The route to Clifton closed to passengers in 1962 and to freight in 1974 when traffic to Hartley Quarry ceased. The first preservation group formed in 1997 and they subsequently acquired the Kirkby Stephen East site. Since then Kirkby Stephen East station building has been repaired and just over one quarter of a mile of railway track has been laid, upon which trains first ran in 2011. The railway may extend the line further in future years.

Contact Details
Website: www.kirkbystepheneast.co.uk
Tel: 01768 371700
Email: suelizjones@hotmail.com
Address: Stainmore Railway Company, Kirkby Stephen East Station, South Road, Kirkby Stephen, Cumbria, CA17 4LA.

Transport Links
By Rail: Kirkby Stephen railway station is just under one mile away.
By Road: Free car parking is available at Kirkby Stephen East (CA17 4LA).

Opening Times
During 2019 the Kirkby Stephen site will open on Saturdays and Sundays, 10.00–16.00 from 20 April until early December. Steam or diesel-hauled trains operate on selected weekends. Please check the website or contact the railway for the latest dates.

Line Mileage and Journey Time
The railway is (just over) a quarter of a mile long and the journey takes about 10 minutes.

Stock List

Type	Number	Builder	Details
Steam	2084 FC TINGEY	Peckett	0-4-0ST
Steam	68009	Hunslet	0-6-0
Steam	910	NER	2-4-0
Diesel	ELIZABETH	Hibberd	0-4-0
Diesel	305	Yorkshire Engine Co.	0-4-0
Diesel	STANTON No. 50	Yorkshire Engine Co.	0-6-0

Attractions

There is a museum, shop, children's play area and wide range of rolling stock to see at the Kirkby Stephen site. 'Driver for a Fiver' may be available in 2019, subject to the completion of railway track work. The Pennine market town of Kirkby Stephen is nearby, including the Temperance Hall Museum of Costume which is less than one mile away from the site. Brough Castle is five miles away and there are a number of walking and cycling routes in the area, some of which are on the former Stainmore Line. In addition, the Eden Valley Railway at Appleby (see page 33) is only eight miles away, making a combined visit possible on a day when both sites are open.

Special Events during 2019

15–16 June: Model Railway Show.
28 July: Westmorland Dales Day with Steam Services.
September: Heritage Open Days.
December: Santa Event.

▲ **Stainmore Railway:** One of a number of industrial diesels at the Stainmore Railway, Yorkshire Engine Co 0-6-0 "Stanton No. 50" stands in the platform at Kirkby Stephen East on 16 February 2019. Behind the train can be seen the restored eastbound trainshed which houses a number of historic vehicles and displays about the station and the former Stainmore Line. The westbound trainshed, the roof of which was removed in 1954, is intended to be restored and eventually reopened to the public as the site develops. **Ian Beardsley**

Tanfield Railway

Introduction and History

The Tanfield Railway is known as the oldest railway in the world, as the line has been in use since the first wagonway was built in the 1720s. This was used to carry coal from local collieries to the River Tyne, where it was loaded onto boats. In the 1830s it was converted from a horse-drawn wagonway to a railway. East Tanfield was the final colliery to use the line and after it closed in 1964 the railway closed and the track was lifted. Nearby Marley Hill engine shed, however, continued to be used by the National Coal Board until 1970. A group formed in the 1960s aiming to preserve the steam railway heritage of the North-East. After Marley Hill engine shed closed in 1970, it was initially used by nearby Beamish Museum as a storage site and they allowed the group to restore steam locomotives and railway items belonging to both organisations. Beamish moved its rolling stock to its new railway when it opened in 1976. A connecting curve was then built from Marley Hill to the Tanfield branch. The first passenger trains in preservation ran for half a mile from Marley Hill in 1977 and the railway was extended north to Sunniside in 1982. It was further extended south along the former trackbed and reached Causey in 1992 and the site of East Tanfield Colliery in 1993.

Contact Details

Website: www.tanfield-railway.co.uk
Tel: 07508 092365
Email: info@tanfield-railway.co.uk
Address: Tanfield Railway, Old Marley Hill, Gateshead, Tyne and Wear, NE16 5ET.

Transport Links

By Rail: The nearest station is Dunston (four miles), Newcastle is six miles away.
By Road: There is free parking at Marley Hill (NE16 5ET).
By Bike: The Tanfield Railway Path runs from Gateshead to Sunniside and Marley Hill.

Opening Times

Trains operate 10.30–16.00 every Sunday all year round, plus Saturdays and Mondays during bank holiday weekends and Thursdays and Saturdays during school summer holidays. On the five weekends before Christmas, North Pole Express trains operate. These need to be booked in advance.

Line Mileage and Journey Time

0.00	Sunniside
0.75	Andrews House
1.75	Causey Arch
2.50	East Tanfield

A return journey takes about one hour.

Stock List

Type	*Number*	*Builder*	*Details*
Steam	4 (9559)	Sentinel	4wVBT
Steam	7007	Robert Stephenson & Hawthorns	0-4-0CT
Steam	WELLINGTON	Black Hawthorn	0-4-0ST
Steam	13 (3732)	Hawthorn Leslie	0-4-0ST
Steam	2 (2859)	Hawthorn Leslie	0-4-0ST
Steam	2711	Hawthorn Leslie	0-4-0ST
Steam	L&HC14	Hawthorn Leslie	0-4-0ST
Steam	1672 IRWELL	Hudswell Clarke	0-4-0ST
Steam	3 (2009)	R & W Hawthorn	0-4-0ST
Steam	21 (7796)	Robert Stephenson & Hawthorns	0-4-0ST
Steam	7409 SIR CECIL A. COCHRANE	Robert Stephenson & Hawthorns	0-4-0ST
Steam	6	Andrew Barclay	0-4-2ST
Steam	3746	Hawthorn Leslie	0-6-0F
Steam	1015	Andrew Barclay	0-6-0ST
Steam	20	Bagnall	0-6-0ST
Steam	STAGSHAW	Hawthorn Leslie	0-6-0ST
Steam	3575	Hawthorn Leslie	0-6-0ST

Steam	RENISHAW IRONWORKS No.6	Hudswell Clarke	0-6-0ST
Steam	16 (7944)	Robert Stephenson & Hawthorns	0-6-0ST
Steam	38 (7763)	Robert Stephenson & Hawthorns	0-6-0ST
Steam	44 (7760)	Robert Stephenson & Hawthorns	0-6-0ST
Steam	47 (7800)	Robert Stephenson & Hawthorns	0-6-0ST
Steam	49 (7098)	Robert Stephenson & Hawthorns	0-6-0ST
Steam	62 (7035)	Robert Stephenson & Hawthorns	0-6-0ST
Steam	20 (2779)	Bagnall	0-6-0ST
Steam	PROGRESS	Robert Stephenson & Hawthorns	0-6-0ST
Steam	38 (1823)	Hudswell Clarke	0-6-0T
Steam	3 TWIZELL	Robert Stephenson & Co	0-6-0T
Diesel	3565	Baguley	2w-2
Diesel	2 (D22)	Armstrong Whitworth	0-4-0
Diesel	6980	Robert Stephenson & Hawthorns	0-4-0
Diesel	7697	Robert Stephenson & Hawthorns	0-4-0
Diesel	7901	Robert Stephenson & Hawthorns	0-4-0
Diesel	1 HUSKY	Robert Stephenson & Hawthorns	0-4-0
Diesel	35	Ruston & Hornsby	0-4-0
Diesel	7746	Robert Stephenson & Hawthorns	0-6-0
Diesel	501	Hunslet	0-6-0
Diesel	4240010	Fowler	0-6-0
Diesel	3716	Hibberd	0-4-0
Diesel	758206	Hunslet	0-4-0
Diesel	54781	Lister Blackstone	0-4-0
Electric	E10 (862)	Siemens	4w
Electric	E9 (1565)	AEG, Berlin	Bo-Bo
Electric	7078	Robert Stephenson & Hawthorns	Bo-Bo
Battery	3872 DEREK SHEPHERD	Hawthorn Leslie	Bo-Bo

Attractions

The railway has a very large collection of industrial locomotives. Marley Hill houses many of these and a number of restored vintage carriages. Engine shed tours are available on Sundays from 21 April to 29 September and afternoon tea 'Director Class' travel on Sundays and Bank Holidays from 7 April to 1 September. There are a number of walking paths in the area, including the Tanfield Railway Path, which follows the railway north and south from Andrews House. Other attractions in the area include the North-East Land, Sea & Air Museum, Newcastle, Sunderland and the East coast. Nearby heritage railways include Beamish (three miles, see page 26), Bowes Railway (six miles, see page 27), North Tyneside Steam Railway (12 miles, see page 47) and Weardale Railway (20 miles see page 59).

Special Events during 2019

31 March: Mothering Sunday event.
7 & 14 April: Easter Eggstravaganza trains.
19–22 April: An Edwardian Easter.
5–6 May: Music at Marley Hill.
18–19 May: Mining Heritage Weekend.
26–27 May: 0-4-0 Locomotives Day on Sunday and NCB Locos Day on Monday 27th.
14–16 June: Legends of Industry Gala.
27–28 July: Teddy Bears' Picnic.
7 & 12 September: Heritage Open Days.
21–22 September: 1940s Weekend.
12–13 October: Run It Weekend.
26–27 October: Tanfield Ghost Train.
Various dates from 23 November: North Pole Express.
26 & 29 December: Mince Pie Specials.

'Kids for a Quid' operates on the May and August bank holidays and during school summer holidays.

▲ **Tanfield Railway:** On 4 February 2017, the Tanfield Railway held their first photographers' charter day including a night shoot. There were only six photographers for the day and ten in the evening! The star of the show was ex Joicey Collieries 0-6-0T No. 3 "Twizell" built in 1891 by Robert Stephenson & Co. It is seen inside Marley Hill Shed alongside Bagnall 0-6-0ST No. 20 and Robert Stephenson & Hawthorns 0-6-0ST No. 49. **Robert Falconer**

▼ **Weardale Railway:** 1980s Scotrail-liveried 47712 is seen at the head of a rake of air-conditioned coaching stock displaying a multitude of liveries from various eras, at the Weardale Railway on 18 December 2015. The locomotive was until recently a long-term resident of Crewe Heritage Centre but is now anticipated to make a commercial return to the main line. **Jimmy Wilson**

Weardale Railway

Introduction and History

The railway first reached Bishop Auckland in 1843 when the line from Shildon to Crook was built. The Wear Valley line from Bishop Auckland to Stanhope opened in 1862 and was extended to Wearhead in 1895. Bishop Auckland became a major junction and at its height, seven routes converged at the station. Passenger services on the Weardale route were withdrawn in 1953, after which the line was cut back from Wearhead to Eastgate to serve the cement works. The heritage and tourist value of the railway was recognised as early as 1983 when intermittent charter trains ran to Stanhope and these became timetabled summer weekend services between 1988 and 1992. In 1993 rail traffic to the cement works ended and British Rail announced its intention to close the line. A preservation group formed in 1993 and trains from Wolsingham to Stanhope returned in 2004. The main line connection at Bishop Auckland was reinstated in 2009 and from 2010 the railway extended to a new station at Bishop Auckland. The railway is now owned by an American railway company, Iowa Pacific Holdings, using the subsidiary British American Railway Services (BARS) and aims to extend a further two and a half miles to Eastgate.

Contact Details

Website: www.weardale-railway.org.uk
Tel: 01388 526203
Email: info@weardale-railway.org.uk
Address: Weardale Railway, Stanhope Station, Station Road, Stanhope, DL13 2YS.

Transport Links

By Rail: Bishop Auckland West station is a five to ten minute walk from Bishop Auckland main line station.
By Road: Free parking is available at Stanhope (DL13 2YS). There is also limited parking at Frosterley (DL13 2SL) and Wolsingham (DL13 3BL).

Opening Times

During 2019 the railway will operate on Saturdays, Sundays and Bank Holidays from 23 March to 3 November 2019 and on Wednesdays 10–24 April, 29 May and 3 July to 11 September.

Line Mileage and Journey Time

0.00	Bishop Auckland West
4.25	Witton-le-Wear
10.75	Wolsingham
14.00	Frosterley
16.00	Stanhope

A return journey takes over two hours.

Stock List

Type	*Number*	*Builder*	*Details*
Steam	40	Robert Stephenson & Hawthorns	0-6-0T
Diesel	31106	Brush Traction	Class 31
Diesel	31190	Brush Traction	Class 31
Diesel	31285	Brush Traction	Class 31
Diesel	31454	Brush Traction	Class 31
Diesel	31459	Brush Traction	Class 31
Diesel	31465	Brush Traction	Class 31
DMU	50980 & 52054	British Railways	Class 108
DMU	55012	GRCW	Class 122

Attractions

The railway travels through Weardale in the North Pennines, which is an Area of Outstanding Natural Beauty. There are a large number of footpaths and bridleways within reach from the railway's stations. Stanhope station is home to a souvenir shop and the No. 40 Café, which serves light refreshments. Other attractions in the area include High Force waterfall, Killhope Lead Mining Museum, Raby Castle and Hamsterley Forest. Nearby heritage railways include Locomotion, Shildon (four miles, see page 41), Beamish (19 miles, see page 26) and the Tanfield Railway (20 miles, see page 56).

Special Events during 2019

2nd Sunday of the month March–September: Afternoon Tea Trains.
4th Sunday of the month March–September: Cream Tea Trains.
23 March: Pie & Peas Evening Special.
13–14 April: Class 31 Diesel Gala.
20 April: Easter Egg Evening Ramble.
18 May & 15 June: Evening Beer & Gin Special.
16 June: Gentlemen's Tea Train, Father's Day.
20 July: Cheese & Wine Evening Special.
17 August: Evening Beer & Gin Special.
14 September: Fish & Chip Evening Special.
5–6 October: Diesel Railcar Gala.
23 November–23 December (selected dates): Train to Christmas Town Specials.

Wensleydale Railway

Introduction and History

The railway was constructed in stages across harsh terrain, with Northallerton to Leeming Bar opening in 1848, extending to Leyburn in 1856 and reaching Garsdale in 1878. It was used to carry passengers, farm produce, quarried stone and coal. The line closed to passengers in 1954, after which it remained open between Northallerton and Redmire for freight workings. The track between Garsdale and Redmire was lifted in the 1960s. In 1992 British Steel decided it was no longer economic to transport limestone by rail and British Rail then announced that it intended to close and sell the line. This, however, was delayed when the Ministry of Defence then used the line to occasionally transport military vehicles. The Wensleydale Railway Association formed in 1990, obtaining a 100-year lease on the line between Northallerton (Castle Hills) and Redmire. The first trains in preservation ran between Leeming Bar and Leyburn in 2003, extending to Redmire in 2004 and to Northallerton West station in 2015, although trains will terminate at Leeming Bar during 2019. The railway aims to extend towards Garsdale, the next step being the Redmire–Bolton Castle section.

Contact Details

Website: www.wensleydalerail.com
Tel: 01677 425805
Email: Written enquiries can be made from the website.
Address: Leeming Bar Station, Leases Road, Leeming Bar, Northallerton DL7 9AR.

Transport Links

By Rail: Northallerton is the nearest railway station and is five and a half miles from Leeming Bar station.
By Road: Car parking is available at Leeming Bar (DL7 9AR), Leyburn (DL8 5ET) and Redmire (DL8 4ES).

Opening Times

During 2019, trains will operate from 9 February on selected dates, mostly being Tuesdays, Fridays and Saturdays. Services depart 10.30–17.00 or 09.45–17.45, depending on which timetable is in operation.

Line Mileage and Journey Time

0.00	Northallerton West
6.00	Leeming Bar
7.75	Bedale
13.50	Finghall Lane
17.75	Leyburn
22.00	Redmire

A return journey takes about two and a half hours.

Stock List

Type	Number	Builder	Details
Steam	92219	British Railways	2-10-0
Diesel	03144	British Railways	Class 03
Diesel	D9523	British Railways	Class 14
Diesel	20166	English Electric	Class 20
Diesel	20169	English Electric	Class 20
Diesel	25313	British Railways	Class 25
Diesel	33035	BRCW	Class 33
Diesel	37250	English Electric	Class 37
Diesel	37674	English Electric	Class 37
Diesel	47715	Brush Traction	Class 47
Diesel	47785	Brush Traction	Class 47
DMU	50256, 50746, 51210 & 56343	Metropolitan Cammell	Class 101
DMU	51572 & 56274	British Railways	Class 108
DMU	51353, 51400, 59500 & 59509	Pressed Steel	Class 117
DMU	55032	Pressed Steel	Class 121
DMU	975874	BREL/Leyland	Railbus
EMU	69335	BREL	Class 422

Attractions

A railway shed has recently been constructed at Leeming Bar and the railway is working towards restoring the Victorian station house. The market town of Bedale will host a Tour de Yorkshire stage during May 2019 and the UCI World Cycling Championship Time Trail will pass through in September 2019. Aysgarth Falls is four miles from Redmire station and as the railway is very close to the Yorkshire Dales National Park, there are many scenic walks in the area, including Redmire to Bolton Castle or Jervaulx Abbey (the railway's website has walking maps and directions).

Special Events during 2019

18, 19, 21, 24–28, 31 May & 1–4 June: Tornado at the Wensleydale.
24–27 May: Wensley Ale.
26 August: Special Dog Train in conjunction with National Dog Day.

In addition to regular railway operating days during 2019, there will be a monthly themed afternoon tea service, plus 'Murder Mystery Trains' and 'Gin & Prosecco Trains' on selected dates, 'Halloween Specials' in October and 'Santa Specials' during December.

Yorkshire Wolds Railway

Introduction and History

The railway between Malton and Driffield opened in 1853, linking the two routes running south from Scarborough, both of which remain in use today. Passenger services between Malton and Driffield ended as early as 1950 although the route continued to carry chalk from local quarries until it was closed in 1958. The Yorkshire Wolds Railway formed in 2008 with the aim of restoring at least part of the route as a heritage railway. Access to the site at Fimber, roughly midway along the railway trackbed, was granted in 2012. The first locomotive arrived in 2013 and the railway opened to the public in 2015, using a short demonstration line. Planning permission has been given to relay one mile of track southwards towards Wetwang and work on this will begin during 2019. A brake van is being restored and when completed it will be used to give passenger rides. The railway is one of the youngest heritage railway to be featured in this book and is a good example of the small and enthusiastic beginnings from which heritage railways start.

Contact Details

Website: www.yorkshirewoldsrailway.org.uk
Tel: 01377 338053
Email: info@yorkshirewoldsrailway.org.uk
Address: Yorkshire Wolds Railway, Fimber Halt, Beverley Road, Fimber, YO25 3HG.

Transport Links

By Rail: The nearest railway stations are Driffield (ten miles) and Malton (11 miles).
By Road: Free car parking is available (YO25 3HG).

Opening Times

The site opens 11.00–17.00 each Sunday and Bank Holidays from 21 April to 27 October inclusive.

Line Mileage and Journey Time

The demonstration line is currently approximately 400 feet long and the journey time is relatively short.

Stock List

Type	*Number*	*Builder*	*Details*
Diesel	5576	English Electric	0-4-0

Attractions

The railway gives cab rides in the diesel locomotive and 'Driver for a Fiver' experiences, which must be booked in advance. There is a visitor centre inside a restored Mark I coach, displaying artefacts and photographs of the line during operation, and a shop selling railway related gifts and refreshments. Nearby attractions include Fimber picnic site, Sledmere House, The Driffield Navigation and the deserted medieval village at Wharram Percy. Pickering, the southern terminus of the North Yorkshire Moors Railway (see page 48), is 20 miles from the Fimber site.

▲ **Wensleydale Railway**: Class 14 No. D9523 is seen arriving at Redmire with a Wensleydale Railway train from Leeming Bar on 7 September 2013. **Robert Pritchard**

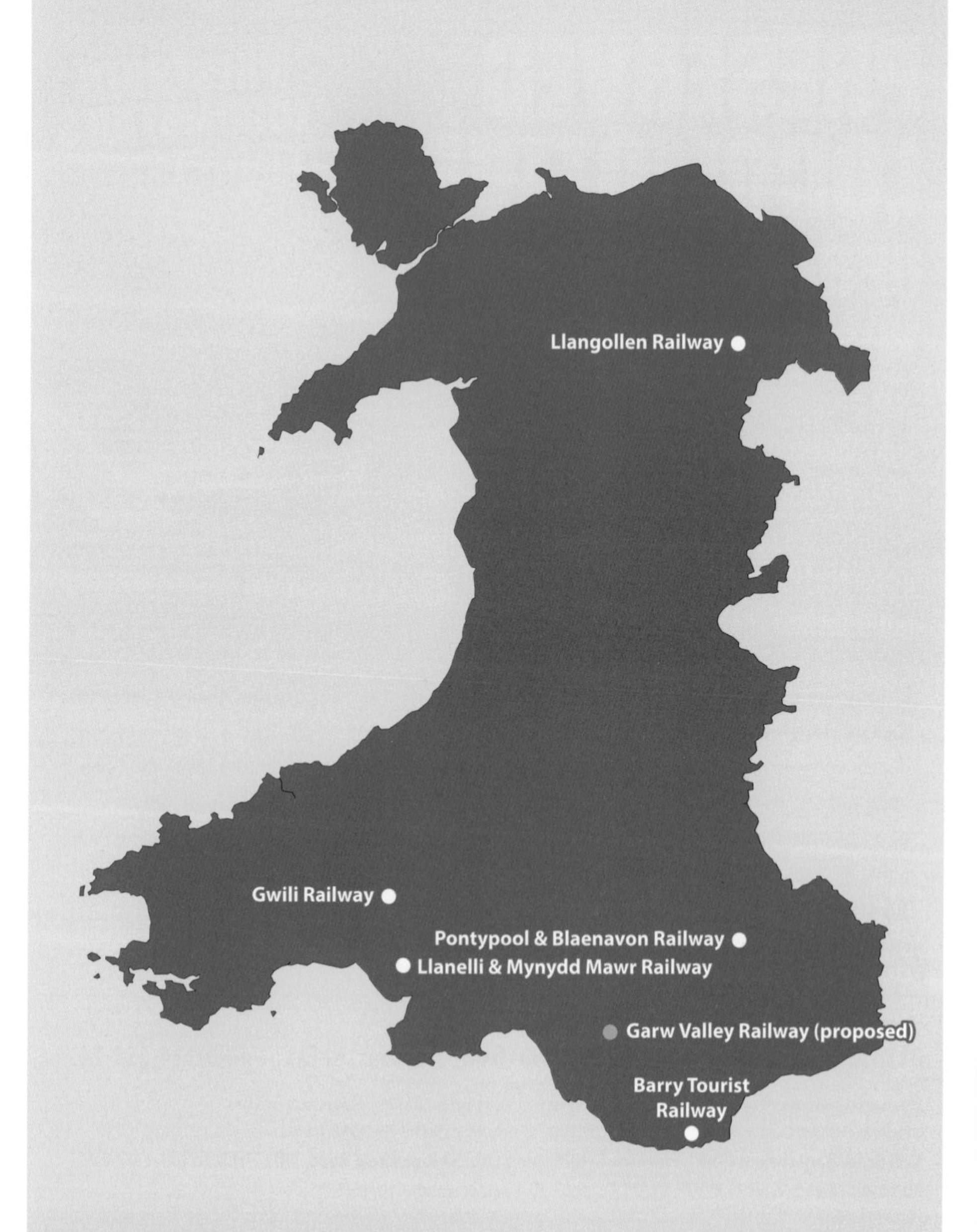
WALES
Llangollen Railway
Gwili Railway
Pontypool & Blaenavon Railway
Llanelli & Mynydd Mawr Railway
Garw Valley Railway (proposed)
Barry Tourist Railway

Region 3 – Wales

Barry Tourist Railway

Introduction and History

The railway first reached Barry and the town's docks in 1889. It was primarily built to create an alternative to Cardiff Docks for exporting minerals, although the railway also carried passengers. The line was cut back to Barry Island when Barry Pier station closed in 1976 and main line trains continue to terminate at Platform 1 of Barry Island station today. The Vale of Glamorgan Railway formed in 1994 and the first preserved trains operated from the Barry Island site in 1998. The railway was extended in stages, with heritage trains first crossing the causeway alongside the Barry Island–Barry Docks single line in 2002. They now continue to two destinations, Gladstone Bridge and a new station, Waterfront, adjacent to the site of the former Woodham's scrapyard. Since 2009 trains have been operated by Cambrian Transport and the railway shares the site with Barry Rail Centre.

Contact Details

Website: www.barrytouristrailway.co.uk
Tel: 01446 748816
Email: enquiries@barrytouristrailway.co.uk
Address: The Station Buildings, Station Approach, Barry Island, Vale of Glamorgan, CF62 5TH.

Transport Links

By Rail: Main line trains connect with the Barry Tourist Railway at Barry Island.
By Road: Parking is available outside Barry Island station (CF62 5TH) and there is free parking nearby.

Opening Times

During 2019 trains operate on these dates: 19–22 April, 4–6 May, 25–27 May, Saturdays and Sundays from 27 July to 25 August plus 26 August and 15 December. Trains depart from Barry Island at 11.35, 13.10, 14.10, and 15.10.

Line Mileage and Journey Time

0.00	Barry Island	0.00	Barry Island
1.00	Waterfront	1.25	Gladstone Bridge

A return journey takes about 45 minutes and includes a guided tour of the workshop, main shed or museum (one of the three facilities).

Stock List

Type	*Number*	*Builder*	*Details*
Steam	SUSAN	Sentinel	4wVBGT
Steam	6686	Armstrong Whitworth	0-6-2T
Steam	5539	GWR	2-6-2T
Steam	92245	British Railways	2-10-0
Diesel	08503	British Railways	Class 08
Diesel	20228	English Electric	Class 20
Electro-Diesel	73118	English Electric	Class 73
DMU	50222, 50338 & 56356	Metropolitan Cammell	Class 101
EMU	61280	British Railways	Class 489

Attractions

The railway can operate private charter trains for a full or a half day and offers driver experiences. The station at Barry Island is also home to Barry War Museum, which opens 14.00–16.00 on Wednesdays and 11.00–16.00 on the second Sunday of the month; admission is free. Nearby attractions include Barry Island Pleasure Park, Porthkerry Country Park, the beach and coast at Whitmore Bay. The city of Cardiff can be reached by train from Barry Island in 30 minutes.

Special Events during 2019

19–22 April: Easter Bunny Weekend; free Easter chocolate bunnies or toy for all children under 16.
4–6 May: Take a Toy Weekend; free toy for youngsters under 16.

25–27 May: Model Train Exhibition Weekend.
4 August: Craft Fair and 10k Race.
11 August: Toy and Train Fair.
15 December: Santa Specials.

Gwili Railway

Introduction and History

The Gwili Railway lies along the route which traversed West Wales from Carmarthen to Aberystwyth. It was originally a broad gauge railway, opening in 1860 to carry both passengers and local goods. Passenger services ceased in 1964 and the line continued to carry produce such as milk until its closure in 1973. The track was lifted in 1975, the same year in which the Gwili Railway Company was formed. The company acquired an eight-mile section of trackbed between Abergwili Junction and Llanpumsaint and the first preserved trains ran from Bronwydd Arms to Cwmdwyfran in 1978. The railway has since extended three times, across the River Gwili to Llwyfan Cerrig in 1987, to Danycoed in 2001 and to the former Abergwili Junction in 2017. Funds are being raised for a new station, car park, carriage shed and museum at Abergwili Junction and the railway aims to extend further north in future years.

Contact Details

Website: www.gwili-railway.co.uk
Tel: 01267 238213
Email: info@gwili-railway.co.uk
Address: Gwili Steam Railway, Bronwydd Arms Station, Bronwydd Arms, Carmarthenshire, SA33 6HT.

Transport Links

All trains depart from and return to Bronwydd Arms Station. There is no public access at Abergwili Junction, Llwyfan Cerrig or Danycoed Halt.
By Rail: Carmarthen railway station is three miles from Brownwydd Arms.
By Road: Car parking is available at Bronwydd Arms station (SA33 6HT).

Opening Times

The railway operates on 200 days each year, the main season being April–October. The standard timetable has trains leaving Bronwydd Arms at 11.00, 13.00 & 15.00 and there are additional trains on some dates, such as during special events.

Line Mileage and Journey Time

0.00	Abergwili Junction
1.50	Bronwydd Arms
3.25	Llwyfan Cerrig
3.75	Danycoed Halt

A return journey takes around one hour 45 minutes.

Stock List

Type	*Number*	*Builder*	*Details*
Steam	7058	Robert Stephenson & Hawthorns	0-4-0ST
Steam	1345	Peckett	0-4-0ST
Steam	HAULWEN	Vulcan Foundry	0-6-0ST
Steam	3829	Hunslet	0-6-0ST
Steam	71516	Robert Stephenson & Hawthorns	0-6-0ST
Steam	7849	Robert Stephenson & Hawthorns	0-6-0ST
Steam	20 (1731)	Hudswell Clarke	0-6-0T
Steam	28	Hunslet	0-6-2T
Diesel	D2178	British Railways	Class 03
DMU	51347, 51401 & 59508	Pressed Steel	Class 117

Attractions

The railway follows a scenic route along the course of the River Gwili. There is a working signal box and gift shop at Bronwydd Arms, a miniature railway at Llwyfan Cerrig and driver footplate experiences are available. The two foot gauge Teifi Valley Railway is about half an hour's drive away. Nearby attractions include Carmarthen with its 800-year-old market, the National Botanic Gardens of Wales and the Brecon Beacons National Park.

Special Events during 2019

19–22 April: Easter Special with entertainers and Easter eggs.
4–5 May: Welsh Food and Craft Festival.
2 June: 4 x 4 and Classic Bike Show.
22–23 June: Steam & Diesel Gala with visiting locomotives.
14 July: Classic Car Show.
Weekends in December: Santa's Magical Steam Trains.

There are regular dining trains with 'Sunday Dining', 'Strawberry Cream Teas' and 'Murder Mystery Evening Dining' events.

Llanelli & Mynydd Mawr Railway

Introduction and History

The first section of the four foot gauge horse-drawn tramway carrying ironstone to Llanelly Docks (as it was spelt at that time) opened in 1803. This was later extended to Cynheidre and Cross Hands; however, it fell into disuse as early as 1844. It was officially re-opened in 1883, although trains had been operating before 1883 and continued to carry minerals and coal until 1989, when Cynheidre Colliery closed. The railway never had a regular passenger service, although it saw regular workmen's services and occasional charter trains. After closure, an initial preservation group was not able to raise sufficient funds to buy the line and it was sold to the local authorities and converted into the Swiss Valley Cycle Route. This is now part of Route 47 of the National Cycle Network. The Llanelli and Mynydd Mawr Railway Company formed in 1999 with the aim of opening a heritage railway. The site of the former Cynheidre Colliery and approximately one mile of trackbed have been purchased. It first opened to the public in late 2017, making it the youngest heritage railway featured in this book. Currently trains operate along a quarter-mile section of track and the railway initially intends to extend northwards, increasing its length to just under one mile. There are also plans to create a visitor centre at Cynheidre and the long-term aim is to extend the railway as far as possible north and south, alongside the existing cycle path.

Contact Details

Website: www.llanellirailway.co.uk
Email: llanellirailway@gmail.com
Address: Llanelli & Mynydd Mawr Railway, Former Cynheidre Colliery, Llanelli, Carmarthenshire, SA15 5YF.

Transport Links

By Rail: The nearest railway station is Llanelli, which is six miles away.
By Road: Free parking is available Cynheidre (SA15 5YF - note this postcode is for the nearby village, turn right before Cynheidre Village sign if travelling from Llanelli).
By Bike: Route 47 of the National Cycle Network passes the Cynheidre site.

Opening Times

During 2019, the railway will operate 10.30–15.00 on 30 March, 27 April, 25 May, 29 June, 31 August, 26 October and 7 & 8 December. Working parties also take place from 10.00 on most Saturday mornings.

Line Mileage and Journey Time

Trains operate for approximately one quarter of a mile and the journey time is relatively short.

Stock List

Type	Number	Builder	Details
Diesel	394014	Ruston & Hornsby	0-4-0
Diesel	10222	Sentinel	0-4-0
Diesel	690	English Electric	0-6-0
DMU	55019	GRCW	Class 122

Attractions

There is a small heritage centre and a static buffet coach selling refreshments at Cynheidre. Guided tours of the site and stock shed are available by advance arrangement, for which donations are suggested. Nature trails are organised in conjunction with a local wildlife group, to explore the area's plant and animal wildlife. Nearby attractions include Gwili Railway (see page 66), Llyn Llech Owain Country Park, Llanelli WWT National Wetland Centre and the National Botanic Gardens of Wales.

Special Events during 2019

30 March: 20th Anniversary Gala.
27 April: Half Term Event.
25 May: Half Term Event.
26 October: Half Term Event.
7–8 December: Christmas Event.

Llangollen Railway

Introduction and History

Llangollen is at the eastern end of the railway which ran across central Wales from Ruabon to Barmouth, opening in full in 1865 and closing to passengers a century later in 1965. It survived for freight use until 1968, soon after which the track was lifted and many of the stations were demolished. The first preservation group formed in 1972 and by 1975 Llangollen station had reopened. The railway extended to Berwyn in 1985, Deeside in 1990, Glyndyfrdwy in 1992, Carrog in 1996 and to the temporary terminus at Corwen East in 2014. A further extension to a new station in the centre of Corwen with a locomotive run round loop is due to be completed during 2019.

Contact Details

Website: www.llangollen-railway.co.uk
Tel: 01978 860979
Email: info@llangollen-railway.co.uk
Address: Llangollen Railway, The Station, Abbey Road, Llangollen, LL20 8SN.

Transport Links

By Rail: Ruabon is the nearest railway station and is six miles from Llangollen.
By Road: Corwen station (LL21 0DN) is the best place to arrive by car as there is ample parking space. There is only limited parking at Carrog (LL21 9BD), no parking at Berwyn or Glyndyfrdwy stations and limited disabled parking only at Llangollen (LL20 8SN).

Opening Times

Daily services operate from April until mid-November, finishing with Santa Specials in December. A variety of timetables operate through the season, please check the website for the latest details.

Line Mileage and Journey Time

0.00	Llangollen
1.50	Berwyn
3.25	Deeside Halt
5.25	Glyndyfrdwy
7.25	Carrog
10.00	Corwen Central

A return journey takes a minimum of 1 hour 40 minutes, the time taken depending on the starting point.

▲ **Gwili Railway:** The Gwili's Railway's Class 117 DMU, 51401, 59508 and 51347, stands at Llwyfan Cerrig after arrival from Bronwydd Arms on 14 August 2010. **Robert Pritchard**

▼ **Llangollen Railway:** Carrog station lay dormant from 1964 until 1996, when it was reopened by the Llangollen Railway. With wagons, carriages and a crane visible in the goods yard, an operational signal box and luggage trolleys on the platform, the period detail belie the date. Class 26 No. D5310 pauses while Class 37 No. 6940 is attached to the rear of the 1255 Llangollen–Corwen service on 23 September 2017. **Andy Chard**

Stock List

Type	Number	Builder	Details
Steam	DESMOND (1498)	Avonside	0-4-0ST
Steam	6430	GWR	0-6-0PT
Steam	7754	GWR	0-6-0PT
Steam	1	Kitson	0-6-0ST
Steam	68030	Hunslet	0-6-0ST
Steam	17 (1338)	Andrew Barclay	0-6-0T
Steam	1873	Hunslet	0-6-0T
Steam	4160	GWR	2-6-2PT
Steam	5199	GWR	2-6-2T
Steam	5532	GWR	2-6-2T
Steam	80072	British Railways	2-6-4T
Steam	4709	Great Western Society	2-8-0
Steam	3802	GWR	2-8-0
Steam	3814	GWR	2-8-0
Steam	45337	Armstrong Whitworth	4-6-0
Steam	61673	B17 SLT	4-6-0
Steam	6880	Betton Grange Society	4-6-0
Steam	5952	GWR	4-6-0
Steam	5551	LMS-Patriot Project	4-6-0
Diesel	2782	Yorkshire Engine Co.	0-4-0
Diesel	1901	English Electric	0-6-0
Diesel	03162	British Railways	Class 03
Diesel	08195	British Railways	Class 08
Diesel	D5310	BRCW	Class 26
Diesel	31271	Brush Traction	Class 31
Diesel	1566	British Railways	Class 47
DMU	50447, 50454 & 50528	BRCW	Class 104
DMU	56456	Cravens	Class 105
DMU	51933, 56223 & 56504	British Railways	Class 108
DMU	50416 & 56171	Wickham	Class 109
DMU	51618	British Railways	Class 127

Attractions

The railway has a large steam and diesel locomotive fleet and offers driver experiences using some of these. There is a railway workshop at Llangollen, where construction of new-build steam loco 6880 "Betton Grange" is under way. The railway runs through part of a UNESCO World Heritage Site and an Area of Outstanding Natural Beauty, following the River Dee which is home to migratory salmon, otters and lampreys. It is also close to the Llangollen Canal and the Berwyn Mountains. The market town of Llangollen has been popular with tourists for centuries and there are many walks, picturesque views and rural areas to explore from the stations along the route. Cambrian Heritage Railways (see page 75) and the Tanat Valley Railway (see page 88) are nearby on the other side of the English border.

Special Events during 2019

23–24 March: Peppa Pig Event.
31 March: Mother's Day Event.
13 April: 1940s Weekend.
16 June: Father's Day Event.
6–7 July: Classic Transport Weekend.
3–4 August: 1960s Event.
17 August: Steam & Jazz Train.
14 September: Oktoberfest.
28–29 September: Diesel Weekend.
10–13 October: Autumn Steam Gala.
27 October: Halloween Train.
December: Santa Specials.

Pontypool & Blaenavon Railway

Introduction and History
The railway from Brynmawr to Blaenavon opened in 1869; passenger services commenced in 1870 and it was subsequently extended south to Pontypool. Passenger traffic ended in 1941 and the last of the coal trains ran from Blaenavon to Pontypool in 1980 when Big Pit closed. The first heritage trains ran in 1983, when the line between Furnace Sidings and Whistle Inn Halt opened. The railway extended south to Blaenavon High Level station in 2010 and along the spur to Big Pit in 2011. There are long-term plans to further extend north to Waunavon and Brynmawr and also to the south, sharing the route with the present cycle path.

Contact Details
Website: www.pontypool-and-blaenavon.co.uk
Tel: 01495 792263
Email: Written enquiries can be made from the website.
Address: Pontypool & Blaenavon Railway, The Railway Station, Furnace Sidings, Garn Yr Erw, Blaenavon, NP4 9SF.

Transport Links
By Rail: The nearest railway stations are Abergavenny and Ebbw Vale Town (both seven miles), however there are good bus connections from Cwmbran (details on P&BR website).
By Road: There is ample free parking at the Furnace Sidings base (NP4 9SF).

Opening Times
Trains operate 10.30–16.00 at weekends from Easter to early September, plus selected Wednesdays during school holidays and on some days during October and December.

Line Mileage and Journey Time
0.00 Coed Avon
0.25 Blaenavon High Level
1.50 Furnace Sidings
2.00 Whistle Inn Halt

0.0 Furnace Sidings
0.5 Big Pit Halt

A round trip takes about one hour five minutes.

Stock List

Type	Number	Builder	Details
Steam	9622	Sentinel	4wVBGT
Steam	1823	Andrew Barclay	0-4-0ST
Steam	FORESTER	Andrew Barclay	0-4-0ST
Steam	ROSYTH No.1	Andrew Barclay	0-4-0ST
Steam	2015	Andrew Barclay	0-4-0ST
Steam	2201	Andrew Barclay	0-4-0ST
Steam	9629	GWR	0-6-0PT
Steam	1 (2074)	Andrew Barclay	0-6-0ST
Steam	SIR JOHN (1680)	Avonside	0-6-0ST
Steam	2 (1421)	Avonside	0-6-0ST
Steam	EMPRESS	Bagnell	0-6-0ST
Steam	71515	Robert Stephenson & Hawthorns	0-6-0ST
Diesel	Blaenavon No. 14	Hudswell Clarke	0-4-0
Diesel	03141	British Railways	Class 03
Diesel	D5627	Brush Traction	Class 31
Diesel	D6916	English Electric	Class 37
DMU	50632 & 52044	British Railways	Class 108
DMU	51351 & 51397	Pressed Steel	Class 117

Attractions
The railway has one of the steepest gradients on a standard gauge heritage railway in the country and the rolling stock includes restored vintage saloons which are used on selected weekends. 'Heritage Railway Experiences' are available, assisting the driver and train guard with their duties. The Pontypool & Blaenavon Model Railway Club is based at the Furnace Sidings site and has railways in several different gauges on display and under construction.

The National Coal Mining Museum and Rhymney Brewery are near to Big Pit station. Blaenavon Heritage Centre and the Ironworks are a ten and 15 minute walk from Blaenavon High Level respectively. Route 492 of the National Cycle Network follows the present railway and much of the disused route between Blaenavon and Pontypool.

Special Events during 2019

26–27 May: Coal Train Weekend.
8–9 June: Model Railway Weekend.
25–26 August: Classic Transport Show.
13–15 September: Steam Gala.
26–27 & 30–31 October: Ghost Train.
30 November, 1, 7–8, 14–15 & 21–22 December: Santa Specials.

▲ **Pontypool & Blaenavon Railway:** Class 31 No. D5627 "Steve Organ G.M." looks immaculately turned out in the early spring sunshine at the Pontypool & Blaenavon Railway on 1 April 2017. Note the cycle path sharing the route with trains, which is a pragmatic solution on a number of heritage railways where the route has become a cycle or walkway. **Alistair Grieve**

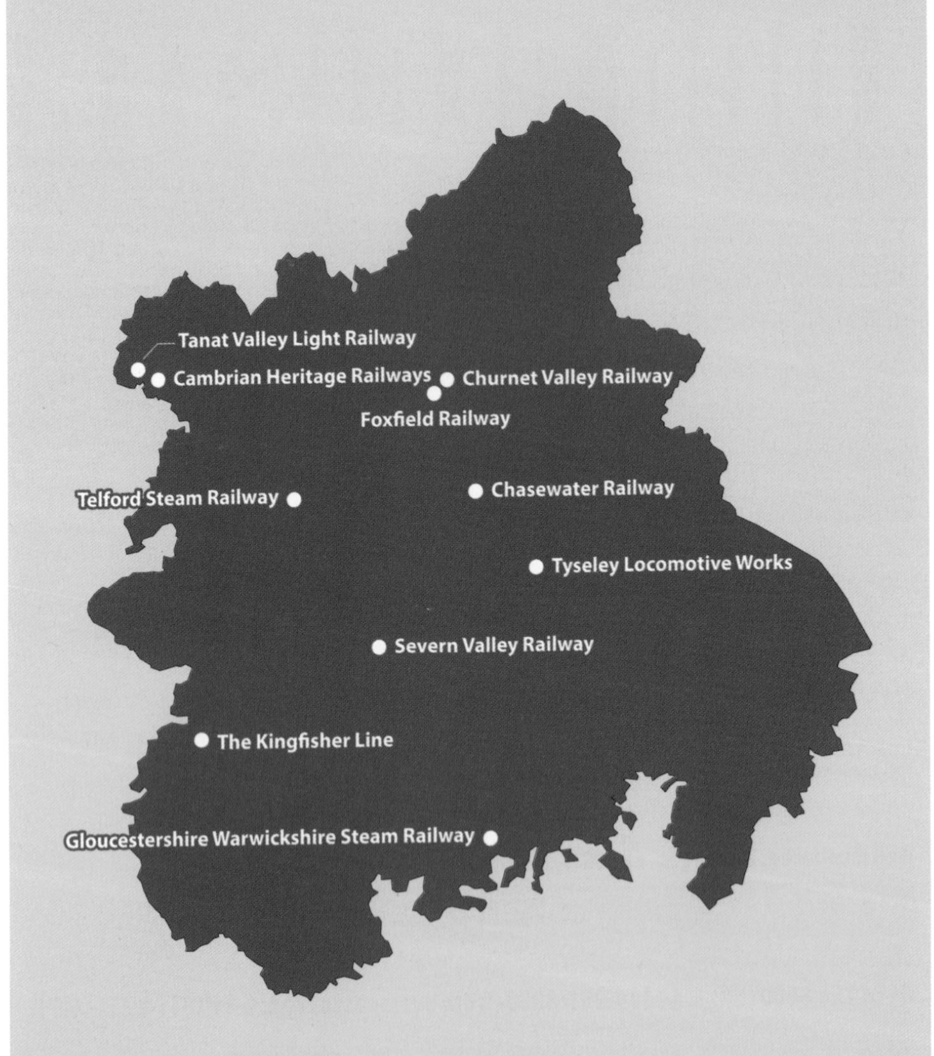
WEST MIDLANDS
Tanat Valley Light Railway
Cambrian Heritage Railways
Churnet Valley Railway
Foxfield Railway
Telford Steam Railway
Chasewater Railway
Tyseley Locomotive Works
Severn Valley Railway
The Kingfisher Line
Gloucestershire Warwickshire Steam Railway

Region 4 – West Midlands

Cambrian Heritage Railways

Introduction and History

The branch line from Gobowen to Oswestry opened in 1848. A separate railway and station opened in Oswestry in 1860, heading south and this included the branch from Llynclys Junction to the quarry at Porthywaen. After the 1923 Grouping, improvements were made to what had become the Cambrian Railways station at Oswestry, enabling the former GWR station to close in 1924. Passenger services between Gobowen and Oswestry ended in 1966; stone trains from Gobowen to Blodwell continued until 1988 and the final weed killing train ran in 1993. A group of enthusiasts formed the Cambrian Railways Society (CRS) in 1972 and leased Oswestry goods yard from British Rail. The society opened a railway museum and from 1997 trains carried passengers on a short stretch of track. In 1998 the separate Cambrian Railways Trust (CRT) formed, aiming to return trains from Gobowen to Blodwell and began negotiations with Railtrack (subsequently Network Rail) to purchase the trackbed. A further group leased the trackbed between Llynclys and Pant after it was purchased by Oswestry Council. They relaid a 1200 m length of track and started operating trains from 2005. Also in 2005, the local council bought Oswestry station and funding was obtained to restore the building and site. The CRS and CRT merged in 2009 forming Cambrian Heritage Railways, which now operates trains from both the Oswestry and Llynclys sites. Work on extending the railway south from Oswestry is progressing and new sections are due to open in stages by mid-2020. The long-term aim is for heritage trains to operate for more than eight miles from Gobowen to Blodwell via Oswestry.

Contact Details

Website: www.cambrianrailways.com
Tel: 01691 728131
Email: enquiries@cambrianrailways.com
Address: Cambrian Heritage Railways, Old Station Building, Oswald Road, Oswestry, Shropshire, SY11 1RE.

Transport Links

By Rail: Gobowen railway station is two and a half miles from the Oswestry site and eight miles from Llynclys.
By Road: Chargeable car parking is available at Oswestry (SY11 1RE) and there is free parking at Llynclys (SY10 8BX).

Opening Times

Oswestry Railway Museum is open 11.00–15.00 Tuesdays–Fridays from Easter to September.
Llynclys Operating Dates: Saturdays and Bank Holidays May–mid-September.
Oswestry Operating Dates: Sundays and Bank Holidays May–mid-September.

Line Mileage and Journey Time

Trains currently operate for three quarters of a mile from Llynclys, for quarter of a mile from Oswestry and the journey time is relatively short.

Stock List

Type	*Number*	*Builder*	*Details*
Steam	2261	Andrew Barclay	0-4-0ST
Steam	2131 OLIVER VELTOM	Peckett	0-4-0ST
Steam	1430	Peckett	0-4-0ST
Steam	885	Andrew Barclay	0-6-0ST
Steam	3770 NORMA	Hunslet	0-6-0ST
Diesel	D893	Hudswell Clarke	0-4-0
Diesel	TELEMON	Drewry	0-4-0
Diesel	CYRIL	Hibberd	0-4-0
Diesel	ALPHA	Hibberd	0-4-0
Diesel	11517	Ruston & Hornsby	0-4-0
Diesel	SCOTTIE	Ruston & Hornsby	0-4-0
Diesel	D1230	English Electric	0-6-0
Diesel	H037	English Electric	0-6-0

Diesel	D3019	British Railways	Class 08
DMU	51512, 51187, 51205 & 56055	Metropolitan Cammell	Class 101

Attractions

There are two sites to visit, both operating passenger trains, although not necessarily on the same dates. The Oswestry site is home to an ornate station building and the Cambrian Railway Museum within the goods shed. Nearby attractions include Oswestry Town Museum, Pontcysyllte Aqueduct, Chirk Castle, the Tanat Valley Light Railway (see page 88) and the Llangollen Railway (see page 68).

Special Events during 2019

31 March: Mother's Day Afternoon Tea.

▲ **Chasewater Railway:** Visiting the Chasewater Railway for its "Made in Staffordshire" Gala on 26 May 2018 was 0-4-0WT, aptly named "Willy the Well Tank", from Bill Parker's Bream workshops. It is seen departing Chasewater Heaths station at the head of a rake of mineral wagons with Bagnall 0-4-0ST No. 2 providing banking. **Martyn Tattam**

Chasewater Railway

Introduction and History

The industrial railways around Cannock Chase opened in the 1860s and were used to carry coal from a number of collieries in the area. This continued until the 1960s when the coal mines and railway network were closed. The first preservation group (Railway Preservation Society, West Midlands District) formed in 1959 and in 1960 it acquired two derelict coaches and a rail-connected base at Hednesford. The first locomotive arrived in 1961 and in 1964 a 25-year lease was signed for a new site, on a section of trackbed on the former Aldridge–Brownhills branch. The first heritage trains ran on this in 1968 when Hawthorne Leslie 0-4-0ST "Asbestos" gave brake van rides. By 1970 all the rolling stock had been transferred from Hednesford to the Brownhills site, where regular operating days were taking place. The railway had to close between 1982 and 1985, as funds were not available for necessary repairs to the railway where it crosses the causeway. These were subsequently carried out and the railway has since reopened and was extended to Norton Lakeside in 1994, Chasewater Heaths in 1995 and Chasetown in 2004.

Contact Details

Website: www.chasewaterrailway.co.uk
Tel: 01543 452623
Email: info@chasewaterrailway.co.uk
Address: Chasewater Country Park, Brownhills West Station, Pool Lane, Burntwood, Staffordshire, WS8 7NL.

Transport Links

By Rail: The nearest railway station is Landywood, which is five miles away.
By Road: There is ample free parking at Brownhills West (WS8 7NL). Note that vehicle access to Brownhills West is only available via the A5 end of Pool Road – follow the brown signs.

Opening Times

The railway opens most Sundays and Bank Holidays, plus selected weekdays from March to October. Trains operate between 11.00 and 16.00 or 17.00, depending on which timetable is operating.

Line Mileage and Journey Time

0.00	Brownhills West
1.00	Norton Lakeside Halt
1.50	Chasewater Heaths
1.75	Chasetown

A return journey takes about one hour.

Stock List

Type	*Number*	*Builder*	*Details*
Steam	5 (9632)	Sentinel	4wVBT
Steam	COLIN McANDREW (1223)	Andrew Barclay	0-4-0ST
Steam	DUNLOP No.6 (2648)	Bagnall	0-4-0ST
Steam	2 (2842)	Bagnall	0-4-0ST
Steam	ASBESTOS (2780)	Hawthorn Leslie	0-4-0ST
Steam	2937	Neilson & Co	0-4-0ST
Steam	6 (917)	Peckett	0-4-0ST
Steam	TEDDY (2012)	Peckett	0-4-0ST
Steam	431	Hudswell Clarke	0-6-0ST
Steam	HOLLY BANK No.3	Hunslet	0-6-0ST
Steam	S100 (1822)	Hudswell Clarke	0-6-0T
Diesel	3097	Bagnall	0-4-0
Diesel	3027	Baguley	0-4-0
Diesel	3410	Baguley	0-4-0
Diesel	3590	Baguley	0-4-0
Diesel	4100013	Fowler	0-4-0
Diesel	4220015	Fowler	0-4-0
Diesel	6678	Hunslet	0-4-0

Diesel	D2911	North British	0-4-0
Diesel	530003 MYFANWY	Robert Stephenson & Hawthorns	0-4-0
Diesel	15097	Simplex	0-4-0
Diesel	15099	Simplex	0-4-0
Diesel	3208	Bagnall	0-4-0
Diesel	01568 HELEN	Thomas Hill	0-4-0
Diesel	DERBYSHIRE STONE No.2 (1891)	Hibberd	0-4-0
Diesel	21 (1612)	Hibberd	0-4-0
Diesel	305306	Ruston & Hornsby	0-4-0
Diesel	3119	Bagnall	0-6-0
DMU	59444	British Railways	Class 116
DMU	59603	British Railways	Class 127

Attractions

At Brownhills West, there is a railway museum with a large collection of exhibits, plus a gift and model shop. The railway travels around and across Chasewater, which is a canal reservoir. The area has a variety of walks, trails and cycle routes. Norton Lakeside is a Site of Special Scientific Interest and there is a nearby wildfowl reserve, which can also be explored on foot or bicycle (trains carry cycles at no extra charge). Nearby attractions include Chasewater Country Park, Wakelake, Beacon Park and the city of Lichfield.

Special Events during 2019

6–7 March: Coal Train Weekend.
26–27 May: 60th Anniversary of RPS West Midlands (forerunner of Chasewater Railway).
28 May: Wizards & Witches Event.
16 June: 1940s Day.
14 July: Brewery Locomotives Day.
28 July: Vintage Fair.
11 August: Charities Day.
12–13 October: Moving The Goods Weekend.
25–26 October: Halloween Special.
December Weekends & Christmas Eve: Santa Specials.

Churnet Valley Railway

Introduction and History

The railways which comprise today's Churnet Valley Railway are the remnants of a number of lines built at different times. The route from Macclesfield to Uttoxeter via Leek opened in 1849 and became known as the Churnet Valley Line, after the course of the river it follows. This carried minerals from local quarries and connected with a number of industrial narrow gauge railways in the area. The line from Stoke-on-Trent to Milton Junction opened in 1864, as part of the Stoke–Congleton route. From Milton Junction to Leekbrook Junction, near Cheddleton, opened in 1867 and the line from Leekbrook Junction to Waterhouses in 1905, where it connected with a narrow gauge line to Hulme End. Passenger services on the Waterhouses branch ended in 1935 and the line was cut back to Cauldon Lowe quarry in 1943. Passenger trains ceased on the Leek–Stoke route in 1956 and on the Macclesfield–Uttoxeter Churnet Valley Line in 1960. The first preservation group formed in the 1970s and Cheddleton became its base from 1977, while freight continued from Stoke-on-Trent to the quarries at Oakmoor until 1988 and to Cauldon Lowe until 1989. The first train in preservation ran for a short distance from Cheddleton in 1996 and since then the railway has been extended in a number of stages. Planning consent has been given to further extend north to Leek and there are plans to extend to Endon in the Stoke-on-Trent direction and return heritage trains to Cauldon Lowe.

Contact Details

Website: www.churnetvalleyrailway.co.uk
Tel: 01538 750755
Email: enquiries@churnetvalleyrailway.co.uk
Address: Churnet Valley Railway, Kingsley and Froghall Station, Froghall, Staffordshire, ST10 2HA.

Transport Links

By Rail: Stoke-on-Trent station is nine miles from Cheddleton and Blythe Bridge is seven miles from Kingsley & Froghall.
By Road: There is free parking at both Cheddleton (ST13 7EE) and Kingsley & Froghall (ST10 2HA) stations.

Opening Times

The railway operates on Sundays in March & October, every Saturday & Sunday April to September and selected other weekdays.

Line Mileage and Journey Time

0.00	Ipstones
5.50	Cheddleton
7.75	Consall
9.75	Kingsley & Froghall

A return journey Froghall–Cheddleton takes about 1 hour 10 minutes, plus a further 1 hour 10 minutes to travel to Ipstones.

Stock List

Type	*Number*	*Builder*	*Details*
Steam	KATIE	Andrew Barclay	0-4-0ST
Steam	2871	Fablok	0-6-0T
Steam	2944	Fablok	0-6-0T
Steam	5197	Lima Locomotive Co	2-8-0
Steam	6046	Baldwin Locomotive Works	2-8-0
Steam	48173	LMS	2-8-0
Diesel	BRIGHTSIDE	Yorkshire Engine Co.	0-4-0
Diesel	6 ROGER H BENNET	Yorkshire Engine Co.	0-6-0
Diesel	D3800	British Railways	Class 08
Diesel	D8057	English Electric	Class 20
Diesel	25322	British Railways	Class 25
Diesel	33021	BRCW	Class 33
Diesel	33102	BRCW	Class 33
Diesel	47524	British Railways	Class 47

Attractions

There is a small museum at Cheddleton station, housed within the original 1849 station building and the site has a loco shed and goods yard. The railway offers steam footplate rides and driver experience courses. Cheddleton Flint Mill is a short walk away from the station. The region is home to Peak Wildlife Park and the market town of Leek, which is on the edge of the Peak District. The Manifold Way is a cycle and footpath along the trackbed of the former Leek & Manifold Light Railway. Nearby heritage railways include Peak Rail (see page 110), the Foxfield Railway (see page 81) and the Ecclesbourne Valley Railway (see page 97).

Special Events during 2019

31 March: Mother's Day Trains & Lunch.
4–6 May: Diesel Gala.
11–12 May: Classic Car Days.
31 May–2 June: Anything Goes and Food & Drink Festival.
5–7 July: Real Ale Trail Event.
23–26 August: Gin & Trains Event.
28–29 September: War in the Valley.
30 November–24 December: Santa & Steam.

The railway operates trains serving Staffordshire cream teas and three course lunches on various dates.

▲ **Churnet Valley Railway:** United States Army Transportation Corps Class S160 No. 5197 heads away from Consal on the Churnet Valley Railway on 4 February 2018. The Cauldon Canal is in the foreground. **Robert Falconer**

▼ **Foxfield Railway:** Recreating the days when Class 14 shunters were placed into industrial use, D9531 "Ernie", visiting from the East Lancashire Railway and wearing its NCB identity, stands beside one of the Foxfield Railway's distinctive headstocks during a photo charter on 13 May 2018. **Martyn Tattam**

Foxfield Railway

Introduction and History

The branch line from Blythe Bridge to Foxfield Colliery in Dilhorne, Staffordshire was built in 1893, taking a circuitous route over steep gradients to keep the railway as far away as possible from Dilhorne Hall. The colliery closed in 1965 and the site was taken over by a mineral processing firm which wanted to retain the railway for carrying minerals. At this time the Foxfield Light Railway Society formed to operate trains over the line, with the agreement of the owning company. No further commercial freight trains operated; however, in 1967 the first heritage trains worked, carrying passengers in converted wagons. Carriages and further locomotives were subsequently acquired and a new station was built at Caverswall Road. The main line connection near Blythe Bridge has been removed and the railway currently operates passenger services to Dilhorne Park; it hopes to extend these to include the steeply graded Foxfield Bank by 2020.

Contact Details

Website: www.foxfieldrailway.co.uk
Tel: 01782 396210
Email: Written enquiries can be made from the website.
Address: Foxfield Railway Station, Caverswall Road, Blythe Bridge, Stoke-on-Trent, ST11 9BG.

Transport Links

By Rail: The nearest station is Blythe Bridge, which is half a mile away.
By Road: Free parking is available at Caverswall Road (ST11 9BG).

Opening Times

The railway operates on Sundays, Bank Holidays and selected other dates from April to October. Trains run 11.30–16.45 or 12.00–15.45, depending on which timetable is in operation.

Line Mileage and Journey Time

0.00	Caverswall Road
2.00	Dilhorne Park

A return journey takes about 45 minutes.

Stock List

Type	*Number*	*Builder*	*Details*
Steam	9535	Sentinel	4wVBGT
Steam	4101	Dübs & Company	0-4-0CT
Steam	1563	Avonside	0-4-0ST
Steam	HAWARDEN (2623)	Bagnall	0-4-0ST
Steam	1827	Beyer Peacock	0-4-0ST
Steam	3581	Hawthorn Leslie	0-4-0ST
Steam	4388	Kerr Stuart	0-4-0ST
Steam	MOSS BAY	Kerr Stuart	0-4-0ST
Steam	11 (2081)	Peckett	0-4-0ST
Steam	HENRY CORT	Peckett	0-4-0ST
Steam	1803	Peckett	0-4-0ST
Steam	6	Robert Heath	0-4-0ST
Steam	7063	Robert Stephenson & Hawthorns	0-4-0ST
Steam	FLORENCE No.2 (3059)	Bagnall	0-6-0ST
Steam	LEWISHAM	Bagnall	0-6-0ST
Steam	WHISTON	Hunslet	0-6-0ST
Steam	1207	Manning Wardle	0-6-0ST
Steam	ACKTON HALL No.3 (1567)	Peckett	0-6-0ST
Steam	WIMBLEBURY	Hunslet	0-6-0ST
Steam	BELLEROPHON	Haydock	0-6-0WT
Steam	2	North Staffordshire Railway	0-6-2T
Diesel	3207	Bagnall	0-4-0
Diesel	WD820	English Electric	0-4-0
Diesel	424841	Ruston & Hornsby	0-4-0
Diesel	111C	Thomas Hill	0-4-0

Diesel	242915	Ruston & Hornsby	0-4-0
Diesel	408496	Ruston & Hornsby	0-4-0
Diesel	2262	Simplex	0-4-0
Diesel	4421	Kerr Stuart	0-4-0
Diesel	CLIVE (486)	Andrew Barclay	0-6-0
Diesel	3150	Bagnall	0-6-0
Diesel	22497	Fowler	0-6-0
Diesel	LUDSTONE (2868)	Yorkshire Engine Co.	0-6-0
Electric	1130	English Electric	0-4-0

Attractions

The railway showcases its industrial history with a large collection of industrial locomotives and wagons. Driving experiences are available, using either steam or diesel locomotives. There is a miniature railway which has steep gradients and a variety of steam, petrol and battery locomotives. This is approximately one quarter of a mile long and operates on selected Sundays. There is a museum at Caverswall Road, which has a large collection of railway exhibits; this opens on Sundays, Bank Holidays and Wednesdays during school holidays from April to October. The site also has a souvenir & model railway shop, a real ale bar and station buffet. Nearby attractions include the Churnet Valley Railway (see page 78), World of Wedgewood and Potteries Museum & Art Gallery in Stoke-on-Trent.

Special Events during 2019

6–7 April: Miniature Mayhem.
14 April: 20th Anniversary Classic & Vintage Rally.
19–22 April: Easter Weekend – Kids travel free!
27–28 April: Diesel Gala.
18–19 May: War Wheels.
14 July: Bikers and Steam.
20–21 July: Summer Festival of Steam.
15 September: Vintage Rally.
28–29 September: Autumn Festival of Steam.
6 October: Autumn Vehicle Rally.
26–27 October: Halloween Ghost Trains.
30 November & 1, 7–8, 14–15, 21–22 & 24 December: Santa Specials.

▲ **Gloucestershire Warwickshire Steam Railway:** BR blue-liveried Class 24 No. 5081 and Class 26 No. D5343 pass Dixton with 2T62, the 12.40 Cheltenham Race Course–Toddington during the GWR diesel gala on 30 July 2016. **Nigel Gibbs**

Gloucestershire Warwickshire Steam Railway

Introduction and History

The railway from Stratford-upon-Avon to Cheltenham via Honeybourne opened in 1906. Passenger services ceased in 1960, although freight and occasional trains to Cheltenham races continued until 1976 when the line closed. The GWSR was formed in 1981, purchasing the trackbed from Cheltenham to Broadway in 1984. The first heritage trains worked on an initial quarter-mile long section. Since then, the railway has extended to Cheltenham Race Course, where the station opened in 2003, and to Broadway in 2018, taking the line to a length of over 13 miles. There are long-term aspirations to extend about four miles further north to Honeybourne and connect with the national rail network and also extend a further three quarters of a mile south to the outskirts of Cheltenham.

Contact Details

Website: www.gwsr.com
Tel: 01242 621405
Email: info@gwsr.com
Address: The Railway Station, Toddington, Gloucestershire, GL54 5DT.

Transport Links

By Rail: The nearest main line railway station is Cheltenham Spa. Stagecoach services D and E operate regularly Monday–Saturday from Cheltenham Spa to Cheltenham Race Course.
By Road: There are car parks at Cheltenham Race Course (GL50 4SH) and Toddington (GL54 5DT) stations. There is limited parking at Winchcombe (GL54 5LD), limited disabled parking only at Broadway station and no parking at Hayles Abbey Halt or Gotherington.

Opening Times

Trains operate regularly from mid-March until late October, plus Santa Specials in December.

Line Mileage and Journey Time

0.00	Broadway
4.00	Toddington
6.50	Winchcombe
10.00	Gotherington
13.50	Cheltenham Race Course

A return journey takes up to three hours.

Stock List

Type	*Number*	*Builder*	*Details*
Steam	1976	Peckett	0-4-0ST
Steam	76077	British Railways	2-6-0
Steam	2807	GWR	2-8-0
Steam	2874	GWR	2-8-0
Steam	3850	GWR	2-8-0
Steam	4270	GWR	2-8-0T
Steam	7820	British Railways	4-6-0
Steam	7903	British Railways	4-6-0
Steam	35006	Southern Railway	4-6-2
Diesel	11230	Drewry	0-6-0
Diesel	372	Yorkshire Engine Co.	0-6-0
Diesel	D2182	British Railways	Class 03
Diesel	D2280	Robert Stephenson & Hawthorns	Class 04
Diesel	2001 (20035)	English Electric	Class 20
Diesel	D8137	English Electric	Class 20
Diesel	5081	British Railways	Class 24
Diesel	D5343	BRCW	Class 26
Diesel	37215	English Electric	Class 37
Diesel	D6948	English Electric	Class 37
Diesel	45149	British Railways	Class 45
Diesel	47105	Brush Traction	Class 47
Diesel	47376	Brush Traction	Class 47

Electro-Diesel	E6036	English Electric	Class 73
DMU	52029	British Railways	Class 107
DMU	51360, 51363, 51372, 51405 & 59510	Pressed Steel	Class 117
DMU	55003	GRCW	Class 122

Attractions
Visitors can see inside the locomotive depot at Toddington. The two foot gauge Toddington Narrow Gauge Railway has steam and diesel locomotives and starts from Toddington station car park, travelling for approximately three quarters of a mile. The Royal Mail Model Railway Team's 'N' and 'OO' gauge model railways, based in a coach at Winchcombe station, are open most weekends and during special event dates. Cheltenham Racecourse is next to its namesake station. Nearby attractions include Berkeley Castle, Blenheim Palace, Sudeley Castle, the Cotswolds and a number of market towns.

Special Events during 2019
22 April: Easter Eggspress.
27–28 April: Wartime in the Cotswolds.
25–27 May: Cotswold Festival of Steam Gala.
9 June: Classic Vehicle Clubs Day.
21–23 June: Steam & Real Ale Weekend.
26–28 July: Heritage Diesel Gala & Classic Bus Rally on 28 July.
Tuesdays during August: Teddy Bear Specials.
10–11 August: Southern Lego Train Club's Cotswold Bricks & Trains Weekend.
11 August: Heritage Engineering Skills Day (especially for young people).
8 September: Classic Vehicle Day.
5–6 October: Autumn Diesel Weekend.
19–20 October: Cotswold Food & Drink Fayre.
30 November, 1, 7–8, 14–15 & 20–24 December: Santa Specials.
14 December: Evening Carols by Steam Train.

The Kingfisher Line

Introduction and History
The railway from Leominster to Kington opened in 1857. It was extended west to New Radnor in 1875 and north along a new branch from Titley to Presteigne, when Titley station became Titley Junction. The final train to carry passengers was a railtour in 1957 to mark the line's centenary, which worked to both termini of New Radnor and Presteigne. Freight continued until 1964 when the line closed. Titley Junction station became a private residence and restoration began in the 1980s. From 2005 trains started to operate on a one-mile stretch of the former railway on selected opening days.

Contact Details
Website: Search for "Titley Junction station" on Facebook
Tel: 01544 340622
Email: kingfisherline@icloud.com
Address: Titley Junction Station, Titley, Herefordshire, HR5 3RX.

Transport Links
By Rail: The nearest stations are Leominster (13 miles) and Knighton (12 miles).
By Road: Parking is available at the station site (HR5 3RX).

Opening Times
Titley Juction station and the railway line are on a private site and access is only available for groups of between 10 and 40 people on some Sundays, by prior arrangement. Due to illness, the site may not open during 2019. Please check the site's Facebook page for the latest information.

Line Mileage and Journey Time
The railway operates for approximately one mile and the journey time is relatively short.

Stock List

Type	*Number*	*Builder*	*Details*
Steam	1738	Peckett	0-4-0ST
Diesel	D2158	British Railways	Class 03

Attractions
There are a number of items of rolling stock and railway interest at this rural Herefordshire site, which is near to the River Arrow and Welsh Borders region. The National Trust sites at Croft Castle and Berrington Hall are also nearby.

Severn Valley Railway

Introduction and History
The railway from Kidderminster to Bridgnorth and Shrewsbury opened in 1862. It closed as a through route in 1963 although freight traffic continued from Kidderminster to Alveley, near Highley, until 1969. The section from Kidderminster to Bewdley survived until early 1970, after which it was cut back to Foley Park, to where freight trains from Kidderminster worked until 1982. The Severn Valley Railway Society formed in 1965, with the initial aim of acquiring five and a half miles of the railway from Bridgnorth to Alveley. This was successful and the first heritage trains operated between Bridgnorth and Hampton Loade in 1970. In the early 1970s the railway sold shares to raise funds to purchase the section from Highley to Foley Park from British Rail. This was also successful and the railway was extended to Bewdley in 1974. After freight services to Foley Park ceased, the final one and a half mile section from Foley Park to Kidderminster was acquired and the new Kidderminster Town station built, allowing through trains from Bridgnorth to return to Kidderminster from 1984. The main line connection at Kidderminster has been reinstated, over which through trains occasionally pass.

Contact Details
Website: www.svr.co.uk
Tel: 01562 757900
Email: contact@svrlive.com
Address: Severn Valley Railway, Number One, Comberton Place, Kidderminster, DY10 1QR.

Transport Links
By Rail: Kidderminster main line station is adjacent to Kidderminster Town (SVR) station.
By Road: There is pay & display parking at Kidderminster (DY10 1QX), Bewdley (DY12 1BG) and Bridgnorth (WV16 5DT). Parking at Arley, Highley & Hampton Loade is very limited and not recommended.

Opening Times
The railway operates every Saturday, Sunday and Bank Holiday and selected other weekdays from 16 February to 31 December. Between 13 April and 29 September, the railway operates every day.

Line Mileage and Journey Time

0.00	Kidderminster Town
3.50	Bewdley
5.00	Northwood Halt
7.00	Arley
9.25	Highley
10.25	Country Park Halt
11.50	Hampton Loade
16.00	Bridgnorth

A return journey takes about three hours.

Stock List

Type	Number	Builder	Details
Steam	1450	GWR	0-4-2T
Steam	4085 DUNROBIN	Sharp Stewart	0-4-4T
Steam	1501	British Railways	0-6-0PT
Steam	5764	GWR	0-6-0PT
Steam	7714	GWR	0-6-0PT
Steam	2047	Manning Wardle	0-6-0ST
Steam	813	Hudswell Clarke	0-6-0ST
Steam	686	Hunslet	0-6-0T
Steam	47383	Vulcan Foundry	0-6-0T
Steam	Catch Me Who Can	Trevithick 200	2-2-0
Steam	43106	British Railways	2-6-0
Steam	46443	British Railways	2-6-0
Steam	7325	GWR	2-6-0
Steam	42968	LMS	2-6-0
Steam	82045	82045 Steam Locomotive Trust	2-6-2T
Steam	4150	GWR	2-6-2T
Steam	4566	GWR	2-6-2T
Steam	80079	British Railways	2-6-4T
Steam	2857	GWR	2-8-0
Steam	48773	North British	2-8-0
Steam	600	North British	2-10-0
Steam	75069	British Railways	4-6-0
Steam	4930	GWR	4-6-0
Steam	7802	GWR	4-6-0
Steam	7812	GWR	4-6-0
Steam	7819	GWR	4-6-0

▲ **Severn Valley Railway:** Class 50 No. 50035 "Ark Royal" crosses the 1861-built Victoria Bridge near Arley on the Severn Valley Railway, with the 1550 Bridgnorth–Kidderminster on 5 October 2018.
Tony Christie

Steam	45110	Vulcan Foundry	4-6-0
Steam	34027	Southern Railway	4-6-2
Diesel	319290	Ruston & Hornsby	0-4-0
Diesel	D2960	Ruston & Hornsby	0-4-0
Diesel	D2961	Ruston & Hornsby	0-4-0
Diesel	08896	British Railways	Class 08
Diesel	D3022	British Railways	Class 08
Diesel	D3201	British Railways	Class 08
Diesel	D3586	British Railways	Class 08
Diesel	08635	British Railways	Class 08
Diesel	09107	British Railways	Class 09
Diesel	D4100	British Railways	Class 09
Diesel	12099	British Railways	Class 11
Diesel	D9551	British Railways	Class 14
Diesel	33108	BRCW	Class 33
Diesel	D7029	Beyer Peacock	Class 35
Diesel	37688	English Electric	Class 37
Diesel	40106	English Electric	Class 40
Diesel	D821	British Railways	Class 42
Diesel	50031	English Electric	Class 50
Diesel	50033	English Electric	Class 50
Diesel	50035	English Electric	Class 50
Diesel	50044	English Electric	Class 50
Diesel	D1013	British Railways	Class 52
Diesel	D1015	British Railways	Class 52
Diesel	D1062	British Railways	Class 52
DMU	50933, 51941, 52064, 56208 & 59250	British Railways	Class 108

Attractions

The SVR is one of Britain's oldest and longest heritage railways and is open for the majority of the year. There are plenty of exhibits at the Engine House Visitor & Education Centre at Highley. The new refreshment room and car park at Bridgnorth are due to open during 2019. The railway has a very large collection of locomotives and the steam and diesel galas usually involve further visiting locomotives. Route 45 of the National Cycle Network travels through Bewdley and along the route of the former Wyre Forest railway line and continues north from Bridgnorth on the former railway to Coalport. Nearby attractions include Severn Valley Country Park, West Midland Safari Park, The Museum of Carpet, Wyre Forest and Hartlebury Castle & Museum.

Special Events during 2019

15–17 March: Spring Steam Gala.
6–7 April: Open House Weekend.
26–28 April: Family Fun Days.
16–18 May: Spring Diesel Festival.
19 May: Mixed Traction Day.
1–2 June: Food & Drink Fayre.
29–30 June & 6–7 July: Step Back to the 1940s.
3 August: Day of Dance.
10–11 August: Steam on the Road.
31 August: Classic Vehicle Day.
1 September: On The Buses.
19–22 September: Autumn Steam Gala.
3–5 October: Autumn Diesel Festival.
26–27 October: Christmas Gift Fayre.

Tanat Valley Light Railway

Introduction and History

The railway from Shrewsbury to the quarries at Nantmawr and Criggion opened in 1866 and following poor revenues and inadequate maintenance it closed in 1880. The route then became part of Cambrian Railways and reopened in 1896. The original Tanat Valley Light Railway (TVLR) from Llanyblodwell to Llangynog in central Wales opened in 1904 for carrying slate; it connected with the quarry branch to Nantmawr. Passenger services on the TVLR ended in 1951 and the line closed in 1964; however, stone traffic from Gobowen to Blodwell Quarry at the beginning of the route continued until 1988. In 2004, the newly formed TVLR Company acquired the route from Blodwell Junction to Nantmawr and ran its first trains in preservation during 2009. There is a rail connection to Cambrian Heritage Railways at Llanddu and there are long term plans for the two railways to work together and operate through trains.

Contact Details

Website: www.nantmawrvisitorcentre.co.uk
Tel: 01691 780042
Email: admin@tvlr.co.uk
Address: Tanat Valley Light Railway, Tan Llwyn, Llangedwyn, Near Oswestry, SY10 9LD.

Transport Links

By Rail: Gobowen is the nearest railway station and is eight miles away.
By Road: Free car parking is available at Nantmawr (SY10 9HW).

Opening Times

During 2019 trains will operate 10.00–16.00 on 23–24 March, 20–22 April, 11–12 May, 27–28 July, 24–25 August, 14–15 & 21–22 September and 19–20 October. The Ruston & Hornsby shunter "Crabtree" will give cab rides and the Class 107 DMU will operate when maintenance is completed.

Line Mileage and Journey Time

0.00	Nantmawr
1.25	Llanddu Junction

Trains currently travel for about a third of a mile from Nantmawr and a return journey takes 10–15 minutes.

Stock List

Type	*Number*	*Builder*	*Details*
Diesel	HE2145	Hunslet	0-4-0
Diesel	338416	Ruston & Hornsby	0-4-0
DMU	51993, 52005, 52012, 52031 & 59791	British Railways	Class 107
EMU	61937, 75642 & 75981	British Railways	Class 309

Attractions

The railway is home to the Richard Morris Collection, an eclectic mix including narrow gauge items, the rail taxi, an Isetta Bubble Car converted to a rail vehicle, a steam monorail and the largest collection of industrial monorail in the country. There is a museum coach and the Clacton café is situated in a Class 309 which was rescued from the closed Coventry Electric Railway Museum. A number of woodland walks, nature trails and picnic spots are within reach from this rural setting in the Welsh-English borders. Cambrian Heritage Railways (see page 75) and the Llangollen Railway (see page 68) are four miles and 17 miles from Nantmawr respectively.

Special Events during 2019

23–24 March: Volunteer & Information Weekend (for current and prospective volunteers).
20–22 April: Easter Egg Hunt.
21–22 September: Heritage Open Days with Crabtree.
19–20 October: Halloween Spectacular.

Telford Steam Railway

Introduction and History

The region is rich in industrial history, with the railways having played in important role in transporting raw materials and locally manufactured goods. The first wooden wagonways in the area were replaced by a cast iron plateway as early as 1769, connecting the mines and sites supplying raw materials to the iron works. The railway between Wellington and Horsehay opened in 1859 and was subsequently extended south-west to Craven Arms in 1867. The Horsehay Company Ltd was established in 1886 and occupied the site of today's steam railway. It fabricated, assembled and disassembled bridges, using its extensive industrial railway network, before transporting the bridges throughout the British Empire. The railway through Horsehay and Dawley closed to passenger services in 1962 and to freight in 1964. The first preservation group, the Telford Horsehay Steam Trust, formed in 1976, restoring its first steam locomotive in 1981 and the steam railway opened to the public in 1984. Since then the heritage railway has been extended to Lawley Village (in 2015) and there are ambitious plans to extend south to a new terminus in the town of Ironbridge.

Contact Details

Website: www.telfordsteamrailway.co.uk
Tel: 01952 503880
Email: Written enquiries can be made from the railway's website.
Address: Telford Steam Railway, The Old Loco Shed, Bridge Road, Horsehay, Telford, TF4 3UH.

Transport Links

By Rail: The nearest railway station is Telford Central, which is three and a half miles away.
By Road: Free parking is available outside the old loco shed or in the main yard (TF4 2NF).

Opening Times

The railway opens on Sundays and Bank Holidays from Easter to October, with trains operating 11.00–16.00. It also opens during December for Christmas Specials.

Line Mileage and Journey Time

0.00	Lawley Village	0.00	Lawley Village
1.25	Spring Village	1.00	Horsehay & Dawley

A return journey on both spurs of the railway starting from Spring Village takes 50 minutes.

Stock List

Type	*Number*	*Builder*	*Details*
Steam	1944	Andrew Barclay	0-4-0F
Steam	3240 BEATTY	Hawthorn Leslie	0-4-0ST
Steam	1990	Peckett	0-4-0ST
Steam	MERLIN	Peckett	0-4-0ST
Steam	ROCKET	Peckett	0-4-0ST
Diesel	27414 TOM	North British	0-4-0
Diesel	183062	Ruston & Hornsby	0-4-0
Diesel	313394	Ruston & Hornsby	0-4-0
Diesel	382824	Ruston & Hornsby	0-4-0
Diesel	525947	Ruston & Hornsby	0-4-0
Diesel	D3429	British Railways	Class 08
Diesel	08757	British Railways	Class 08
Diesel	37263	English Electric	Class 37
DMU	50479, 50531 & 59228	BRCW	Class 104
DMU	51950 & 52062	British Railways	Class 108

Attractions

Steam trains run on most operating days and diesel services on other dates. The railway has a two foot gauge steam tram, a model railway, miniature railway, gift shop and tea room. A variety of hands-on railway experiences are available, including a guard experience, driving a steam locomotive, diesel locomotive or steam tram. The Phoenix Model Engineering Society operate a miniature railway alongside Telford Steam Railway and this is open on the last Sunday of each month and Bank Holiday Mondays. Nearby attractions include Wonderland Telford, Cosford RAF Museum, Blists Hill Victorian Town and Ironbridge Gorge museums.

Special Events during 2019

December: Polar Express Train Ride.

Tyseley Locomotive Works

Introduction and History

The steam locomotive depot at Tyseley opened in 1908 and has remained in continuous use as a traction maintenance depot since. When former GWR locomotive 7029 'Clun Castle' was purchased by a rail enthusiast in 1966, it was moved to Tyseley, which became its new home. The final British Railways steam locomotives allocated to Tyseley left the depot in 1967 and as preservationists acquired further steam locomotives, these were brought to Tyseley. The heritage operation grew and became known as Birmingham Railway Museum, while continuing to share the site, as it does with Tyseley DMU depot today. The first main line steam train ran in 1999 and the organisation subsquently split into two, with Tyseley Locomotive Works storing and maintaining steam locomotives and Vintage Trains promoting main line trains. Vintage Trains became a train operating company in its own right in 2018. Tyseley Locomotive Works is open to the public on a small number of dates each year, during which trains operate along a short stretch of track.

Contact Details

Website: www.vintagetrains.co.uk
Tel: 0121 708 4960
Email: tickets@vintagetrains.co.uk
Address: Tyseley Locomotive Works, 670 Warwick Road, Birmingham, B11 2HL.

Transport Links

By Rail: Tyseley railway station is adjacent to the works, a short walk away.
By Road: No on-site parking is available and visitors are encouraged to travel by public transport.

Opening Times

There will be two open weekends at Tyseley Locomotive Works during 2019, taking place on 22–23 June and 28–29 September; steam-hauled trains will carry passengers. These will be the only dates in 2019 when the site is open to the public.

Line Mileage and Journey Time

Trains carry passengers for approximately one quarter of a mile and the journey time is relatively short.

Stock List

Type	*Number*	*Builder*	*Details*
Steam	3 (3597)	Hawthorn Leslie	0-4-0ST
Steam	No 1 (2004)	Peckett	0-4-0ST
Steam	No.1 Cadbury	Avonside	0-4-0T
Steam	9600	GWR	0-6-0PT
Steam	7760	North British	0-6-0PT
Steam	L94 (7752)	North British	0-6-0PT
Steam	Fred (7289)	Robert Stephenson & Hawthorns	0-6-0ST
Steam	4121	GWR	2-6-2T
Steam	4588	GWR	2-6-2T
Steam	2885	GWR	2-8-0
Steam	3278	American Locomotive Co	2-8-0
Steam	7029	British Railways	4-6-0
Steam	4965	GWR	4-6-0
Steam	5043	GWR	4-6-0
Steam	5080	GWR	4-6-0
Steam	5593	North British	4-6-0
Steam	71000	British Railways	4-6-2
Diesel	299099	Ruston & Hornsby	0-4-0
Diesel	13029	British Railways	Class 08

Diesel	08616	British Railways	Class 08
Diesel	40118	English Electric	Class 40
Diesel	47773	Brush Traction	Class 47

Attractions

Tyseley Locomotive Works has an operational turntable and is home to a large collection of locomotives, including new-build projects. Nearby attractions include Blakesley Hall and the city of Birmingham. The Severn Valley Railway (see page 85) is 20 miles away.

Special Events during 2019

22–23 June: Open Day.
28–29 September: Open Day.

▲ **Tyseley Locomotive Works:** A trio of Great Western locomotives stand around the turntable at Tyseley on 29 October 2017. From left to right are 4073 Class 4-6-0 No. 5080 "Defiant", sister 4073 Class No. 5043 "Earl of Mount Edgcumbe" and 5700 Class 0-6-0PT No. 9600. **Robert Falconer**

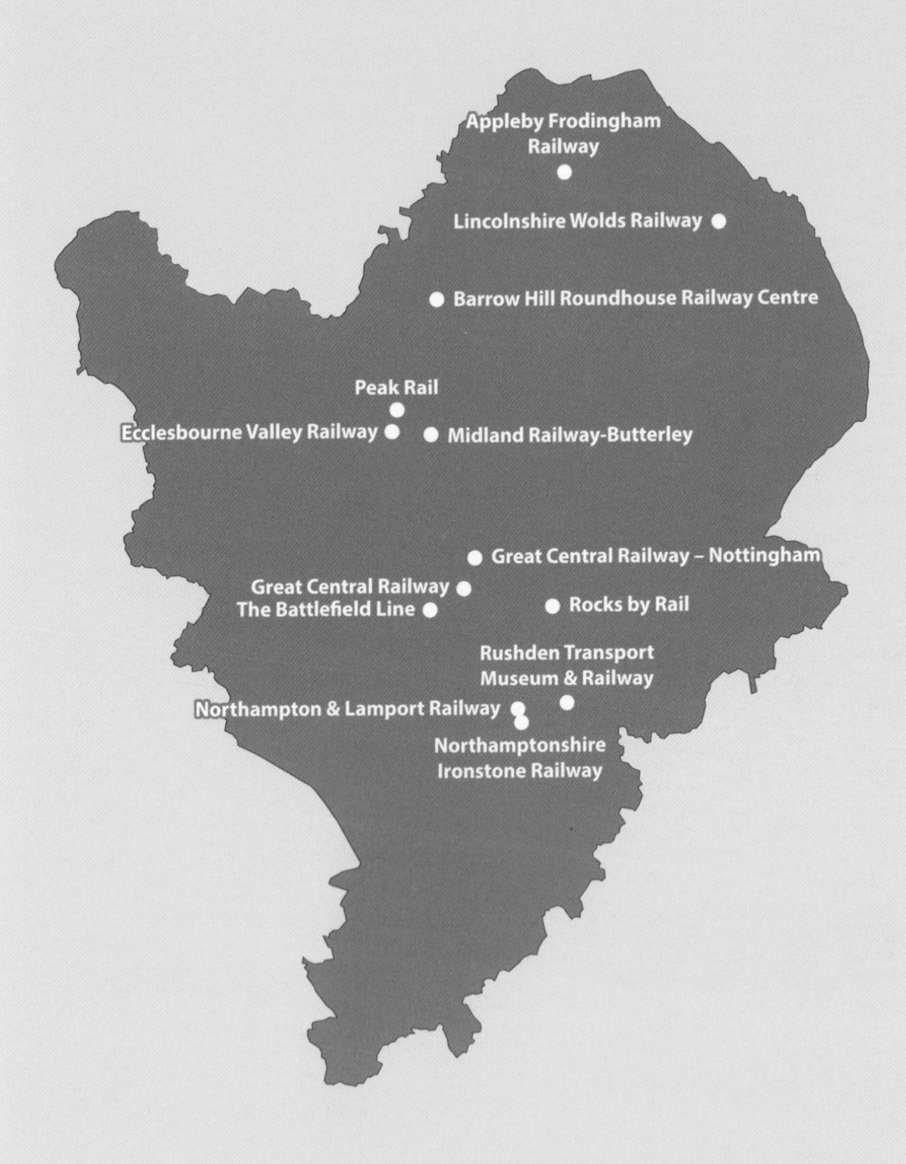
EAST MIDLANDS
Appleby Frodingham Railway
Lincolnshire Wolds Railway
Barrow Hill Roundhouse Railway Centre
Peak Rail
Ecclesbourne Valley Railway
Midland Railway-Butterley
Great Central Railway – Nottingham
Great Central Railway
The Battlefield Line
Rocks by Rail
Rushden Transport Museum & Railway
Northampton & Lamport Railway
Northamptonshire Ironstone Railway

Region 5 – East Midlands

Appleby Frodingham Railway

Introduction and History

The steelworks at Scunthorpe and the extensive railway complex within them were established in the mid-19th Century. The site remains an operational steelworks today and contains more than 100 miles of working track, over which railtours operate on selected dates throughout the year. Since 1990, these have been operated by the Appleby Frodingham Railway Preservation Society (AFRPS), which owns a diesel multiple unit and a number of steam and diesel locomotives for this purpose, giving a very different experience to that of other heritage railways.

Contact Details

Website: www.afrps.co.uk
Tel: Tours are booked through Brigg Tourist Information, tel 01652 657053.
Email: brigg.tic@northlincs.gov.uk
Address: AFRPS, Brigg Tourist Information Centre, The Buttercross, Market Place, Brigg, DN20 8ER.

Transport Links

By Rail: The nearest railway station is Scunthorpe, which is one mile from the site.
By Road: Car parking is available at the steelworks, which is accessed from Brigg Road, Scunthorpe (DN16 1XA).

Opening Times

Railtours of the steelworks operate on selected Saturdays from 30 March. No charge is made for the tours; however, a donation is suggested to cover costs.

Line Mileage and Journey Time

The railway is not linear and consists of an extensive track layout around the steelworks. Railtours travel for varying distances, usually covering about 15 miles and taking up to four hours.

Stock List

Type	*Number*	*Builder*	*Details*
Steam	8 (2369)	Andrew Barclay	0-4-0ST
Steam	1 (1438)	Peckett	0-4-0ST
Steam	3 (1919)	Avonside	0-6-0ST
Steam	22 (3844)	Hunslet	0-6-0ST
Steam	3138	Fablok	0-6-0T
Diesel	1 (2661)	Yorkshire Engine Co.	0-6-0
Diesel	1 (2877)	Yorkshire Engine Co.	0-6-0
DMU	56207 & 59245	British Railways	Class 108

Attractions

Railtours are operated either by locomotives hauling brake vans or the diesel multiple unit. On some tours a restored buffet carriage is used to provide refreshments. Note that for safety reasons children under the age of 10 cannot travel on brake van tours and children under 5 cannot travel on any tour. Steam locomotive driver experiences are available, which are unique in that these take place around an operational steelworks. Nearby attractions include North Lincolnshire Museum in Scunthorpe, Elsham Hall, Gardens & Country Park and Normanby Hall Country Park.

Special Events during 2019

There are occasional diesel locomotive events, please check the website for details.

Barrow Hill Roundhouse Railway Centre

Introduction and History

The railway through Chesterfield and Staveley opened in 1841, as part of the North Midland Railway's route from Derby to Rotherham and Leeds. A locomotive depot was built at Staveley in 1865, followed by the roundhouse in 1870. After 121 years of continuous use, British Rail closed the roundhouse in 1991, after which the condition of the buildings and site deteriorated. In 1989 the Barrow Hill Engine Shed Action Group formed with the aim of saving the roundhouse from demolition. The group lobbied for the building to be given Grade II listed status and this was granted in 1991. After the project received funding from a number of organisations and much restoration work was undertaken, the site first opened to the public in 1998, with diesel-hauled brake van rides being provided. The site has a museum and a large collection of locomotives, some of which reside there long-term and others travel to and from other locations. It remains connected to the main line, enabling occasional charter trains to travel directly for special events.

Contact Details

Website: www.barrowhill.org
Tel: 01246 475554
Email: enquiries@barrowhill.org
Address: Barrow Hill Limited, Campbell Drive, Barrow Hill, Chesterfield, S43 2PR.

Transport Links

By Rail: The nearest station is Chesterfield, which is four miles away. There is a free bus from Chesterfield station and town centre on some special event days.
By Road: There is ample free parking on site (S43 2PR).

Opening Times

The roundhouse and museum open 10.00–16.00 on Saturdays and Sundays from 2 March until early December.

Line Mileage and Journey Time

Trains operate on a stretch of the former Springwell branch on selected dates. The return trip is approximately one mile and takes about ten minutes.

Stock List

Type	Number	Builder	Details
Steam	HENRY (2491)	Hawthorn Leslie	0-4-0ST
Steam	E B WILSON (1795)	Manning Wardle	0-4-0ST
Steam	8217	GER	0-6-0
Steam	68006	Hunslet	0-6-0ST
Steam	2000	Peckett	0-6-0ST
Steam	VULCAN (3272)	Vulcan Foundry	0-6-0ST
Steam	41708	Midland Railway	0-6-0T
Steam	5164	GWR	2-6-2T
Steam	506	Great Central Railway	4-4-0
Steam	1000	Midland Railway	4-4-0
Electric	81002	BRCW	Class 81
Electric	82008	Beyer Peacock	Class 82
Electric	E3035	English Electric	Class 83
Electric	85006	British Railways	Class 85
Electric	89001	BREL	Class 89
Diesel	01515	Thomas Hill	0-4-0
Diesel	02003	Yorkshire Engine Co.	Class 02
Diesel	D2868	Yorkshire Engine Co.	Class 02
Diesel	03066	British Railways	Class 03
Diesel	07012	Ruston & Hornsby	Class 07
Diesel	D4092	British Railways	Class 10
Diesel	D5910	Baby Deltic Project	Class 23
Diesel	26007	BRCW	Class 26
Diesel	27066	BRCW	Class 27
Diesel	45060	British Railways	Class 45
Diesel	45105	British Railways	Class 45

Diesel	45118	British Railways	Class 45
Diesel	D9009	English Electric	Class 55
Diesel	D9015	English Electric	Class 55
Diesel	55019	English Electric	Class 55
EMU	HAZEL & CAR No. 87	Metropolitan Cammell	5 Bel
EMU	62364 & 76762	BREL	Class 421
EMU	62266, 62321, 76527 & 76528	BREL	Class 423

Harry Needle Railroad Company is based at Barrow Hill. Members of its locomotive fleet will be present, but are omitted from the stocklist as this is a commercial operator whose locomotives regularly move to and from the site.

Attractions

The roundhouse, with its 24-road turntable, is the only surviving operational roundhouse in Great Britain. The shear legs (lifting gear) can be seen, along with a large display of locomotives, an operational signal box, display rooms and various railway exhibits. The Deltic Preservation Society's maintenance depot and museum is adjacent to the roundhouse and opens 10.00–16.00 on Saturdays and during some special events. Peak Rail (see page 110), the Midland Railway-Butterley (see page 104) and the Ecclesbourne Valley Railway (see page 97) are all less than 20 miles away. Other attractions in the area include Cliffe Park, Abbeydale Industrial Hamlet, Chesterfield and Sheffield.

Special Events during 2019

20 April: Easter Event.
16–18 May: Real Ale Beer & Music Festival.
29 June: World War One Peace Event.
8–19 July: Archaeology Dig.
17 August: Science Day.
21–22 September: Steampunk Event.
26–27 October: Halloween Event.
7 December: Christmas Event.

▲ **Barrow Hill Roundhouse Railway Centre:** It could almost be the 1970s or '80s inside Barrow Hill Roundhouse on 10 December 2016. Class 03 No. 03066 stands on the turntable with Class 33 No. 33018 to the left and Class 40 No. 40012 to the right. **Robert Falconer**

The Battlefield Line

Introduction and History

The Battlefield Line was part of the Ashby and Nuneaton Joint Railway which opened in 1873, linking Nuneaton to the Leicestershire coalfields. Before the 1923 Grouping, it was jointly operated by the London & North Western Railway and the Midland Railway. British Rail operated the final passenger train over the route in 1965, after which the line closed. The preservation era began in 1969 when the Shackerstone Railway Society formed, shortly before the track was lifted in 1970. The first heritage train worked from Shackerstone to Market Bosworth in 1973 and in 1992 the line was extended to Shenton. The railway takes its name from Bosworth Battlefield near Shenton, where the final battle of the War of the Roses took place.

Contact Details

Website: www.battlefieldline.co.uk
Tel: 01827 880754
Email: enquiries@battlefieldline.co.uk
Address: The Shackerstone Railway Society Ltd, Shackerstone Station, Leicestershire, CV13 6NW.

Transport Links

By Rail: Nuneaton and Hinckley railway stations are seven and six miles from Shenton station respectively. Polesworth and Atherstone stations are both nine miles from Shackerstone.
By Road: There is ample parking at all three stations, which is free at Shakerstone (CV13 0BS) and Market Bosworth (CV13 0PF); charges apply at Shenton (CV13 6DJ).
By Boat: Narrowboats can moor at Ashby Canal Bridge 52 (a ten minute walk to Shackerstone station), Bridge 42 at Bosworth Marina (a five minute walk to Market Bosworth station) and Shenton Aqueduct or Bridge 35 (both a five minute walk to Shenton station).

Opening Times

Trains operate on selected days from late March to the end of December, including every Saturday and Sunday from April to October and during December. The timetables vary through the year and a different timetable operates for special events.

Line Mileage and Journey Time

0.00	Shackerstone
2.50	Market Bosworth
4.25	Shenton

A return journey takes about one hour.

Stock List

Type	Number	Builder	Details
Steam	1859 SIR GOMER	Peckett	0-6-0ST
Steam	7537 RICHARD III	Robert Stephenson & Hawthorns	0-6-0T
Diesel	2 NANCY	Ruston & Hornsby	0-4-0
Diesel	422 HOT WHEELS	Andrew Barclay	0-6-0
Diesel	594 BIG MOMMA	Andrew Barclay	0-6-0
Diesel	D2867	Yorkshire Engine Co.	Class 02
Diesel	04110	Robert Stephenson & Hawthorns	Class 04
Diesel	12083	British Railways	Class 11
Diesel	2002 (20063)	English Electric	Class 20
Diesel	D7523	British Railways	Class 25
Diesel	33008	BRCW	Class 33
Diesel	33019	BRCW	Class 33
Diesel	33208	BRCW	Class 33
Diesel	45015	British Railways	Class 45
Diesel	47640	Brush Traction	Class 47
Diesel	58012	BREL	Class 58
Diesel	58023	BREL	Class 58
Diesel	58048	BREL	Class 58
Electro-Diesel	73114	English Electric	Class 73
DMU	51131	British Railways	Class 116
DMU	51321	BRCW	Class 118

DMU	55005	GRCW	Class 122
DEMU	975386	British Railways	Class 202
EMU	65321 & 77112	British Railways	Class 416

Attractions
Footplate rides, murder mystery evenings, dining and driver experiences are available on various dates. There is a working pottery business, glassmaking studio and shop on the site of Shenton station; Bosworth Battlefield is one mile from Shenton. The Ashby Canal runs alongside the railway and boats can be hired and moored at the marina, which is a short walk from Market Bosworth station. Other attractions nearby include Conkers World of Adventure & Discovery, Ashby de la Zouch Castle, Tamworth Castle and Twycross Zoo.

Ecclesbourne Valley Railway

Introduction and History
The branch from Duffield to Wirksworth opened in 1867 and passenger services were withdrawn 80 years later in 1947. Wirksworth station was demolished in 1967 to enable the area to be used as a stone terminal and the line continued to be used for transporting local stone until freight traffic ceased in 1989. The track remained in place and the route opened as a heritage railway in 2002. Initially heritage trains ran for half a mile from Wirksworth and they now make the 18-mile round trip to Duffield and up the steep 1 in 27 incline of the Ravenstor extension. The railway is currently fundraising to build a new station at Wirksworth.

Contact Details
Website: www.e-v-r.com
Tel: 01629 823076
Email: ticketoffice@e-v-r.com
Address: Ecclesbourne Valley Railway, Station Road, Coldwell Street, Wirksworth, DE4 4FB.

Transport Links
By Rail: There is a main line rail connection at Duffield; cross the footbridge to Platform 3 for the EVR.
By Road: Car parking is available at Wirksworth (DE4 4FB) and Duffield (DE56 4EQ) where there is a car park for both the EVR and national rail users.

Opening Times
Trains operate most weekends and on selected other days throughout the year. There are no services on Tuesdays.

Line Mileage and Journey Time
0.00 Ravenstor
0.50 Wirksworth
4.00 Idridgehay
5.25 Shottle
9.00 Duffield

A return journey takes about 1 hour 30 minutes.

Stock List

Type	Number	Builder	Details
Steam	2217	Andrew Barclay	0-4-0
Steam	3 (2360)	Andrew Barclay	0-4-0
Steam	68012	Bagnall	0-6-0ST
Steam	102	Hudswell Clarke	0-6-0T
Diesel	319284	Ruston & Hornsby	0-4-0
Diesel	402803	Ruston & Hornsby	0-4-0
Diesel	MEGAN	Thomas Hill	0-4-0
Diesel	Tom	Thomas Hill	0-4-0
Diesel	10275	Rolls Royce Sentinel	0-6-0
Diesel	08605	British Railways	Class 08
Diesel	08704	British Railways	Class 08

▲ **The Battlefield Line:** Class 47 No. 47640 "University of Strathclyde" awaits departure from Shackerstone on the Battlefield Line with a service for Shenton on 19 September 2009.
Robert Pritchard

▼ **Ecclesbourne Valley Railway:** Derby Lightweight DMU 79900 "Iris" pauses at Shottle on the Ecclesbourne Valley Railway with the 13.15 Duffield–Wirksworth on 22 August 2015. Class 119 DMBC 51073 can be seen at the rear.
Alan Yearsley

Diesel	D9537	British Railways	Class 14
Diesel	31206	Brush Traction	Class 31
Diesel	31601	Brush Traction	Class 31
Diesel	33103	BRCW	Class 33
Electro-Diesel	73210	English Electric	Class 73
DMU	50170, 50253, 51505 & 59303	Metropolitan Cammell	Class 101
DMU	50599 & 51567	British Railways	Class 108
DMU	51073	GRCW	Class 119
DMU	55027 & 55031	Pressed Steel	Class 121
DMU	55006	GRCW	Class 122
DMU	79018 & 79612	British Railways	Derby Lightweight
DMU	79900	British Railways	Derby Lightweight
EMU	68500 & 68506	British Railways	Class 489

Attractions
The railway has a large collection of heritage multiple units and offers both steam and diesel footplate experiences. The Ravenstor branch has an unusally steep 1 in 27 gradient and at Wirksworth there is a miniature railway which runs parallel to the standard gauge line. The region has many attractions including the Peak District, Matlock, Matlock Bath and Carsington Water. Other nearby railway attractions include Peak Rail (see page 110), Crich Tramway Village, Midland Railway-Butterley (see page 104) and Steeple Grange Light Railway.

Special Events during 2019
16–17 March: Multiple Memories Railcar Gala.
19–22 April: Easter Weekend Event.
26–28 April: Spring Diesel & Ale Bash.
25–27 May: Kids go Free Weekend.
25 May & 8 June: Jazz & Real Ale on Rails.
15–16 June: Steam in the Valley Weekend.
30 June: Classic Bus & Coach Rally.
10–11 August: Summer Diesel Gala.
6 September: Cider & Folk Music on the Train.
19–20 October: Wirksworth Model Railway Exhibition.
26 October: Wirksworth Wizarding Weekend.
December: Santa Experiences.

Great Central Railway

Introduction and History
The Great Central Railway from London Marylebone to Rugby, Leicester and Nottingham opened to freight in 1898 and to passenger services in 1899, providing a new route from the North to the South East. Express trains ended in 1960 and the smaller stations, including Rothley and Quorn and Woodhouse, closed in 1963. Through services ended in 1966 when the line south of Rugby was severed and it closed fully in 1969, when Rugby–Nottingham Arkwright Street services ceased. The first preservation group, the Main Line Steam Trust, formed in the early 1970s and acquired the station and trackbed at Loughborough. The first heritage trains worked in 1973, with steam-hauled services to Quorn. In 1976 the section from Loughborough to Rothley was secured and with the assistance of the local council, the trackbed from Loughborough to Belgrave & Birstall was acquired. A new station at Leicester North was built immediately south of the former Belgrave & Birstall station, with trains terminating there from 1990. The line became Britain's only double track heritage railway in 2000, with the facility for test trains to operate at 60mph, although the maximum speed for passenger carrying heritage trains is 25mph. In 2015 the branch from Swithland to the former quarry site at Mountsorrel reopened and infrequent services now operate to a newly constructed halt. Plans are under way to merge with the Great Central Railway, Nottingham (see page 102), creating an 18-mile railway. The bridge over the Network Rail line near Leicester was reinstated in 2017 and funds are currently being raised for repairs to the railway bridge crossing the Grand Union Canal to enable to the merger.

Contact Details

Website: www.gcrailway.co.uk
Tel: 01509 632323
Email: sales@gcrailway.co.uk
Address: Great Central Railway, Great Central Road, Loughborough, LE11 1RW.

Transport Links

By Rail: Loughborough (main line station) is one mile from Loughborough Central.
By Road: Parking is available at Loughborough (LE11 1RW, roadside parking), Quorn & Woodhouse (LE12 8AG), Rothley (LE7 7LD) and Leicester North (LE4 3BR).

Opening Times

Trains operate every weekend and on selected weekdays and Bank Holidays, with services between approximately 09.30 and 16.30, depending on which timetable is in use.

Line Mileage and Journey Time

0.00	Loughborough Central
2.00	Quorn and Woodhouse
4.75	Rothley
7.75	Leicester North

0.00	Rothley
1.50	Mountsorrel Halt

A return journey takes about 1 hour 30 minutes.

Stock List

Type	*Number*	*Builder*	*Details*
Steam	9370	Sentinel	4wVBT
Steam	68067	Hudswell Clarke	0-6-0ST
Steam	3809	Hunslet	0-6-0ST
Steam	47406	Vulcan Foundry	0-6-0T
Steam	4 (7684)	Robert Stephenson & Hawthorns	0-6-0T
Steam	78018	British Railways	2-6-0
Steam	78019	British Railways	2-6-0
Steam	46521	British Railways	2-6-0
Steam	63601	Great Central Railway	2-8-0
Steam	48305	LMS	2-8-0
Steam	48624	Southern Railway	2-8-0
Steam	92214	British Railways	2-10-0
Steam	45305	Armstrong Whitworth	4-6-0
Steam	73156	British Railways	4-6-0
Steam	6990	British Railways	4-6-0
Steam	45491	LMS	4-6-0
Steam	777	North British	4-6-0
Steam	70013	British Railways	4-6-2
Steam	34039	Southern Railway	4-6-2
Diesel	28	Andrew Barclay	0-4-0
Diesel	D2989	Ruston & Hornsby	Class 07
Diesel	08694	British Railways	Class 08
Diesel	08907	British Railways	Class 08
Diesel	13101	British Railways	Class 08
Diesel	D3690	British Railways	Class 08
Diesel	10119	British Railways	Class 10
Diesel	D8098	English Electric	Class 20
Diesel	D5185	British Railways	Class 25
Diesel	D5401	BRCW	Class 27
Diesel	D5830	Brush Traction	Class 31
Diesel	D6535	BRCW	Class 33
Diesel	37714	English Electric	Class 37
Diesel	D123	British Railways	Class 45
Diesel	1705	Brush Traction	Class 47
Diesel	50017	English Electric	Class 50
DMU	50193, 50203, 50266, 50321, 51427 & 56342	Metropolitan Cammell	Class 101
DMU	59575	Metropolitan Cammell	Class 111

DMU	59276	British Railways	Class 120
DMU	51616 & 51622	British Railways	Class 127
EMU	70576	British Railways	Class 411

Attractions

There is a museum at Loughborough Central station and a walkway from which the signal box and part of the engine shed can be seen (the shed itself is restricted). Quorn and Woodhouse station has a tea room housed in an authentic recreated air raid shelter. The railway offers a number of dining trains, plus steam and diesel driving experiences. The Charnwood Forest Garden Railway is adjacent to Rothley station and operates at weekends and Bank Holidays. Nearby attractions include Stonehouse Family Farm & Motor Museum, Charnwood Museum, Bradgate Park and Gorse Hill City Farm in Leicester.

Special Events during 2019

13–14 April: Diesel Gala.
19–22 April: Easter Vintage Festival.
27 April: Heritage Bus Rally.
11–12 May: Goods Galore Gala & Vintage Vehicle Festival.
31 May–2 June: 1940s Wartime Event.
14–16 June: Model Event.
12–14 July: Vintage Ford Owners Club.
20–21 July: Morris Minor Owners Club.
3–4 August: Summer Vintage Vehicle Festival.
6–8 September: Diesel Gala.
13–15 September: Piston & Pumps Festival.
3–6 October: Autumn Steam Gala.
31 October: Steam & Scream.
16–17 November: Last Hurrah Steam Gala.
December (various dates): Santa Steam and Christmas Holiday Trains.

Trains will operate on the Mountsorrel branch on: 31 March, 17, 24 & 28 April, 26 May, 30 June, 28 July, 7, 14 & 25 August, 29 September and 27 October.

▲ **Great Central Railway:** BR Standard Class 2MT 2-6-0 78018, is seen near Loughborough on the Great Central Railway on 2 September 2018. **Tony Christie**

Great Central Railway – Nottingham

Introduction and History

The railway from London Marylebone to Rugby and Nottingham opened in 1898 and details of the route's history, decline and early preservation efforts are given in the Great Central Railway listing above. The section from Loughborough to Ruddington survived beyond the 1969 closure as an unsignalled single line to the British Gypsum site at Hotchley Hill and the Ministry of Defence (MoD) depot on the spur at Ruddington. Freight traffic continued until the 1980s when the MoD depot closed and the route was never formally closed by British Rail. In the early 1990s a group of transport enthusiasts created a museum on the former MoD site and operated trains on a short section of track. Negotiations began to return trains to the route and purchase the line from British Rail. Gypsum traffic resumed; however, the railway had been severed at East Leake, separating the freight and heritage operations. This was reconnected and passenger services returned to Rushcliffe Halt in 2003. Freight trains now use the route on weekdays, via the main line connection at Loughborough, and heritage trains operate at weekends. Nottingham Express Transit (tram service) occupies the former railway north of Ruddington, preventing a northern extension; however, plans are under way to connect to the Great Central Railway at Loughborough (see the above listing).

Contact Details

Website: www.gcrn.co.uk
Tel: 0115 940 5705
Email: info@gcrn.co.uk
Address: Great Central Railway – Nottingham, Mere Way, Ruddington, Nottinghamshire, NG11 6JS.

Transport Links

By Rail: Nottingham railway station is six miles from Ruddington and East Midlands Parkway is six miles from Rushcliffe Halt.
By Road: Parking is available at Ruddington (NG11 6JS) and Rushcliffe Halt (LE12 6HX).

Opening Times

The railway operates 10.45–16.15 every Sunday and Bank Holiday from April to October and on selected other dates, including each Saturday from June to August and during December.

Line Mileage and Journey Time

0.00	Ruddington
3.50	Rushcliffe Halt
8.75	Loughborough

A return journey takes 1 hour 30 minutes.

Stock List

Type	Number	Builder	Details
Steam	Julia (1682)	Hudswell Clarke	0-6-0ST
Steam	5 (2015)	Manning Wardle	0-6-0ST
Steam	1762	Manning Wardle	0-6-0ST
Steam	2009	Manning Wardle	0-6-0ST
Steam	56 (7667)	Robert Stephenson & Hawthorns	0-6-0ST
Steam	63 CORBY	Robert Stephenson & Hawthorns	0-6-0ST
Steam	1631	American Locomotive Co.	2-8-0
Steam	2138	American Locomotive Co.	2-8-0
Steam	2364	Baldwin Locomotive Works	2-8-0
Steam	8274	North British	2-8-0
Diesel	D2959	Ruston & Hornsby	0-4-0
Diesel	No.2 MARBLAEGIS	Ruston & Hornsby	0-4-0
Diesel	03118	British Railways	Class 03
Diesel	13180	British Railways	Class 08
Diesel	08784	British Railways	Class 08
Diesel	08922	British Railways	Class 08
Diesel	D8154	English Electric	Class 20
Diesel	37009	English Electric	Class 37

Diesel	41001	BREL	Class 43 Prototype
Diesel	46010	British Railways	Class 46
Diesel	47292	British Railways	Class 47
Diesel	56097	BREL	Class 56
DMU	50645 & 50926	British Railways	Class 108
DMU	51138 & 51151	British Railways	Class 116
DMU	59501 & 59522	Pressed Steel	Class 117

Attractions

There is plenty to explore at Ruddington, including a miniature railway, a large model railway, the standard gauge railway workshop, a children's play area, café and gift shop. Nottingham Area Bus Society is also based at the Ruddington site and has a large collection of vintage buses and coaches. Steam and diesel driving experiences are available along the route. The railway is home to the 125 Group which has restored a prototype InterCity 125 power car and is raising funds to build a new depot at Ruddington. The Great Central Railway is located close to the southern end of the railway. Attractions in nearby Nottingham include Green's Mill & Science Centre, Stonebridge City Farm, the National Justice Museum and City of Caves.

Special Events during 2019

21–22 April: Easter Eggspress Steam Specials.
28 April: Road Transport Event.
5–6 & 26–27 May & 25–26 August: Bank Holiday Specials.
29–30 June: Model Rail 2019.
14 July: Nottingham Area Bus Society Gathering & Running Day.
11 August: Stewart Classic Vehicle Register Summer Gathering.
14–15 September: Autumn Diesel Event.
6 October: Road Transport Event.
26–27 October: Anything Goes Weekend.
2 November: GCRN Firework Spectacular.
Saturdays & Sundays 30 November–22 December: Santa Specials.
27–28 December: Winter Holiday Trains.
29 December: Mixed Traffic Gala.

Lincolnshire Wolds Railway

Introduction and History

Trains first worked on the railway from Grimsby to Louth in 1847 and it was opened to passengers in 1848. All stations on the route except North Thoresby were closed to passengers in 1961, followed by North Thoresby and Louth stations, which were closed in 1970 when the line was singled. It was retained for freight traffic until 1980, when British Rail closed the line and then promptly demolished the stations and lifted the track. The first preservation group formed in the late 1970s, initially opposing the proposed closure, and in 1984 they established a base at Ludborough station. Since then much of the trackbed has been purchased by the LWR and 2009 saw the first heritage trains from Ludborough to North Thoresby. The railway is currently being extended south towards the outskirts of Louth and the long-term aim is to extend further north and south, restoring as much as possible of the route from Grimsby to Louth.

Contact Details

Website: www.lincolnshirewoldsrailway.co.uk
Tel: 01507 363881
Email: Written enquiries can be made from the LWR website.
Address: Lincolnshire Wolds Railway, Ludborough Station, Station Road, Ludborough, Lincolnshire, DN36 5SQ.

Transport Links

By Rail: Grimsby Town is the nearest railway station and is nine miles from the Ludborough base.
By Road: Free parking is available at Ludborough station (DN36 5SH).

Opening Times

Trains operate most Sundays from late March to October, leaving Ludborough hourly from 10.45 to 15.45. A different timetable may operate on special event dates.

Line Mileage and Journey Time

0.00	Ludborough
1.75	North Thoresby

A return journey takes 35 minutes.

Stock List

Type	Number	Builder	Details
Steam	SPITFIRE	Andrew Barclay	0-4-0ST
Steam	1749 FULSTOW	Peckett	0-4-0ST
Steam	LION	Peckett	0-4-0ST
Steam	7597	Robert Stephenson & Hawthorns	0-6-0T
Steam	1313	Motala Verkstad	4-6-0
Diesel	4210131	Fowler	0-4-0
Diesel	4210145	Fowler	0-4-0
Diesel	375713	Ruston & Hornsby	0-4-0
Diesel	414303	Ruston & Hornsby	0-4-0
Diesel	421418	Ruston & Hornsby	0-4-0
Diesel	5308	Hunslet	0-4-0
Diesel	DEBBIE (3151)	Bagnall	0-6-0
Diesel	D3167	British Railways	Class 08

Attractions

The railway museum at Ludborough has free admission and opens when trains operate. Guided tours around the engine shed are available on these days and most Tuesdays and Saturdays when volunteers are working (please check before visiting). Footplate rides and signal box experiences are available for an additional charge. The railway is near to the market town of Louth, the coastal resort of Cleethorpes and the larger town of Grimsby.

Special Events during 2019

31 March: Mother's Day Special.
19–22 April: Easter Special.
25–27 May: Steam Punk Weekend.
16 June: Father's Day Special.
24–26 August: Anything Goes (steam & diesel).
31 August–1 September: 1940s Weekend.
14–15 September: Lincolnshire Heritage Weekend.
29 September: Diesel Day.
27 October: Halloween Special.
14–15 & 21–22 December: Santa Specials.

Midland Railway-Butterley

Introduction and History

The railway between Pye Bridge and Ambergate opened in 1875, linking the present day routes from Chesterfield to Nottingham and Derby to Matlock. Passenger services ended in 1947 and the line closed in 1968 after freight traffic ceased. The track was then lifted and Butterley station was demolished. In the late 1960s Derby Corporation and Derbyshire County Council planned to create a museum dedicated to the Midland Railway and three steam locomotives were purchased. A site was found on the closed Pye Bridge–Ambergate line; however, the organisations withdrew from the project due to a lack of funds. The Midland Railway Project Group was a volunteer group which collected and restored railway items. It revived the project in the early 1970s. Butterley became its base and Swanwick Junction was to be the site of the museum. The first open day was held in 1975. One mile of track was laid and the first preserved trains departed from the newly-constructed Butterley station in 1981. The railway has since been extended west to Hammersmith, where the A38 severs the trackbed, and east to Ironville, where the main line connection has been reinstated. New stations have been constructed and there has been considerable development of heritage attractions on the site.

Contact Details

Website: www.midlandrailway-butterley.co.uk
Tel: 01773 570140
Email: Written enquiries can be made from the website.
Address: Butterley Station, Ripley, Derbyshire, DE5 3QZ.

Transport Links

By Rail: The nearest station is Alfreton, which is four miles away.
By Road: Free parking is available at Butterley (DE5 3QZ).

Opening Times

The railway operates on Saturdays, Sundays and selected weekdays, with trains usually operating between 11.00 and 16.00.

Line Mileage and Journey Time

0.00	Hammersmith
0.25	Butterley
1.00	Swanwick Junction
2.75	Ironville Junction
3.00	End of Line

A return journey from Butterley takes 45–70 minutes, depending on which timetable is operating.

Stock List

Type	Number	Builder	Details
Steam	4 (454)	Naismyth Wilson	0-4-0
Steam	STANTON No.24 (1875)	Andrew Barclay	0-4-0CT
Steam	109	Markham & Co	0-4-0ST
Steam	LYTHAM ST. ANNES (2111)	Peckett	0-4-0ST
Steam	VICTORY (1547)	Peckett	0-4-0ST
Steam	WHITEHEAD	Peckett	0-4-0ST
Steam	7214	Robert Stephenson & Hawthorns	0-4-0ST
Steam	1 (7817)	Robert Stephenson & Hawthorns	0-4-0ST
Steam	68007	Hudswell Clarke	0-6-0ST
Steam	47445	Hunslet	0-6-0T
Steam	47564	Hunslet	0-6-0T
Steam	47357	North British	0-6-0T
Steam	23 (BR No. 47327)	North British	0-6-0T
Steam	158A	Midland Railway	2-4-0
Steam	80098	British Railways	2-6-4T
Steam	73129	British Railways	4-6-0
Steam	6233	LMS	4-6-2
Steam	46203	LMS	4-6-2
Diesel	D2858	Yorkshire Engine Co.	Class 02
Diesel	D2138	British Railways	Class 03
Diesel	08331	British Railways	Class 08
Diesel	08590	British Railways	Class 08
Diesel	12077	British Railways	Class 11
Diesel	20048	English Electric	Class 20
Diesel	D8059	English Electric	Class 20
Diesel	D8188	English Electric	Class 20
Diesel	20205	English Electric	Class 20
Diesel	D7671	British Railways	Class 25
Diesel	31108	Brush Traction	Class 31
Diesel	5580	Brush Traction	Class 31
Diesel	31418	Brush Traction	Class 31
Diesel	D5814	Brush Traction	Class 31
Diesel	37190	English Electric	Class 37
Diesel	40012	English Electric	Class 40
Diesel	D4	British Railways	Class 44
Diesel	45133	British Railways	Class 45
Diesel	D182	British Railways	Class 46
Diesel	47761	British Railways	Class 47

Diesel	47401	Brush Traction	Class 47
Diesel	D1516	Brush Traction	Class 47
Diesel	D1048	British Railways	Class 52
Electric	27000	British Railways	Class 77
DMU	51118 & 56097	GRCW	Class 100
DMU	51907 & 56490	British Railways	Class 108
DMU	50015, 50019, 56006 & 56015	British Railways	Class 114
DMU	59659	British Railways	Class 115
DMU	51591, 51610, 51625 & 59609	British Railways	Class 127
DMU	55513 & 55533	BREL/Leyland	Class 141
EMU	29666 & 29670	Metropolitan Cammell	MSJ&A
EMU	70824	Metropolitan Cammell	Class 491
EMU	70855, 76298 & 76322	British Railways	Class 491

Attractions

There is plenty to explore at Swanick Junction; the West Shed Experience (railway museum), a second railway museum in the Matthew Kirtley Building, the demonstration signal box, the Victorian railwayman's church, the Road Transport Gallery and the National Fork Truck Heritage Centre. Smaller railways present include the Golden Valley Light Railway and a miniature railway. At Butterley, there is a garden railway, a model railway and carriage shed. Butterley Country Park is adjacent to the railway and other nearby attractions include Crich Tramway Village and Duffield Castle.

Special Events during 2019

4–6 May: Victorian Train Weekend.
25 May–2 June: Butterley Lego Event.
26–28 July: Indietracks Music Event.
24–26 August: Victorian Train Weekend.
21–22 & 28–29 September: Teddy Bears' Weekend.
26 October–3 November: Halloween Half Term.
2 November: Fireworks Night.
23–24 & November & 1, 7–8, 11, 14–15, 18, 20–24 December: Santa Specials.

Northampton & Lamport Railway

Introduction and History

The railway between Northampton and Market Harborough opened in 1859 to carry passengers and local goods. Passenger services were withdrawn in 1960; however, through traffic returned between January and May 1969 and again from 1972 to 1973. The first preservation group formed in 1981 and organised a final charter train to travel the length of the line before it closed in August 1981. The group's name was later changed to the Northampton & Lamport Railway and a base was established at Pitsford and Brampton, the first station north of Northampton. The first trains ran in late 1995 and the heritage railway formally opened in 1996. The railway is in the process of being extended south, with half a mile of track having been laid; funding has been secured to complete this and build a new station adjacent to The Windhover pub. There are also plans to extend north, which will require repairs to the bridge crossing the River Nene.

Contact Details

Website: www.nlr.org.uk
Tel: 01604 820327
Email: enquiries@nlr.org.uk
Address: Northampton & Lamport Railway, Pitsford & Brampton Station, Pitsford Road, Chapel Brampton, NN6 8BA.

Transport Links

By Rail: The nearest station is Northampton, which is five miles away.
By Road: Free parking is available Pitsford & Brampton Station.
By Bike: Arrive on the Brampton Valley Way, a foot and cycle path following the railway and trackbed between Northampton and Market Harborough.

▲ **Great Central Railway – Nottingham**: The Great Central Railway – Nottingham is home to the only surviving prototype High Speed Train power car. On 24 May 2015 41001 is seen arriving at Rushcliffe Halt on its first public service in decades, with compatible preserved Mark III coaches which have since been repainted into BR blue and grey livery to match the locomotive. **Paul Gerrard**

▼ **Midland Railway-Butterley:** BREL/Leyland 2-car railbus 141113 (55513 + 55533) arrives at Swanwick Junction on the Midland Railway-Butterley, with a Butterley–Swanwick Junction service on 5 April 2017. **Steve Donald**

Opening Times

Trains depart on the hour from 11.00 to 16.00 on Sundays from 24 March to 27 October and on selected other dates for special events. During the operating season the station is usually open 11.00–16.00 on Wednesdays and Saturdays when trains aren't in service, subject to availability of volunteers.

Line Mileage and Journey Time

From Pitsford & Brampton, the railway travels approximately half a mile to the south and three quarters of a mile to the north. A round trip from Pitsford & Brampton takes about half an hour.

Stock List

Type	*Number*	*Builder*	*Details*
Steam	776	Andrew Barclay	0-4-0ST
Steam	2104	Peckett	0-4-0ST
Steam	2130	Peckett	0-4-0ST
Steam	45	Kitson	0-6-0ST
Steam	1378 WESTMINSTER	Peckett	0-6-0ST
Steam	3862	GWR	2-8-0
Steam	5967	GWR	4-6-0
Diesel	146C	Fowler	0-4-0
Diesel	21	Fowler	0-4-0
Diesel	764	Ruston & Hornsby	0-4-0
Diesel	1	Ruston & Hornsby	0-4-0
Diesel	53	Ruston & Hornsby	0-6-0
Diesel	31289	Brush Traction	Class 31
Diesel	47205	British Railways	Class 47

Attractions

At Pitsford & Brampton station, visitors can browse the gift shop and second-hand book shop. The Brampton Valley Way foot and cycle path follows the course of the present day railway and the disused sections between Northampton and Market Harborough. Other attractions in the area include Abington Museum, Delapre Abbey and the large town of Northampton.

Special Events during 2019

31 March: Mothering Sunday Cream Teas.
20–22 April: Easter Egg Specials.
28 April: Kids for a Quid.
4–6 May: Brampton Bear Specials.
25 May & 9 June: Brake Van Rides.
16 June: Father's Day Cream Teas.
25–26 August: Themed Character Days.
31 August: Kids for a Quid.
19–20 October: Gala Weekend.
26–27 October: Halloween Event.
24 & 30 November and 1, 7–8, 14–15 & 21–22 December: Santa Specials.

Northamptonshire Ironstone Railway

Introduction and History

When iron ore deposits were found in the area during the mid-19th Century, these were excavated and initially transported using a network of industrial narrow gauge railways. These later fell into disuse after the minerals became uneconomical to extract. The Rushden Railway Society formed in December 1971 with the intention of purchasing and restoring two Peckett industrial steam locomotives, which were previously used in the ironstone industry. At the same time, residential development was planned for the area and Northampton Development Corporation wanted to preserve the disused ironstone railway and the nearby Iron Age fort. The society gained access to the site, gradually restored it and laid the standard gauge railway. There is now approximately one and a half miles of track; however, not all of this is currently in use as renewal works are required.

Contact Details

Website: www.nir.org.uk
Tel: 01604 702031
Email: Written enquiries can be made from the website.
Address: Northamptonshire Ironstone Railway, Hunsbury Hill Road, Camp Hill, Northampton, NN4 9UW.

Transport Links

By Rail: Northampton is the nearest station and is three miles away.
By Road: Parking is available at the railway (NN4 9UW).

Opening Times

The railway operates 10.00–15.30 on Sundays and Bank Holidays from April to October. The site can be viewed on days when trains are not in service.

Line Mileage and Journey Time

Trains currently operate on a section of approximately a quarter of a mile in length and the journey time is relatively short.

Stock List

Type	Number	Builder	Details
Steam	BELVEDERE	Sentinel	4wVBGT
Steam	MUSKETEER	Sentinel	4wVBGT
Steam	750	Hudswell Clarke	0-4-0ST
Diesel	CHARLES WAKE	Fowler	0-4-0
Diesel	3967	Hibberd	0-4-0
Diesel	D697	Hudswell Clarke	0-4-0
Diesel	16	Hunslet	0-4-0
EMU	70284, 70510 & 70296	British Railways	Class 411
EMU	14351, 14352 & 15396	British Railways	Class 415
EMU	69304	British Railways	Class 422
EMU	13004	British Railways	4DD

Attractions

The standard gauge industrial railway has a number of sharp curves and steep gradients and there are also two garden railways of different gauges. The railway shares the site with the Ironstone Heritage Museum and Hunsbury Hill Country Park, which includes a children's play area and an Iron Age fort. Nearby attractions include Abington Museum, Abington Park, Delapre Abbey and the Northampton & Lamport Railway which is eight miles away (see page 106).

Special Events during 2019

April: Easter weekend.
April: St George's Day Event.
September: Heritage Days.
December: Santa Specials.

Peak Rail

Introduction and History

The railway from Derby to Ambergate opened in 1840 and was extended north to Rowsley in 1849, including the section that Peak Rail now occupies. The route across the more challenging terrain from Rowsley to Manchester was later completed in 1860. Local passenger services ceased in 1967 when Matlock Bath, Darley Dale, Rowsley, Bakewell and Millers Dale stations closed and the line between Matlock and Millers Dale closed in 1968, when St Pancras–Manchester express services ended. The northern section of the route has remained in continuous use with freight services to Peak Forest. The Peak Railway Preservation Society formed in 1975 and initially opened the Buxton Steam Centre with a short running track, which later closed. Peak Rail relocated to Darley Dale in the 1980s and the first heritage trains worked to Matlock Riverside in 1991. The line was extended north to a new station at Rowsley South in 1997 and south to Matlock in 2011, when the railway was reconnected with the main line network. There are plans to extend further north to the original station in Rowsley and also to Bakewell. It has long been hoped that the railway could one day return to Buxton, which would require a number of major obstacles to be overcome.

Contact Details

Website: www.peakrail.co.uk
Tel: 01629 580381
Email: peakrail@peakrail.co.uk
Address: Peak Rail, Matlock Station, Matlock, Derbyshire, DE4 3NA.

Transport Links

By Rail: At Matlock, cross from the main line Platform 1 to Platform 2 for Peak Rail.
By Road: Pay & display parking is available at Matlock (DE4 3NA) and free parking at Darley Dale (DE4 2EQ) and Rowsley South (DE4 2LF).
By Bike: The traffic-free Monsal Trail follows the railway from Matlock to Rowsley and beyond.

Opening Times

The railway operates on Saturdays, Sundays and selected weekdays from mid-February until early November. Trains operate between approximately 11.00 and 17.00, depending on which timetable is in operation.

Line Mileage and Journey Time

0.00	Matlock
2.25	Darley Dale
3.25	Rowsley South

A return journey takes about one hour.

Stock List

Type	Number	Builder	Details
Steam	72	Vulcan Foundry	0-6-0ST
Steam	68006	Hunslet	0-6-0ST
Steam	150 (3892)	Robert Stephenson & Hawthorns	0-6-0ST
Steam	45 Colwyn	Kitson	0-6-0ST
Steam	65	Hudswell Clarke	0-6-0T
Steam	6634	GWR	0-6-2T
Steam	5553	GWR	2-6-2T
Steam	5224	GWR	2-8-0T
Diesel	2 JAMES (2675)	Yorkshire Engine Co.	0-4-0
Diesel	RS8	ICI South Central Workshops	0-4-0
Diesel	BIGGA (102C)	Thomas Hill	0-4-0
Diesel	2654	Yorkshire Engine Co.	0-4-0
Diesel	2679	Yorkshire Engine Co.	0-4-0
Diesel	265V	Thomas Hill	0-4-0
Diesel	284V	Thomas Hill	0-4-0
Diesel	3777	Hibberd	0-4-0
Diesel	9222	Hunslet	0-4-0
Diesel	27097	North British	0-4-0

Diesel	WD7229	Vulcan Foundry	0-4-0
Diesel	803	Brush Traction	0-6-0
Diesel	2940	Yorkshire Engine Co.	0-6-0
Diesel	6295	Hunslet	0-6-0
Diesel	10180	Sentinel	0-6-0
Diesel	27932	North British	0-6-0
Diesel	D1186	Hudswell Clarke	0-6-0
Diesel	D2953	Andrew Barclay	Class 01
Diesel	D2854	Yorkshire Engine Co.	Class 02
Diesel	D2866	Yorkshire Engine Co.	Class 02
Diesel	03027	British Railways	Class 03
Diesel	03099	British Railways	Class 03
Diesel	03113	British Railways	Class 03
Diesel	03901	British Railways	Class 03
Diesel	D2139	British Railways	Class 03
Diesel	03180	British Railways	Class 03
Diesel	D2199	British Railways	Class 03
Diesel	D2205	Vulcan Foundry	Class 04
Diesel	D2229	Vulcan Foundry	Class 04
Diesel	D2272	Robert Stephenson & Hawthorns	Class 04
Diesel	D2284	Robert Stephenson & Hawthorns	Class 04
Diesel	D2289	Robert Stephenson & Hawthorns	Class 04
Diesel	D2337	Robert Stephenson & Hawthorns	Class 04
Diesel	D2587	Hunslet	Class 05
Diesel	06003	Andrew Barclay	Class 06
Diesel	07001	Ruston & Hornsby	Class 07
Diesel	13000	British Railways	Class 08
Diesel	08016	British Railways	Class 08
Diesel	08830	British Railways	Class 08
Diesel	09001	British Railways	Class 09
Diesel	D9500	British Railways	Class 14
Diesel	D9525	British Railways	Class 14
Diesel	D7659	Beyer Peacock	Class 25
Diesel	31270	Brush Traction	Class 31
Diesel	37152	English Electric	Class 37
Diesel	D8	British Railways	Class 44
Diesel	46035	British Railways	Class 46
Diesel	50029	English Electric	Class 50
Diesel	50030	English Electric	Class 50
Diesel	58022	BREL	Class 58
Diesel	PWM650	Ruston & Hornsby	Class 97
Diesel	PWM654	Ruston & Hornsby	Class 97
EMU	75102	British Railways	Class 307
EMU	61287 & 75407	British Railways	Class 414

The stock list includes locomotives belonging to the Heritage Shunters Trust, which has a large collection of diesel shunting locomotives, based at Rowsey South.

Attractions

Darley Dale has a small museum displaying the history of the line. The Rowsley site has a 60-foot working turntable and a number of heritage railway groups are based there. These include the Heritage Shunters Trust with its extensive collection of shunting locomotives, the Renown Repulse Restoration Group which is restoring two Class 50 locomotives, 50029 & 50030 and the LMS Carriage Association. There are many attractions in Matlock Bath and the surrounding Peak District, including the Peak District Lead Mining Museum and Chatsworth House to the north. Nearby heritage railways include the Ecclesbourne Valley Railway (see page 97), the Churnet Valley Railway (see page 78) and the Midland Railway-Butterley (see page 104).

Special Events during 2019

20–22 April: Easter Event.
Selected dates in December: Santa Specials.

Rocks by Rail

Introduction and History

Rocks by Rail, also known as The Living Ironstone Museum, demonstrates historic mineral extraction techniques and includes an operational railway. The site was connected to the Midland Railway branch line from Ashwell Junction to Cottesmore, which was completed in 1882 to transport quarried iron ore, and remained in use until 1974. The three-foot gauge tramway and rope incline allowed loaded stone and minerals to be let down the steep slope and into rail wagons for onward transport to steelworks. The railway today is used to demonstrate the techniques used and carries passengers in restored brake vans.

Contact Details

Website: www.rocks-by-rail.org
Tel: 07974 171068
Email: curator@rocks-by-rail.org
Address: Rocks By Rail Living Ironstone Museum, Cottesmore, Oakham LE15 7FF.

Transport Links

By Rail: The nearest railway station is Oakham, which is five miles away.
By Road: The site has ample car parking (at LE15 7FF) and is near to the village of Cottesmore.

Opening Times

Rocks by Rail is open 10.00–16.00 on Tuesdays and Thursdays all year round, plus some Bank Holidays and Sundays from Easter until mid-October. The on-site café opens on selected Thursdays, Sundays and Bank Holidays from Easter until late October. Steam-hauled brake van rides usually operate on the third Sunday of the month and trains are due to work on the following dates during 2019, some of which are diesel days (see Special Events below): 21–22 April, 5–6, 19 & 26–27 May, 16 & 30 June, 14 July, 11, 25–26 August, 15 & 29 September and 13 October.

Line Mileage and Journey Time

The railway line is three quarters of a mile long and the journey takes about ten minutes.

Stock List

Type	*Number*	*Builder*	*Details*
Steam	2110	Peckett	0-4-0
Steam	776	Andrew Barclay	0-4-0ST
Steam	1931	Andrew Barclay	0-4-0ST
Steam	2088 SIR THOMAS ROYDEN	Andrew Barclay	0-4-0ST
Steam	3865 SINGAPORE	Hawthorn Leslie	0-4-0ST
Steam	287	Hunslet	0-4-0ST
Steam	1257 UPPINGHAM	Peckett	0-4-0ST
Steam	1759	Peckett	0-4-0ST
Steam	2350 BELVOIR	Andrew Barclay	0-6-0ST
Steam	3138	Hawthorn Leslie	0-6-0ST
Steam	1972	Avonside	0-6-0ST
Steam	2668 CRANFORD No.2	Bagnall	0-6-0ST
Steam	1308	Hudswell Clarke	0-6-0ST
Steam	2521	Yorkshire Engine Co.	0-6-0ST
Diesel	4220007	Fowler	0-4-0
Diesel	5578	GEC Traction Ltd	0-4-0
Diesel	27656	North British	0-4-0
Diesel	10201 BETTY	Rolls Royce Sentinel	0-4-0
Diesel	10204 JEAN	Rolls Royce Sentinel	0-4-0
Diesel	10207 GRAHAM	Rolls Royce Sentinel	0-4-0
Diesel	306092	Ruston & Hornsby	0-4-0
Diesel	411319	Ruston & Hornsby	0-4-0
Diesel	421436	Ruston & Hornsby	0-4-0
Diesel	544997	Ruston & Hornsby	0-4-0
Diesel	186V	Thomas Hill	0-4-0
Diesel	1382	Yorkshire Engine Co.	0-6-0
Diesel	DE5	Yorkshire Engine Co.	0-6-0

Attractions

The museum has a good collection of industrial steam and diesel locomotives and wagons, plus an exhibition building and workshop which visitors can view. There is a cab and model of the huge dragline crane "Sundew", which was the largest of its type in the world when built. 'Driver for a Fiver' sessions are available on the first Sunday of the month, giving the opportunity to drive one of the diesel locomotives with dual controls. On Bank Holidays from April to August steam-hauled brake van rides and demonstration diesel-hauled quarry freight trains operate. Nearby attractions include Rutland Water which has an aqua park and nature reserve, and the market towns of Oakham, Melton Mowbray and Stamford.

Special Events during 2019

21 April: Easter Bunny Hunt.
30 June: Quarry Diesel Day.
29 September: Quarry Diesel Day.
13 October: Museum Gala Open Day.

Diesel 'Driver for a Fiver' experiences are available on 7 April, 2 June, 7 July, 4 August, 1 September and 6 October.

Rushden Transport Museum & Railway

Introduction and History

Rushden railway station was the only intermediate station on the short branch from Wellingborough to Higham Ferrers, which opened in 1894 and closed to passenger services in 1959. The line remained open for freight and seasonal passenger traffic until the final train ran in 1969. This consisted of a Class 25 collecting 12 wagons from Higham station; the railway track was lifted soon afterwards. Rushden Historical Transport Society (RHTS) formed in 1976 and leased Rushden station from 1984. Rushden Transport Museum opened in 1986 and in 1996 the site was purchased by the RHTS. The first heritage train ran from Rushden in 2009, exactly 50 years after passenger services ended. In June 2017 RHTS acquired Rushden goods shed from Northamptonshire County Council and plan to develop the site as a heritage community hub. The railway has been extended to a length of half a mile and there are plans to extend it a further half-mile towards Higham Ferrers.

Contact Details

Website: www.rhts.co.uk
Tel: 0300 3023 150
Email: secretary@rhts.co.uk
Address: Rushden Transport Museum, Station Approach, Rushden, Northamptonshire, NN10 0AW.

Transport Links

By Rail: The nearest railway station is Wellingborough, which is six miles from Rushden.
By Road: There is limited car parking at Rushden station (NN10 0AW); however, free parking is available nearby on Rectory Road and at the small car park on John Clark Way. During events the museum has access to a larger car park on John Clark Way, which includes disabled parking.

Opening Times

Rushden Transport Museum opens 14.00–16.00 on Saturdays and Sundays from April to October. On standard operating days, trains usually depart from Rushden station at 11.00, 11.45, 12.30, 13.15, 14.00, 14.45, 15.30 & 16.00.

Line Mileage and Journey Time

The train operates for half a mile from Rushden station and the journey time is relatively short.

Stock List

Type	*Number*	*Builder*	*Details*
Steam	2323	Andrew Barclay	0-4-0ST
Steam	EDMUNDSONS	Andrew Barclay	0-4-0ST
Steam	2654	Bagnall	0-6-0ST
Steam	THE BLUE CIRCLE	Aveling & Porter	2-2-0WT

Diesel	10159	Sentinel	0-4-0
Diesel	03179	British Railways	Class 03
DMU	55029	Pressed Steel	Class 121

Attractions

The Rushden site is home to the Victorian railway station, the Transport Museum, a Gresley buffet coach and a real ale bar which opens each evening and from midday at weekends. Other attractions in the area include Wellingborough Museum, Irchester Country Park, Irchester Narrow Gauge Railway Museum and the Northampton & Lamport Railway (see page 106) which is 20 miles away.

Special Events during 2019

30 March: Oompah Band & German Bier Festival.
31 March: Mother's Day.
6–7 April: Radio Controlled Vehicles Weekend.
21–22 April: Easter Bunny Surprise.
22 June: Armed Forces Day.
6–7 July: Teddy Bears' Picnic.
24–26 August: Sausage & Cider Weekend.
7–8 September: Model Weekend.
22 September: Food Festival.
27–29 September: Beer Festival.
19–20 October: 1940s Weekend.
26 October: Halloween Event.

▲ **Peak Rail:** Former NCB 0-6-0ST No. 72 has just arrived in Platform 2 at Peak Rail's Darley Dale station, in charge of the 1328 Rowsley South–Matlock service on 1 September 2018. **John Stretton**

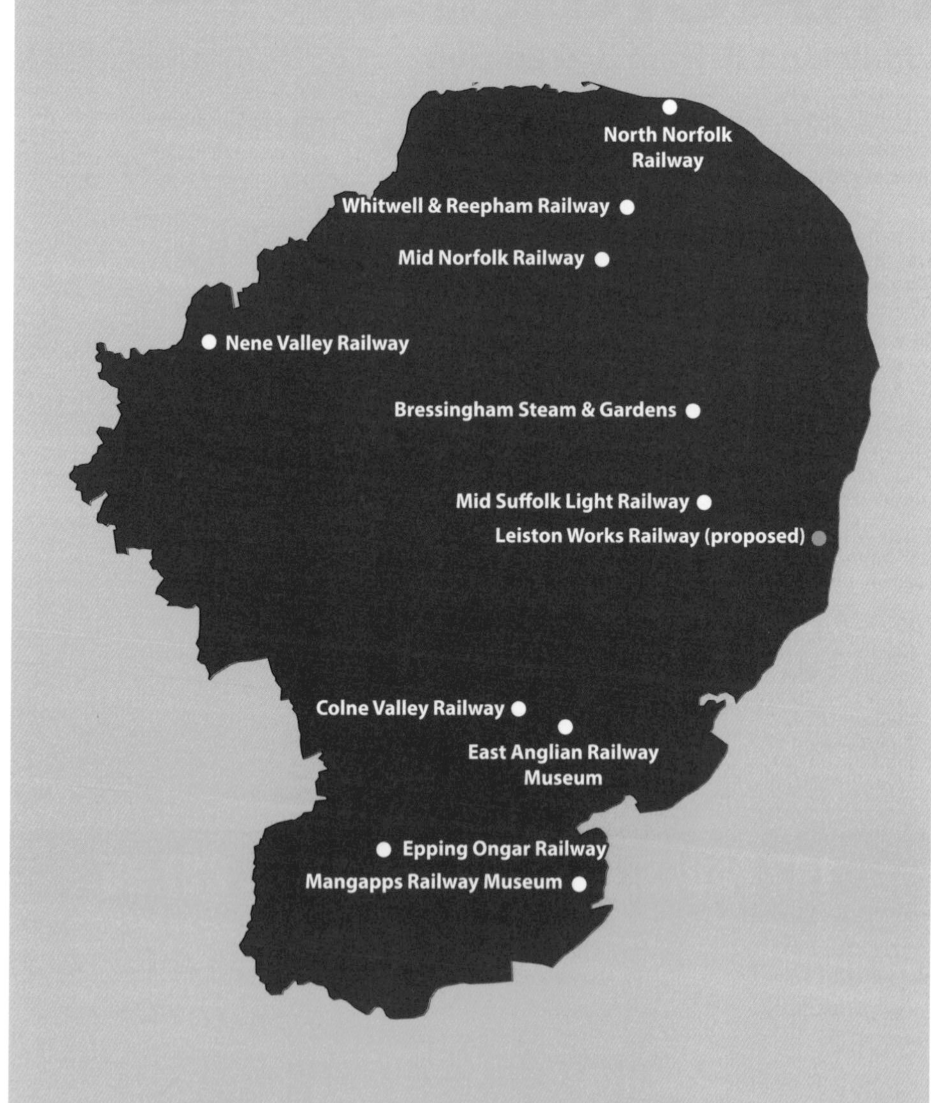
EASTERN
North Norfolk Railway
Whitwell & Reepham Railway
Mid Norfolk Railway
Nene Valley Railway
Bressingham Steam & Gardens
Mid Suffolk Light Railway
Leiston Works Railway (proposed)
Colne Valley Railway
East Anglian Railway Museum
Epping Ongar Railway
Mangapps Railway Museum

Region 6 – Eastern

Bressingham Steam & Gardens

Introduction and History

Bressingham was established by Alan Bloom after he purchased the 220-acre estate of Bressingham Hall in 1946. The first of a number of traction engines arrived in 1961 and the first narrow gauge railway was laid in 1965. The site now houses a steam museum, gardens, a nursery and a number of different railways, all of which are open to the public. The railways consist of a standard gauge demonstration line (approximately one quarter of a mile long), the Fen Railway (2 foot gauge, one and a half miles long), the Garden Railway (10¼ inch gauge, three quarters of a mile) and the Waveney Valley Railway (15 inch gauge, one and a half miles long).

Contact Details

Website: www.bressingham.co.uk
Tel: 01379 686900
Email: Written enquiries can be made from the website.
Address: Bressingham Steam & Gardens, Low Road, Bressingham, Diss, Norfolk, IP22 2AA.

Transport Links

By Rail: The nearest railway station is Diss, which is three and a half miles away.
By Road: Free parking for cars and coaches is available on site (IP22 2AA).

Opening Times

The gardens and railway are open 10.30–17.00 (last entry 16.00) from 29 March until October. They are closed outside of these times, except for occasional special events, which are listed on the website.

Line Mileage and Journey Time

The standard gauge demonstration line is approximately a quarter of a mile long and the journey time is relatively short.

Stock List

Type	Number	Builder	Details
Steam	6841 WILLIAM FRANCIS	Beyer Peacock	0-4-0+0-4-0
Steam	7070 MILLFIELD	Robert Stephenson & Hawthorns	0-4-0CT
Steam	1472	Andrew Barclay	0-4-0F
Steam	25 (6087)	Neilson & Co	0-4-0ST
Steam	GRANVILLE (BR No. 30102)	LSWR	0-4-0T
Steam	3193	Hunslet	0-6-0ST
Steam	32662	LBSCR	0-6-0T
Steam	87	GER	0-6-0T
Steam	5865	Norwegian State Railways	2-10-0
Steam	490	GER	2-4-0
Steam	377 KING HAAKON VII	Norwegian State Railways	2-6-0
Steam	80 THUNDERSLEY	LT&SR	4-4-2T

Attractions

Bressingham has four different railways, each with a different gauge, together giving over four miles of railway journeys available. There is a collection of working and static steam and traction engines, gardens to visit and an adjacent garden centre. Bressingham is also the home of the Dad's Army Appreciation Society and a Dad's Army Museum. Various driving experiences are available, driving trains of different gauges and traction engines. Other attractions in the region include Banham Zoo, the market town of Diss and the fens and coastlines of Norfolk.

Special Events during 2019

21 April: Paddington Visits.
4–6 May: Heritage Steam Gala.
12 May: 1940s Day.
26 May: Rover Car Rally.
1 June: Narrow Gauge East.

6–7 July: Steampunk Weekend.
27–28 July: Fire Rally & Marshall from Paw Patrol visits on 27th and Fireman Sam visits 28th.
10 August: East Anglia Garden Rail Show.
10–11 August: Steam in Miniature.
1 September: Model Railway Day.
22 September: Vintage Farming Day.
25–26 October: Halloween Evenings.

Colne Valley Railway

Introduction and History

The railway from Chappel & Wakes Colne on the present day Sudbury branch, to Haverhill, opened in a number of stages. It reached Halstead in 1860, extending to Castle Hedingham in 1861, to Yeldham in 1862, to Haverhill in 1863 and it was connected to the Stour Valley Railway at Haverhill in 1865. Passenger services were withdrawn in 1960, followed by freight in 1965 and much of the railway infrastructure was demolished soon after. The land at the Hedingham site was bought in 1973; a heritage railway organisation was formed and the first trains ran in 1976. The surviving Hedingham railway station was carefully relocated from its original location one mile away and has been renamed Castle Hedingham. The railway has recently secured its long-term future and in 2019, a new car park, entrance building and interactive museum will open.

Contact Details

Website: www.colnevalleyrailway.co.uk
Tel: 01787 461174
Email: info@colnevalleyrailway.co.uk
Address: Colne Valley Railway, Castle Hedingham, CO9 3DZ.

Transport Links

By Rail: Sudbury and Braintree are the nearest railway stations and both are nine miles away.
By Road: Ample free car parking is available at Castle Hedingham station (CO9 3DZ).

Opening Times

The Castle Hedingham site and museum open every day from 6 April and trains will operate on the following dates:

Sundays & Bank Holiday Mondays 24 March–27 October: (steam-hauled).
Saturdays 23 March–2 November: (diesel railcar).
Wednesdays during Essex School Holidays: (steam-hauled, except Halloween).

Line Mileage and Journey Time

Castle Hedingham is in the centre of the railway, which operates for slightly less than one mile and a return trip takes about half an hour.

Stock List

Type	*Number*	*Builder*	*Details*
Steam	1875	Avonside	0-4-0ST
Steam	1	Hawthorn Leslie	0-4-0ST
Steam	190	Hunslet	0-6-0ST
Steam	200	Hunslet	0-6-0ST
Steam	60 JUPITER	Robert Stephenson & Hawthorns	0-6-0ST
Steam	45163	Armstrong Whitworth	4-6-0
Steam	45293	Armstrong Whitworth	4-6-0
Steam	35010	Southern Railway	4-6-2
Diesel	D2041	British Railways	Class 03
Diesel	D2184	British Railways	Class 03
Diesel	14901	British Railways	Class 14
DMU	55033	Pressed Steel	Class 121
DMU	55508 & 55528	BREL/Leyland	Class 141
DMU	79978	AC Cars	Railbus
EMU	75023	British Railways	Class 307
EMU	75881	British Railways	Class 308
EMU	71205 & 78037	BREL	Class 312

Attractions

The Brewster Interactive Museum, a larger shop and improved facilities will open during 2019. The site has four different sized railways; the standard gauge line, a 7¼ inch gauge miniature railway with steam and diesel locomotives, a garden railway and a model railway. Train driver experience courses and Pullman dining trains are available on selected dates. Heritage railways within the region include the East Anglian Railway Museum (see page 120), the Mid Suffolk Light Railway (see page 124) and the Epping Ongar Railway (see page 121). Other attractions in the area include Hedingham Castle, Long Melford Country Park and Coggeshall Grange Barn.

Special Events during 2019

14 April: Colne Valley at War (1940s themed event).
28 April: Paw Patrol visit.
2 June: Peter Rabbit visit.
30 June: Gruffalo visit.
21 July: Peppa Pig visit.
18 August: Wallace & Grommitt visit.
25 August: Bus & Commercial Vehicle Rally.
8 September: Paddington Bear visit.
6 October: PJ Masks visit.
27 October: Paw Patrol visit.
29–31 October: Halloween at Hedingham (Diesel Ghost Train).
December Saturdays & Sundays: Steam with Santa.

▲ **Epping Ongar Railway:** A preserved Pressed Steel DMU formed of Class 117 DMS No. M51384 and Class 121 DTS No. W56287 waits at North Weald on the Epping Ongar Railway on 22 April 2017. **Tony Christie**

East Anglian Railway Museum

Introduction and History

The Stour Valley Railway Preservation Society formed in 1968 to preserve the railway from Long Melford to Sudbury. This was not successful and the line now terminates at Sudbury. However, in 1969 the society instead leased the derelict goods yard, shed, signal box and station buildings at nearby Chappel & Wakes Colne from British Rail. In 1970 a Hunslet steam loco first carried passengers along a short stretch of relaid track and in the years that followed, the buildings and various items of rolling stock were restored. In 1983 the engine restoration workshop was built. In 1986 the society became the East Anglian Railway Museum focusing on the railway history of the area and in 1987 the site was purchased from British Rail. Today it is easily accessible by rail, with one platform of Chappel & Wakes Colne being the museum's home and the other platform is used by Marks Tey to Sudbury main line services.

Contact Details

Website: www.earm.co.uk
Tel: 01206 242524
Email: information@earm.co.uk
Address: East Anglian Railway Museum, Chappel & Wakes Colne Station, Colchester, Essex, CO6 2DS.

Transport Links

By Rail: Cross the footbridge at Chappel & Wakes Colne station. If arriving by a Greater Anglia train service, present your ticket and receive a 10% museum discount (except on special event dates).
By Road: Free car parking is available at the museum (CO6 2DS).

Opening Times

The site is open 10.00–16.30 every day except Christmas Day and Boxing Day, although the museum and railway occasionally close during special events, such as beer festivals.

Line Mileage and Journey Time

The railway demonstration line is approximately one quarter of a mile and the journey time is relatively short.

Stock List

Type	Number	Builder	Details
Steam	11 (1047)	Andrew Barclay	0-4-0ST
Steam	2542 JUBILEE	Bagnall	0-4-0ST
Steam	2039	Peckett	0-4-0ST
Steam	54	Robert Stephenson & Hawthorns	0-6-0ST
Steam	LAMPORT No.3	Bagnall	0-6-0ST
Steam	69621	GER	0-6-2T
Diesel	144 JOHN PEEL	Andrew Barclay	0-4-0
Diesel	D72229	Drewry	0-4-0
Diesel	4220039 7	Fowler	0-4-0
Diesel	2029	Simplex	0-4-0
Diesel	D2279	Robert Stephenson & Hawthorns	Class 04
DMU	51213 & 56358	Metropolitan Cammell	Class 101
DMU	79963	Waggon und Maschinenbau	Railbus

Attractions

The museum has a wealth of railway-related attractions, including the heritage centre with various interactive exhibits, the restored goods shed filled with railway memorabilia, the restoration shed where locomotives and rolling stock are being restored and the active Grade I listed signal box. There is miniature railway, which operates on selected dates and can be ridden or driven for £5. The 'Railway Experience Course' includes driving a steam engine, operating the signal box, working as a crossing keeper and guard. There is an escape room experience for four to eight people and an on site café and pub. If arriving by train from Marks Tey, you will cross Chappel Viaduct, which is one of the largest viaducts and brick built structures in the country. The Colne Valley Railway (see page 118) is 12 miles away and the Epping Ongar Railway (see below) is relatively close. Other nearby attractions include Clare Castle Country Park, Long Melford Country Park and Colchester Zoo.

Special Events during 2019

6–7 April: Spring Steam Gala.
19–22 April: Days Out with Thomas.
11 May, 17 August & 2 November: Kids Run The Railway.
26–27 May: Transport Extravaganza.
29 May: Half Term Diesel Day.
30 October: Half Term Diesel Day.

Epping Ongar Railway

Introduction and History

The railway from London reached Ongar in 1865 and steam trains used the route until 1957, when the railway become part of London Underground's Central Line. Passenger numbers declined until the Underground line between Epping and Ongar was closed in 1994. Fortunately, much of the infrastructure remained in place, facilitating the transition into a heritage railway and the line reopened as such in 2004. The railway doesn't currently operate into Epping (London Underground) station, but there are plans to extend there, which would provide a direct rail connection.

Contact Details

Website: www.eorailway.co.uk
Tel: 01277 365200
Email: enquiries@eorailway.co.uk
Address: Epping Ongar Railway, Ongar Station, Station Approach, Ongar, Essex, CM5 9BN.

Transport Links

By Rail: London Underground Central Line services terminate at Epping, where a connecting heritage bus service (number 339) travels to North Weald station.
By Road: There is no public parking at Ongar or North Weald stations, except limited disabled spaces which must be booked in advance. Car parking is available at Epping Underground station (CM16 4HW), from where the connecting heritage bus service starts (see above).

Opening Times

Trains operate on Saturdays, Sundays and Bank Holidays from 6 April to 27 October and on selected other weekdays, with services between approximately 10.00 and 16.30.

Line Mileage and Journey Time

0.00	Ongar
1.75	Blake Hall
1.50	North Weald
5.75	Epping Ongar Boundary
6.00	Epping

A return journey takes about 1 hour 30 minutes.

Stock List

Type	*Number*	*Builder*	*Details*
Steam	No. 1	Metropolitan Railway	0-4-4T
Steam	3883 LORD PHIL	Hunslet	0-6-0ST
Steam	3837	Hawthorn Leslie	0-6-0ST
Steam	3437	Hawthorn Leslie	0-6-0ST
Steam	4141	GWR	2-6-2T
Steam	4953	GWR	4-6-0
Diesel	RH398616	Ruston & Hornsby	0-4-0
Diesel	03119	British Railways	Class 03
Diesel	03170	British Railways	Class 03
Diesel	20001	English Electric	Class 20
Diesel	31438	Brush Traction	Class 31
Diesel	D6729	English Electric	Class 37
Diesel	45132	British Railways	Class 45
Diesel	47635	British Railways	Class 47

DMU	51342 & 51384	Pressed Steel	Class 117
DMU	56287	Pressed Steel	Class 121
DEMU	60110 & 60810	British Railways	Class 205
EMU	69013 & 70235	British Railways	Class 412

Attractions

The Epping Ongar Miniature Railway Group has a 7¼ inch gauge railway and is based at the railway (see www.eomrg.co.uk). Driver and signal box experiences are available. The Penny Salon Micro Gallery can be found at Ongar station; North Weald Airfield and Museum is a short walk from North Weald station and Epping Forest is also nearby. Other heritage railways in the area include the Colne Valley Railway (see page 118) and Mangapps Railway Museum (see below).

Special Events during 2019

19–22 April: Easter Egg Hunt.
27–28 April: Spring Diesel Gala.
7–9 June: Steam Gala.
22–23 June: 1940s Steam Weekend.
10–11 August: Vintage Steam Weekend.
17–18 August: Family Fun Day.
December: Santa Specials.

Mangapps Railway Museum

Introduction and History

The Mangapps Railway Museum is situated on a private site and, unlike most heritage railways and museums, it is not on the site of a former railway. All the station buildings, signal boxes, infrastructure and rolling stock have been brought from other sites. The site includes a museum with a large collection of railway exhibits, many of which are from East Anglia and the Great Eastern Railway. An operational railway line has been created and this is used by a variety of locomotives, including examples of industrial steam, industrial diesel and main line diesel locomotives.

Contact Details

Website: www.mangapps.co.uk
Tel: 01621 784898
Address: Mangapps Railway Museum, Southminster Road, Burnham-on-Crouch, Essex, CM0 8QG.

Transport Links

By Rail: The nearest station is Burnham-on-Crouch, which is just over one mile away.
By Road: There is parking on-site (CM0 8QG).

Opening Times

The Railway opens 11.30–17.00 on Saturdays, Sundays and Bank Holidays from March to October and every day during August. Trains depart every hour from 12.15 to 16.15.

Line Mileage and Journey Time

The railway is over half a mile long and a return journey takes about 20 minutes.

Stock List

Type	*Number*	*Builder*	*Details*
Steam	1619	Andrew Barclay	0-4-0ST
Steam	8 (2157)	Andrew Barclay	0-4-0ST
Steam	2087	Peckett	0-4-0ST
Steam	2613	Bagnall	0-6-0PT
Steam	MINNIE	Fox Walker	0-6-0ST
Steam	80078	British Railways	2-6-4T
Diesel	ELLAND No 1	Hudswell Clarke	0-4-0
Diesel	11104	Drewry	0-6-0
Diesel	03018	British Railways	Class 03
Diesel	03081	British Railways	Class 03

Diesel	03089	British Railways	Class 03
Diesel	03399	British Railways	Class 03
Diesel	D2325	Robert Stephenson & Hawthorns	Class 04
Diesel	31105	Brush Traction	Class 31
Diesel	31233	Brush Traction	Class 31
DMU	51381	Pressed Steel	Class 117
EMU	75033 & 75250	British Railways	Class 302

Attractions
The Mangapps site has two stations, a sizeable collection of locomotives, wagons and a museum housing a substantial number of railway artefacts, including many signals and an operable lever frame. Other attractions in the area include National Trust Danbury Commons & Blakes Wood, Northey Island and Dengie National Nature Reserve.

Mid Norfolk Railway

Introduction and History
The railway between Wymondham and Dereham opened in 1847. It was extended to King's Lynn in 1848 and to Wells-next-the-Sea in 1857. The decline began when passenger services between Dereham and Wells ended in 1964 and the line from Wymondham to Dereham was singled in 1965. Passenger services between Dereham and King's Lynn ceased in 1968, followed by Wymondham–Dereham in 1969. Freight services continued to use the line from Wymondham to Dereham and in 1974 a group formed and began campaigning for passenger trains to return. This resulted in at least one charter train operating on the line each year between 1978 and 1988, although the line closed north of Dereham in stages during the 1980s. The preservation group leased Hardingham station and yard in 1983, at which time it initially established a museum and base. In 1989 this closed and a number of groups merged in 1990, creating the beginning of today's Mid Norfolk Railway. The first heritage trains ran from Yaxham in 1995 and trains returned to Dereham in 1997. In 1998 the Wymondham–Dereham section was purchased and through trains from the main line were reinstated. The railway was extended north to Hoe in 2013 and in spring 2018 passenger services reached Worthing Crossing. It is being extended further north towards North Elmham and County School, with a long-term aim of reaching Fakenham.

Contact Details
Website: www.mnr.org.uk
Tel: 01362 851723
Email: Written enquiries can be made from the website.
Address: Dereham Railway Station, Station Road, Dereham, Norfolk, NR19 1DF.

Transport Links
By Rail: Wymondham railway station is just under one mile from Wymondham Abbey station.
By Road: Parking is available at Dereham station (NR19 1DF) and is very limited at Wymondham Abbey.

Opening Times
The railway operates on Saturdays, Sundays and Bank Holidays from mid-March to mid-October, plus selected weekdays, including each Wednesday from May to September.

Line Mileage and Journey Time
0.00	Wymondham Abbey
3.00	Kimberley Park
6.25	Thuxton
8.75	Yaxham
10.50	Dereham
12.25	Hoe
15.00	Worthing Crossing

A return journey takes about 1 hour 45 minutes.

Stock List

Type	Number	Builder	Details
Steam	9596	Sentinel	4wVBGT
Steam	2 (7818)	Robert Stephenson & Hawthorns	0-4-0ST
Diesel	D2334	Robert Stephenson & Hawthorns	Class 04
Diesel	08847	British Railways	Class 08
Diesel	D8069	English Electric	Class 20
Diesel	31255	Brush Traction	Class 31
Diesel	33202	BRCW	Class 33
Diesel	47367	Brush Traction	Class 47
Diesel	47596	Brush Traction	Class 47
Diesel	50019	English Electric	Class 50
DMU	56301	GRCW	Class 100
DMU	51226, 51434, 51499, 51503,56347 & 59117	Metropolitan Cammell	Class 101
DMU	51942 & 56270	British Railways	Class 108
DMU	55009	GRCW	Class 122
EMU	75120	British Railways	Class 307
EMU	68004	British Railways	Class 419
EMU	69318	British Railways	Class 422

Attractions
The Mid Norfolk is one of Britain's longer heritage railways and offers regular high tea and cream tea days, as well as diesel driver experience days. The North Norfolk Railway (see page 128), narrow gauge Bure Valley Railway and Bressingham Steam & Gardens (see page 117) are nearby. Other attractions in the area include Lenwade Dinosaur Adventure and Gressenhall Farm and Workhouse. Wymondham Abbey is a short walk from the railway's southern terminus and there is plenty to explore in Wymondham and Dereham.

Special Events during 2019
5–7 April: Spring Diesel Event.
12 May: Classic Bus Day.
16 June: Classic Car Day.
28–30 June: Summer Steam Event.
19 July: Evening Jazz Train from Wymondham Abbey.
3–4 August: 1940s Weekend – Railway at War.
23–26 August: Ales by Rails – Dereham Beer & Music Festival.
6 September: Evening Jazz Train from Wymondham Abbey.
27–29 September: Autumn Diesel Event.
13 October: Classic Car Day.
December: Polar Express Train Rides.

Mid Suffolk Light Railway

Introduction and History
The light railway, with reduced speed and safety requirements, from Haughley near Stowmarket to Laxfield, opened to goods traffic in 1904 and to passenger services in 1908. It was intended for the railway to continue to Halesworth on the present day Ipswich–Lowestoft line, but a lack of finances meant that it only reached Laxfield. The railway was effectively bankrupt before it opened and was never profitable, leading to its closure in 1952. The track was lifted in 1953. In 1991 a group of railway enthusiasts formed and initially created a railway museum close to the current Brockford site. The station at Brockford was re-established, a short stretch of track was laid and the first heritage trains worked in 2002. Planning approval has been granted to extend the railway by 500 m along the trackbed, which will more than double its current length. Work on this started during 2018 and the railway is raising funds for the extension and a new station which will be called Aspall Halt.

Contact Details
Website: www.mslr.org.uk
Tel: 01449 766899
Email: events@mslr.org.uk
Address: Mid Suffolk Railway, Brockford Station, Wetheringsett, Stowmarket, Suffolk, IP14 5PW.

◀ **Mid Suffolk Light Railway:** LNER Class Y7 0-4-0T No. 985 propels its train towards Brockford station on the Mid Suffolk Light Railway on 1 April 2018. This locomotive was built by the LNER to a North Eastern Railway design. **Peter Foster**

▼ **Nene Valley Railway:** Class 31 No. 31271 is seen at the head of 1M48, the 12.50 Peterborough NVR–Wansford at Castor on the Nene Valley Railway on 10 April 2016. This locomotive has recently moved to the Llangollen Railway in Wales. **Jamie Squibbs**

Transport Links

By Rail: The nearest railway station is Stowmarket, which is nine miles away.
By Road: Free car parking is available at Brockford (IP14 5PW).

Opening Times

During 2019 the railway will open on 21–22 April, 5–6 May, 25 May, every Sunday and Bank Holiday from 26 May to 26 August inclusive, 7–8 September and selected weekends during December. Trains depart from Brockford every 20 minutes from 11.00 until about 16.30.

Line Mileage and Journey Time

Trains travel for a quarter of a mile from Brockford station and a return journey takes about 20 minutes.

Stock List

Type	*Number*	*Builder*	*Details*
Steam	2565	Bagnall	0-4-0ST
Steam	1604	Hudswell Clarke	0-4-0ST
Steam	985	LNER	0-4-0T
Steam	SIRAPITE	Aveling & Porter	0-4-0WT
Steam	2525	Cockerill	0-4-0WT
Diesel	294266	Ruston & Hornsby	0-4-0
Diesel	ALSTON	Ruston & Hornsby	0-4-0

Attractions

Unlike many other heritage railways, there is no ex-British Rail coaching stock. Instead, vintage carriages are used, including the recently restored Victorian four wheel coach and the 1865 Great Eastern Railway First Class smoking coach No. 140. Visitors can explore the Arts Council accredited railway museum which tells the story of the railway and see the carriage and wagon workshop which houses active renovation projects. Tours of the workshop are available, subject to staffing. There is a café, shop, the Kitchener Arms restored real ale bar coach and train driver experiences are also available. Attractions in the region include Suffolk Owl Sanctuary and the Museum of East Anglian Life in Stowmarket. The East Anglian Railway Museum (see page 120) and Colne Valley Railway (see page 118) are both about 35 miles away.

Special Events during 2019

21–22 April: Easter Bunny hunts for children.
5–6 May: Middy in the War Years, with displays of life during WW2, re-enactors, vehicles and music.
25 May: Maverick on the Rails, celebrating American roots music and its rail connections.
7 July: Land Rover Day.
21 July: Vintage Tractor & Ploughing Event.
25–26 August: Hornby Collectors Day and Model Mania.
7–8 September: Country Railway Gala.
7–8, 14–15 & 21–22 December: Santa Specials.

Nene Valley Railway

Introduction and History

The railway from Blisworth (near Northampton), on the present day West Coast Main Line, to Peterborough opened in 1845 and was the first railway to reach Peterborough. Wansford subsequently grew in importance, becoming a junction with four lines converging after the railway to Stamford was built in 1867 and the route to Seaton in 1879. Passenger trains from Peterborough to Rugby via Seaton ceased in 1966 although freight continued until 1972. In 1969 a group that was to become the Peterborough Railway Society (PRS) formed and after the Peterborough Development Corporation purchased the railway in 1974, it was leased to the PRS. The first trains in preservation ran between Orton Mere and Wansford in 1977, using continental locomotives and rolling stock, a theme which continues with some of the railway's rolling stock today. The railway was extended from Orton Mere to Peterborough in 1986 and from Wansford to Yarwell Junction in 2007. The main line connection remains and is used for transferring visiting locomotives and occasional railtours. There are aspirations to extend the railway towards Elton on the original route to Blisworth.

Contact Details

Website: www.nvr.org.uk
Tel: 01780 784444
Email: adminassistant@nvr.org.uk
Address: Nene Valley Railway Ltd, Wansford Station, Stibbington, Peterborough, PE8 6LR.

Transport Links

By Rail: The nearest railway station is Peterborough, which is just over one mile away.
By Road: Free parking is available at Wansford (PE8 6LR) and Orton Mere (PE2 7DA) stations. Alternatively, there is chargeable parking in Ferry Meadows Country Park (PE2 5UU) adjacent to Overton station or Pleasure Fair Meadow car park (PE2 9NR) near Peterborough NVR station.

Opening Times

Trains operate on selected weekends and Wednesdays from 10.00 or 11.00 to 16.00, depending on which timetable is in operation.

Line Mileage and Journey Time

0.00	Peterborough NVR
1.50	Orton Mere
2.50	Overton for Ferry Meadows
6.25	Wansford
7.25	Yarwell Junction

A return journey takes about 1 hour 30 minutes, but slightly less when the railcar is operating.

Stock List

Type	*Number*	*Builder*	*Details*
Steam	1626	Cockerill	0-4-0VBT
Steam	DEREK CROUCH	Hudswell Clarke	0-6-0ST
Steam	75006	Hunslet	0-6-0ST
Steam	75008 SWIFTSURE	Hunslet	0-6-0ST
Steam	JACKS GREEN	Hunslet	0-6-0ST
Steam	656	Danske Statsbaner	0-6-0T
Steam	THOMAS	Hudswell Clarke	0-6-0T
Steam	5619	GWR	0-6-2T
Steam	64305	DB, Germany	2-6-2T
Steam	1178	Motala Verkstad	2-6-2T
Steam	73050	British Railways	4-6-0
Steam	101	Motala Verkstad	4-6-0
Steam	34081	British Railways	4-6-2
Diesel	BARABEL	Sentinel	0-4-0
Diesel	DL83	Sentinel	0-6-0
Diesel	D9520	British Railways	Class 14
Diesel	9529	British Railways	Class 14
Diesel	45041	British Railways	Class 45
DMU	1212	Hagglund and Soner	Swedish Railcar

Attractions
The viewing platform at Wansford gives access to the restoration work in progress and shed tours are available (advance arrangement may be needed). There is also a second-hand book carriage, café and gift shop. The railway offers driving experiences using either steam or diesel locomotives. At nearby Peterborough is the city's Cathedral and Railworld, which has a variety of railway and wildlife exhibits. Ferry Meadows Country Park is close to Overton station and Thorpe Meadows, with a sculpture walk and rowing lake, is also nearby.

Special Events during 2019
9–10 March: Southern Steam Event.
13 April: Steam, Folk & Morris Event.
20–21 April: Who's at Wansford.
4–6 May: May Bank Holiday Branch Line Weekend.
11–12 May: Steampunk.
25–27 May: May Bank Holiday Branch Line Weekend.
19 May: Thomas' Big Adventure.
15–16 June: Steam and Vintage Rally.
13 July: 'Allo 'Allo Jolly Fisherman.
28–30 September: Flying Scotsman.
25–26 October: The Wizard's Express.
The Jolly Fisherman (Fish & Chip Specials): 8 March, 3 May, 7 June, 19 July, 2 August & 18 October.
Ride behind Thomas: 19 May, 8–9 June, 6–7 July, 10–11 August, 28–29 September & 19–20 October.
December: Santa Steam.

North Norfolk Railway

Introduction and History
The railway between Cromer and Melton Constable opened in 1887 as part of the Midland and Great Northern Joint Railway network. Despite public protest beforehand, the line was closed in 1959. The North Norfolk Railway (NNR) formed in 1965. The first two steam locomotives were delivered in 1967 and services between Sheringham and Holt began in 1975. A major milestone was achieved in 2010 when Sheringham East level crossing was reinstated, reconnecting the NNR with the national rail network. There is a long-term plan to join the NNR with the Mid Norfolk Railway, creating the Norfolk Orbital Railway, a rail circuit that would include the current routes of the MNR and NNR.

Contact Details
Website: www.nnrailway.co.uk
Tel: 01263 820800
Email: enquiries@nnrailway.co.uk
Address: North Norfolk Railway, Station Approach, Sheringham, Norfolk, NR26 8RA.

Transport Links
By Rail: Main line connection at Sheringham; the two stations are adjacent, separated by a road.
By Road: Car parking is available at Sheringham (NR26 8RA, charges apply), Weybourne (NR25 7HN) and Holt (NR25 6AJ) stations. Parking space at Weybourne is limited.

Opening Times
Trains operate all year round, with limited services during January to March and November. The NNR website shows the latest timetables, which differ through the year.

Line Mileage and Journey Time
0.00 Sheringham
2.75 Weybourne
3.25 Kelling Heath Halt
5.00 Holt

A return journey takes about 50 minutes.

Stock List

Type	*Number*	*Builder*	*Details*
Steam	985	LNER	0-4-0T
Steam	564	GER	0-6-0
Steam	1982	Hunslet	0-6-0ST
Steam	1700	Hudswell Clarke	0-6-0ST
Steam	1744	North British	0-6-2T
Steam	76084	British Railways	2-6-0
Steam	53809	Robert Stephenson & Co	2-8-0
Steam	92203	British Railways	2-10-0
Steam	90775	North British	2-10-0
Steam	8572	Beyer Peacock	4-6-0
Diesel	D2051	British Railways	Class 03
Diesel	D2063	British Railways	Class 03
Diesel	D3935	British Railways	Class 08
Diesel	D3940	British Railways	Class 08
Diesel	12131	British Railways	Class 11
Diesel	20227	English Electric	Class 20
Diesel	25057	British Railways	Class 25
Diesel	D5631	Brush Traction	Class 31
Diesel	D6732	English Electric	Class 37
DMU	51188, 51192, 51228, 56062 & 56352	Metropolitan Cammell	Class 101
DMU	56182	BRCW	Class 104

Attractions

The William Marriott Museum, which tells the story of East Anglia's railways, and the North Norfolk Model Engineering Club's miniature railway are both located at Holt station. The Mid Norfolk Railway (see page 123) and the narrow gauge Bure Valley Railway are about eight and ten miles from the NNR respectively. Sheringham town centre, the Norfolk Coastal Path, Sheringham Park and a number of other National Trust sites are near to the railway.

Special Events during 2019

5–7 April: That's Yer Lot Gala
4–6 May: Days Out with Thomas.
26–27 May: Dad's Army Live.
14–16 June: Mixed Traction Gala.
6 July: Bus Rally.
7 July: Vintage Transport Day.
19–21 July: Beer Festival.
3–4 August: S&D Weekend.
30 August–1 September: Autumn Steam Gala.
14–15 September: '40s Weekend.
19–31 October: Halloween.
30 November, 1, 7–8, 14–15 & 20–24 December: Santa Specials.
26 December–5 January 2020: Mince Pie Specials.

Whitwell & Reepham Railway

Introduction and History

The Midland & Great Northern Joint Railway (M&GNJR) from Norwich City to Melton Constable opened in 1882; Whitwell & Reepham station was situated roughly half way along the rural route. The Great Eastern Railway had opened a more conveniently located station in Reepham in 1881, creating competition from the beginning. After declining use, passenger services to Whitwell & Reepham ceased in 1959. Regular freight ended in 1964 and the track was lifted in 1985 after freight traffic finished. From 1993, much of the trackbed became part of Marriott's Way, a traffic-free cycle and footpath which runs through both former stations in Reepham and is named after William Marriott, Chief Engineer of the M&GNJR. The derelict Whitwell & Reepham station site was offered for sale by Norfolk County Council in 2006 and bought by a rail enthusiast who restored it and relaid railway track in the yard behind the station, extending for a short distance to the south. The first heritage trains ran when the station reopened in 2009 and it now has a growing collection of railway rolling stock. There are plans to extend the railway north for a number of miles towards Themelthorpe Curve.

Contact Details

Website: www.whitwellstation.com
Tel: 01603 871694
Email: info@whitwellstation.com
Address: Whitwell & Reepham Station, Whitwell Road, Reepham, Norfolk, NR10 4GA.

Transport Links

By Rail: The nearest stations are on other heritage railways. Aylsham on the narrow gauge Bure Valley Railway is nine miles away, Dereham on the Mid Norfolk Railway (see page 123) is 11 miles away and Norwich station is 15 miles away.
By Road: Car parking is available at Whitwell & Reepham.
By Bike: Whitwell & Reepham station is situated on the Marriott's Way route. Cycle hire is available at the site.

Opening Times

The station opens every day except Mondays during the winter months and trains operate each weekend. Steam trains operate 12.30–16.00 on the first Sunday of the month. On Saturdays and the other Sundays diesel trains work on demand 10.00–17.00.

Line Mileage and Journey Time

The railway is approximately half a mile long and the journey time is relatively short.

Stock List

Type	*Number*	*Builder*	*Details*
Steam	2199 VICTORY	Andrew Barclay	0-4-0ST
Steam	945 ANNIE	Andrew Barclay	0-4-0ST
Steam	AGECROFT No.3 (7681)	Robert Stephenson & Hawthorns	0-4-0ST
Diesel	1 (3733)	Baguley	0-4-0
Diesel	D2700	North British	0-4-0
Diesel	466629 TIPOCKITY	Ruston & Hornsby	0-4-0
Diesel	518494 SWANWORTH	Ruston & Hornsby	0-4-0
Diesel	D1171	Hudswell Clarke	0-6-0
DMU	51370 & 51412	Pressed Steel	Class 117
EMU	70527	British Railways	Class 411

Attractions

The site includes the restored station building, a signal box which is being renovated and a museum with exhibits relating to the station and the railway's history. There is a model and miniature railway club based at the site. Bicycles are available for hire from the site, which is directly on the 26-mile-long traffic-free Marriott's Way through rural Norfolk. The region is also home to the North Norfolk Railway (see page 128), the Mid Norfolk Railway (see page 123), the historic city of Norwich and a number of coastal destinations.

Special Events during 2019

6–7 April: 1940s Weekend.
14 April: 1940s Era Sale with collectors, enthusiasts, and re-enactors.
21 April: Easter Egg Hunt.
9–14 August: Reepham Festival '19.
20 October: 1940s Era Sale with collectors, enthusiasts, and re-enactors.

▲ **North Norfolk Railway:** Metropolitan Cammell Class 101 DMU 101693, formed of DMBS 51192 and DTSL 56352, is seen near Sheringham forming the 1440 to Holt on 21 June 2017. **Glen Batten**

SOUTH-EAST

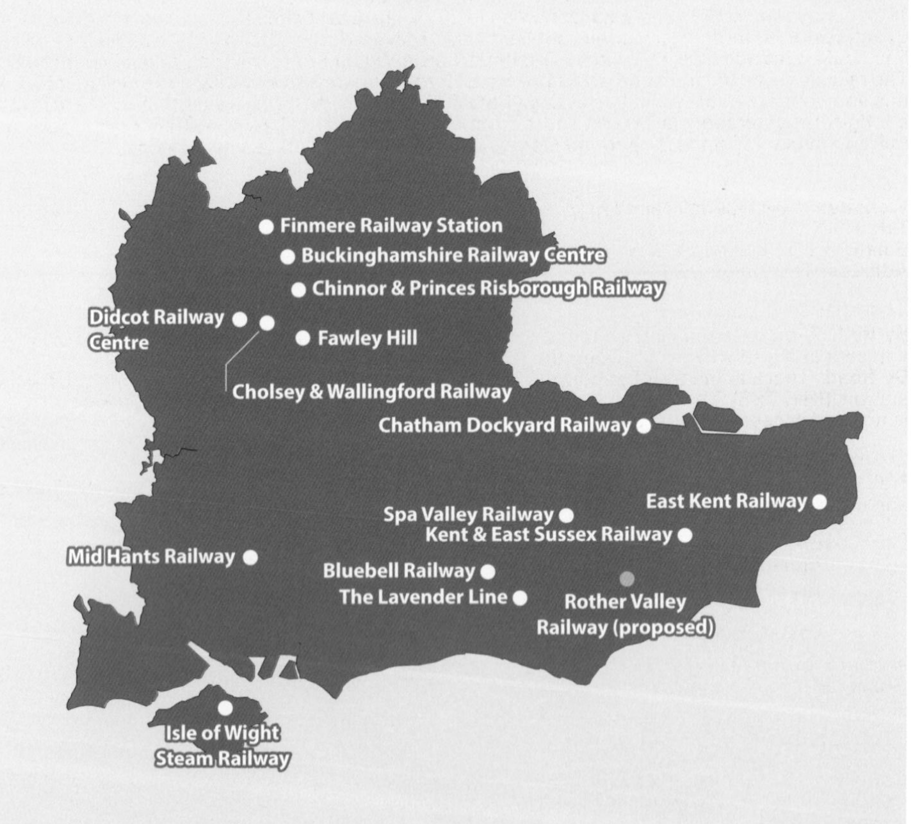

Finmere Railway Station
Buckinghamshire Railway Centre
Chinnor & Princes Risborough Railway
Didcot Railway Centre
Fawley Hill
Cholsey & Wallingford Railway
Chatham Dockyard Railway
East Kent Railway
Spa Valley Railway
Kent & East Sussex Railway
Mid Hants Railway
Bluebell Railway
The Lavender Line
Rother Valley Railway (proposed)
Isle of Wight Steam Railway

Region 7 – South-East

Bluebell Railway

Introduction and History

This railway was the first of two routes between Oxted and Lewes and was built by the London, Brighton & South Coast Railway, opening in 1882. Closure of the East Grinstead–Lewes route was proposed in 1954 and effected in 1958, with the Haywards Heath–Horsted Keynes route surviving until 1963. A preservation group formed in 1959 and in 1960 the Bluebell Railway became one of the first standard gauge preserved railways in the world to operate trains, initially from Sheffield Park to Bluebell Halt, with the line extending north to Horsted Keynes in 1962, Kingscote in 1994 and East Grinstead in 2013. The East Grinstead extension required vast quantities of 30 foot deep landfill rubbish to be excavated from the railway cutting, before the line could continue over the impressive Imberhorne Viaduct to rejoin the national rail network. The railway owns the trackbed of the line from Horsted Keynes to Ardingly and plans to reinstate this and connect to the main line at Copyhold Junction, north of Haywards Heath. There is also a long-term aspiration to extend south from Sheffield Park to Lewes, which would make the railway unique in connecting to the main line network at three different locations.

Contact Details

Website: www.bluebell-railway.co.uk
Tel: 01825 720800
Email: info@bluebell-railway.co.uk
Address: The Bluebell Railway, Sheffield Park Station, East Sussex, TN22 3QL.

Transport Links

By Rail: There is a rail connection at East Grinstead; the main line and Bluebell stations are adjacent and a short walk between the two is needed.
By Road: There is plenty of parking space at Sheffield Park (TN22 3QL) and Horsted Keynes station (RH17 7BB). There is pay and display parking near to East Grinstead (RH19 1EB) and there is no road access at Kingscote.

Opening Times

Trains operate most weekends in February and March, then every day from April to October and most days in December.

Line Mileage and Journey Time

0.00	Sheffield Park
4.50	Horsted Keynes
8.50	Kingscote
10.75	East Grinstead

A return journey takes 1 hour 40 minutes from Sheffield Park or about two hours from East Grinstead.

Stock List

Type	*Number*	*Builder*	*Details*
Steam	3 CAPTAIN BAXTER	Fletcher Jennings	0-4-0T
Steam	96 NORMANDY	LSWR	0-4-0T
Steam	263	SECR	0-4-4T
Steam	65	SECR	0-6-0
Steam	592	SECR	0-6-0
Steam	30541	Southern Railway	0-6-0
Steam	24 STAMFORD	Avonside	0-6-0ST
Steam	4	Manning Wardle	0-6-0ST
Steam	641	Manning Wardle	0-6-0ST
Steam	FENCHURCH (32636)	LBSCR	0-6-0T
Steam	55 STEPNEY	LBSCR	0-6-0T
Steam	58850	North London Railway	0-6-0T
Steam	31027	SECR	0-6-0T
Steam	178	SECR	0-6-0T

Steam	323 BLUEBELL	SECR	0-6-0T
Steam	1959 (30064)	Vulcan Iron Works	0-6-0T
Steam	32473	LBSCR	0-6-2T
Steam	1638	Southern Railway	2-6-0
Steam	31618	Southern Railway	2-6-0
Steam	84030	Bluebell Railway SC2P	2-6-2T
Steam	80064	British Railways	2-6-4T
Steam	80100	British Railways	2-6-4T
Steam	80151	British Railways	2-6-4T
Steam	92240	British Railways	2-10-0
Steam	9017	GWR	4-4-0
Steam	928	Southern Railway	4-4-0
Steam	32424	Bluebell Railway Atlantic Group	4-4-2
Steam	488	LSWR	4-4-2T
Steam	73082	British Railways	4-6-0
Steam	75027	British Railways	4-6-0
Steam	847	Southern Railway	4-6-0
Steam	34059	Southern Railway	4-6-2
Steam	21C123 (BR No.34023)	Southern Railway	4-6-2
Diesel	957	Howard	0-4-0
Diesel	10241	Rolls Royce Sentinel	0-4-0
Diesel	D4106	British Railways	Class 09

Attractions

The Bluebell Railway has the largest collection of British steam locomotives after the National Railway Museum. This, along with the engine shed and museum at Sheffield Park and carriage & wagon works with its viewing gallery at Horsted Keynes, give plenty of railway interest. Attractions in the region include Sheffield Park Gardens and Standen House & Garden (both National Trust), Bluebell Vineyard which is two miles from Sheffield Park and Sackville College at East Grinstead. The Royal Botanic Gardens' Wakehurst site is a few miles from Horsted Keynes.

Special Events during 2019

18–22 April: Easter Weekend & Easter Egg Hunt.
17–18 May: Trains after Dark.
25–27 May: Science Technology Engineering & Maths Event at Sheffield Park.
14–16 June: Road meets Rail – Traction engines, steam trains & Sussex Ales Beer Festival.
29–30 June: Model Railway Weekend.
27 July: Toy & Rail Collectors Fair.
10–11 August: Steam through the Ages.
24–26 August: Teddy Bears' Picnic.
11–13 October: Giants of Steam Autumn Gala.
26 October–3 November: Witches and Wizards Event.

Buckinghamshire Railway Centre

Introduction and History

The Buckinghamshire Railway Centre is based at Quainton Road railway station, which opened in 1868 on the route from London to Verney Junction via Aylesbury. It grew in significance after becoming part of the Great Central Railway in 1899. However, passenger services no longer stopped at the station from 1963 and in 1966 the route was closed to passenger traffic. The Quainton Road Society was formed in 1969 and in 1971 it absorbed the London Railway Preservation Society with its collection of railway exhibits. Today the 25-acre site has one of the country's largest collections of locomotives, rolling stock and railway memorabilia and a short operational steam railway. The station remains connected to the national railway network and freight trains continue to pass through the site.

Contact Details

Website: www.bucksrailcentre.org
Tel: 01296 655720
Email: office@bucksrailcentre.org
Address: Buckinghamshire Railway Centre, Station Road, Quainton, Aylesbury, Bucks, HP22 4BY.

Transport Links

By Rail: Aylesbury Vale Parkway is the nearest railway station and is less than five miles away.
By Road: There is ample free parking for cars and coaches (HP22 4BY).

Opening Times

The Centre is open 10.30–17.00 on Sundays 7 April–29 September inclusive, when trains will operate. It opens 10.30–16.30 Monday–Wednesday within the same period, without trains operating. Trains also operate on Bank Holidays and 17, 20 & 24 February, 10, 17, 19–22 April, 1–2 & 29–30 June, 31 July, 7, 14, 21 & 28 August, 7–8 & 21–22 September, 27 & 30 October–3 November and 7–8, 14–15 & 21–22 December.

Line Mileage and Journey Time

The railway is just under half a mile in length and the journey time is relatively short.

Stock List

Type	*Number*	*Builder*	*Details*
Steam	6515	Sentinel	4wT
Steam	1477	Andrew Barclay	0-4-0F
Steam	2243	Andrew Barclay	0-4-0F
Steam	699	Andrew Barclay	0-4-0ST
Steam	2469	Bagnall	0-4-0ST
Steam	1742	Hudswell Clarke	0-4-0ST
Steam	3717	Hawthorn Leslie	0-4-0ST
Steam	3718	Hawthorn Leslie	0-4-0ST
Steam	1159	Peckett	0-4-0ST
Steam	2105	Peckett	0-4-0ST
Steam	807	Aveling & Porter	0-4-0T
Steam	9366	Sentinel	0-4-0T
Steam	1900	Peckett	0-4-0T
Steam	3567	Aveling & Porter	0-4-0WT
Steam	7715	GWR	0-6-0PT
Steam	9466	Robert Stephenson & Hawthorns	0-6-0PT
Steam	3890	Hunslet	0-6-0ST
Steam	3782	Hunslet	0-6-0ST
Steam	2498	Yorkshire Engine Co.	0-6-0ST
Steam	1334	Hudswell Clarke	0-6-0T
Steam	24564	North British	0-6-0T
Steam	3020	LNWR	2-2-2
Steam	30585	LSWR	2-4-0WT
Steam	7200	GWR	2-8-2T
Steam	6989	British Railways	4-6-0
Steam	3405	North British	4-8-4

▲ **Bluebell Railway:** The Bluebell Railway's SECR Class H 0-4-4T No.263 passes a bank of bluebells in Lindfield Wood, between Sheffield Park and Horsted Keynes, with an afternoon "Golden Arrow" dining service on 6 May 2018. **Jon Bowers**

▼ **Didcot Railway Centre:** GWR 1400 Class 0-4-2T No. 1466, the first engine to be taken into preservation by the Great Western Society, stands alongside 4073 Class No. 5051 "Drysllwyn Castle" and 6959 Class No. 6998 "Burton Agnes Hall" during the GWR shed experience weekend at Didcot Railway Centre, also on 6 May 2018. **David Dew**

Diesel	20067	Fowler	0-4-0
Diesel	2102	Hibberd	0-4-0
Diesel	3271	Hibberd	0-4-0
Diesel	3765	Hibberd	0-4-0
Diesel	2067	Hunslet	0-4-0
Diesel	K4428	Hunslet	0-4-0
Diesel	425477	Ruston & Hornsby	0-4-0
Diesel	463153	Ruston & Hornsby	0-4-0
Diesel	459518	Ruston & Hornsby	0-6-0
Diesel	D2298	Robert Stephenson & Hawthorns	Class 04
DMU	51886, 51899 & 59761	British Railways	Class 115

Attractions
The museum and visitor centre have extensive exhibits including a royal dining coach from 1901 and one of the most complete sets of British Rail goods vehicles. Visitors can ride the 1 km-long miniature railway and look at the projects awaiting renovation in the restoration sheds. The Travelling Post Office tells the story of moving mail by rail and visitors can try sorting mail. Steam engine driver experiences are available. Nearby attractions include Quainton Windmill, Waddesden Manor, Buckinghamshire County Museum and the town of Aylesbury.

Special Events during 2019
June 1 & 2: 1940s Event.
June 29 & 30 and September 7 & 8: Day Out with Thomas.
September 21 & 22: Traction Engine Rally.

Chatham Dockyard Railway

Introduction and History
Chatham Dockyard was a Royal Navy dockyard which was established in the mid-16th Century. A standard gauge railway within the dockyard was built in 1865 to move materials within the site and serve the shipbuilding yards. This was connected to the main line network in 1877. A narrow gauge railway and locomotives were introduced in 1871; however, this had ceased operating by the 1930s. At its peak, it is estimated that there were approximately 17 miles of railway within the dockyard; this had reduced to about two miles when the Royal Navy dockyard closed in 1984. The site opened the following year as Chatham Historic Dockyard, a maritime museum. The Chatham Dockyard Railway runs demonstration trains through the site. The railway is not able to carry passengers.

Contact Details
Website: www.dockyardrailway.co.uk
Tel: 01634 823800
Email: nkils2@hotmail.co.uk
Address: Chatham Historic Dockyard, Main Gate, Chatham, ME4 4TY.

Transport Links
By Rail: The nearest stations are Chatham and Gillingham (Kent); both are just over a mile away.
By Road: Parking is available at the dockyard site (ME4 4TY).

Opening Times
During 2019 the dockyard opens 10.00–16.00 daily from 2 February to 24 November. Trains will operate during these weekends: 9–10 & 16–17 March, 6–7 & 21–22 April, 25–26 May, 15–16 June, 6–7 July, 3–4 August, 7-8 & 21–22 September and 2–3 November.

Line Mileage and Journey Time
The dockyard has nearly two miles of track and demonstration trains usually use approximately three quarters of a mile of this. A return journey takes about 25 minutes.

Stock List

Type	Number	Builder	Details
Steam	INVICTA (2220)	Andrew Barclay	0-4-0ST
Steam	1903	Peckett	0-4-0ST
Steam	AJAX (7042)	Robert Stephenson & Hawthorns	0-4-0ST
Diesel	WD42	Andrew Barclay	0-4-0
Diesel	THALIA (2503)	Drewry	0-4-0
Diesel	ROCHESTER CASTLE (FH3738)	Hibberd	0-4-0

Attractions

The dockyard railway operates demonstrations using steam cranes, steam and diesel locomotives and wooden wagons, most of which pre-date the 1923 railway Grouping. Special steamings can be arranged in advance for photographers, railway enthusiasts or private functions. Trains travel through the dockyard, which is a maritime museum covering an 80 acre site, including warships, a historic RNLI lifeboat collection and Victorian ropery. Additional attractions nearby include Fort Amherst, Chatham Ski & Snowboard Centre and Diggerland Kent.

Special Events during 2019

April: Easter Specials.
21–22 April: Festival of Steam and Transport.
21–22 September: Salute to the 1940s.
October: Halloween Special.

Chinnor & Princes Risborough Railway

Introduction and History

The branch line from Princes Risborough to Watlington opened in 1872, with intermediate stations at Chinnor and Aston Rowant. Passenger services ceased in 1957 although trains carrying goods and parcels continued until early 1961, after which the track beyond Chinnor was lifted. The station and platform at Chinnor were demolished in the 1970s; trains continued to work to Chinnor Cement Works until 1989 when Class 47 47258 hauled the final revenue-earning service. The Chinnor & Princes Risborough Railway Association took over the route in 1990 and in 1994 it purchased the freehold for the line, built a new station and platform and ran its first trains from Chinnor. The railway was extended in 1995 and again in 1996 when it reached the former main line junction at Princes Risborough. In 2018 the railway extended into Platform 4 of Princes Risborough station, returning passenger services to the branch for the first time since 1957. There are aspirations to extend the railway south-west along the former Watlington branch in the future.

Contact Details

Website: www.chinnorrailway.co.uk
Tel: 07979 055366
Email: Written enquiries can be made from the website.
Address: Chinnor & Princes Risborough Railway, Station Approach, Station Road, Chinnor, OX39 4ER.

Transport Links

By Rail: The railway operates from Princes Risborough station. Cross to Platform 4 for Chinnor services.
By Road: Free parking is available opposite Chinnor station (OX39 4BZ).

Opening Times

During 2019 trains operate every Sunday from 31 March to 27 October and on selected other dates for special events.

Line Mileage and Journey Time

0.00	Princes Risborough
3.75	Chinnor

A return journey takes about 50 minutes.

Stock List

Type	Number	Builder	Details
Diesel	IRIS (459515)	Ruston & Hornsby	0-6-0
Diesel	08825	British Railways	Class 08
Diesel	D3018	British Railways	Class 08
Diesel	D8568	Clayton	Class 17
Diesel	97205 (31163)	Brush Traction	Class 31
Diesel	37227	English Electric	Class 37
DMU	51375 (977992)	Pressed Steel	Class 117
DMU	55023 & 55024	Pressed Steel	Class 121
EMU	61736, 61737 & 70573	British Railways	Class 411

Attractions

The railway's Chinnor base is home to the Cambrian Tea Room and a shop selling railway books, models and souvenirs. The historic market town of Princes Risborough is home to a number of 17th and 18th Century buildings, including the National Trust-owned Manor House, which is less than a mile from the station. The railway is on the edge of the Chiltern Hills, an Area of Outstanding Natural Beauty, which has a large number of walks, hills and woodlands that can be explored.

Special Events during 2019

31 March: Mothering Sunday (Mums travel half price).
5–7 April: Vintage Diesel Gala.
26 May: Steam & Classic Cars.
15 June & 21 September: Real Ale & Steam and Gin & Cheese Tasting & Steam.
16 June: Father's Day (Dads travel free).
20 & 27 October: Spooks & Ghouls.
December: Santa Specials & Mince Pie Specials.

There are also a number of Kids for £1 days and a variety of dining trains through the year.

▲ **Chinnor & Princes Risborough Railway:** Pressed Steel Class 121 single-car DMU No. 55023 sets off with the 1300 departure from Chinnor on a very wintry 17 March 2018. **Tony Christie**

Cholsey & Wallingford Railway

Introduction and History

The branch line from Cholsey to Wallingford opened 1866. It was originally planned for the railway to continue to Watlington and meet the branch from Princes Risborough, part of which forms the Chinnor & Princes Risborough Railway today, but this was not built. Passenger services ceased in 1959; freight trains to Wallingford station continued until 1965, after which the station was closed and the land sold. Traffic continued to the malting plant to the south of Wallingford until 1981. A final railtour ran from London Paddington to Wallingford in May 1981, before British Rail closed the junction at Cholsey. The C&WR Preservation Society was then formed and the first trains in preservation ran in 1985 from a temporary platform in Wallingford. The railway returned to Cholsey station in 1994, with trains working into a dedicated bay platform, although there is no main line rail connection.

Contact Details

Website: www.cholsey-wallingford-railway.com
Tel: 01491 835067
Email: Written enquiries can be made from the website.
Address: Cholsey & Wallingford Railway, Wallingford Station, 5 Hithercroft Road, Wallingford, Oxfordshire, OX10 9GQ.

Transport Links

By Rail: Heritage trains depart from Platform 5 at Cholsey station. Through tickets to Wallingford can be purchased from GWR stations (the Wallingford Rover).
By Road: Free parking is available at Wallingford (OX10 9GQ) and there is a small pay & display car park outside Cholsey station (OX10 9QD).

Opening Times

Trains operate 11.00–16.30 on selected weekends and bank holidays throughout the year and are steam hauled on some dates.

Line Mileage and Journey Time

0.00	Cholsey
2.25	Wallingford

A return journey takes about 45 minutes.

Stock List

Type	*Number*	*Builder*	*Details*
Steam	NORTHERN GAS BOARD No. 1	Peckett	0-4-0ST
Diesel	3270	Hibberd	0-4-0
Diesel	08022 LION	British Railways	Class 08
Diesel	08060 UNICORN	British Railways	Class 08
Diesel	08123	British Railways	Class 08

Attractions

The railway has a number of locomotives with an industrial and shunting history. Wallingford station has a café and shop with many railway-related items and second-hand books. In Wallingford, there is a 15th Century market place, a castle, views of the River Thames and a local museum. Cholsey Church is the burial place of Agatha Christie and is a short walk from Cholsey station. Didcot Railway Centre (see below) is six miles away and the Chinnor & Princes Risborough Railway is 16 miles away (see page 138).

Special Events during 2019

21–22 April: Easter Running Days.
4 May: Ale Rail Tour.
5–6 May: Spring Bank Holiday Event.
30 August–1 September: Bunkfest Folk, Music & Beer Festival.
7–8, 14–15 & 21–22 December: Santa Specials.

Didcot Railway Centre

Introduction and History

There has been a railway at the site since the original broad gauge line was built in 1839. Didcot station first opened in 1844 and it has been an important junction, depot and stabling point since. The depot became surplus to British Rail's requirements and closed in 1965; however, in 1967 the Great Western Society gained access to the site and has used it since to restore, exhibit and demonstrate an array of rolling stock and items of railway interest. The site is in the middle of the triangle of busy railway lines at Didcot and includes a number of short railway lines on which a variety of traction hauls passenger trains.

Contact Details

Website: www.didcotrailwaycentre.org.uk
Tel: 01235 817200
Email: info@didcotrailwaycentre.org.uk
Address: Didcot Railway Centre, Didcot, Oxfordshire, OX11 7NJ.

Transport Links

By Rail: The subway inside Didcot Parkway railway station leads directly to the Centre.
By Road: Car parking is available at Didcot Parkway (OX11 7NJ) or the nearby larger Foxhall Road site (OX11 7NR) and both are chargeable. Note that as the Railway Centre is entirely surrounded by railway lines, the route to the Centre includes crossing a footbridge or using the station subway, both of which involve stairs.

Opening Times

The Centre opens 10.30–16.00 (17.00 on some summer dates) on all Saturdays & Sundays and every day from 16 February to 6 October and 26 October to 3 November.

Line Mileage and Journey Time

The section carrying passengers is a quarter of a mile long and the journey time is relatively short. The locomotive roster for this railway in shown on the Centre's website.

Stock List

Type	*Number*	*Builder*	*Details*
Steam	1340	Avonside	0-4-0ST
Steam	1338	Kitson	0-4-0ST
Steam	1 BONNIE PRINCE CHARLIE	Robert Stephenson & Hawthorns	0-4-0ST
Steam	5	George England	0-4-0WT
Steam	1466	GWR	0-4-2T
Steam	3650	GWR	0-6-0PT
Steam	3738	GWR	0-6-0PT
Steam	1363	GWR	0-6-0ST
Steam	2409	Hunslet	0-6-0ST
Steam	6697	Armstrong Whitworth	0-6-2T
Steam	FIRE FLY (replica)	Fire Fly Trust	2-2-2
Steam	5322	GWR	2-6-0
Steam	4144	GWR	2-6-2T
Steam	5572	GWR	2-6-2T
Steam	6106	GWR	2-6-2T
Steam	3822	GWR	2-8-0
Steam	5227	GWR	2-8-0T
Steam	7202	GWR	2-8-2T
Steam	IRON DUKE	Resco Railways	4-2-2
Steam	1014	Great Western Society	4-6-0
Steam	2999	Great Western Society	4-6-0
Steam	7808	GWR	4-6-0
Steam	4079	GWR	4-6-0
Steam	5051	GWR	4-6-0
Steam	5900	GWR	4-6-0
Steam	6023	GWR	4-6-0
Steam	6998	British Railways	4-6-0
Gas Turbine	18000	Brown Boveri	A1A-A1A

Diesel	DL26	Hunslet	0-6-0
Diesel	604	British Railways	Class 08
Diesel	D9516	British Railways	Class 14
Steam Railcar	93	GWR	Steam Railmotor
DMU	22	GWR	Railcar

Attractions

The Centre has a large and varied collection of locomotives. Visitors can see the engine shed, carriage display shed, transfer shed with broad and standard gauge railways and the signalling centre with a modern panel and mechanical levers which can be pulled. The site is close to the centre of Didcot; the city of Oxford is 12 miles away and nearby heritage railways include the Cholsey & Wallingford (six miles, see page 140), the Chinnor & Princes Risborough (19 miles, see page 138) and the Swindon & Cricklade (29 miles, see page 177).

Special Events during 2019

5–7 April: Official Launch for No. 2999 'Lady of Legend'.
19–22 April: The Impossible Dream.
2 June: Transport Rally.
7–9 June: Hall and Saint in Steam Together.
15 June: 175th Anniversary Celebrations.
7 July: Teddy Bears' Picnic.
20–21 July: Star Tugs Weekend.
21–22 September: Victorian Weekend.
27 October: Apple Day.

East Kent Railway

Introduction and History

The East Kent Light Railway, as it was originally known, was built in stages between 1911 and 1917, primarily to carry coal. It ran from Shepherdswell to Wingham and Richborough. The first passengers were carried in 1916; however, passenger services between Eastry and Sandwich Road ended as early as 1928 and the remaining passenger services ceased in 1948. The stretch from Shepherdswell to Tilmanstone Colliery continued to carry coal until 1986 and finally closed in 1987. The preservation era began in 1985 when the East Kent Railway Society formed; the first trains ran in 1993. There are plans to extend the railway along the trackbed towards Coldred.

Contact Details

Website: www.eastkentrailway.co.uk
Tel: 01304 832042
Email: Written enquiries can be made from the EKR website.
Address: East Kent Railway Trust, Station Road, Shepherdswell, Dover, CT15 7PD.

Transport Links

By Rail: The main line station at Shepherdswell is next to the EKR station.
By Road: There is plenty of free parking at Shepherdswell station (CT15 7PD).

Opening Times

The railway operates on Sundays and Bank Holidays from April to October, plus Saturdays in July and August. Santa train services also run on Saturdays and Sundays in December until Christmas.

Line Mileage and Journey Time

0.00	Shepherdswell
1.50	Eythorne

A return journey takes just under one hour.

Stock List

Type	Number	Builder	Details
Steam	2004 ST DUNSTAN	Avonside	0-6-0ST
Diesel	416002	Fowler	0-4-0
Diesel	01530	Thomas Hill	0-4-0
Diesel	01543	Thomas Hill	0-4-0
Diesel	D1197	English Electric	0-6-0
Diesel	427	Ruston & Hornsby	0-6-0
Diesel	08676	British Railways	Class 08
Diesel	08685	British Railways	Class 08
Diesel	08742	British Railways	Class 08
Diesel	08799	British Railways	Class 08
Diesel	08804	British Railways	Class 08
Diesel	NS687	English Electric	Dutch 600 Series
DEMU	60100 & 60800	British Railways	Class 205
DEMU	54000	BREL	Class 210
EMU	11161 & 11187	Southern Railway	4 Cor
EMU	62385	BREL	Class 421
EMU	70904, 76397 & 76398	British Railways	Class 423
EMU	76875	BREL	Class 423

Attractions

Steam trains are due to the return on selected dates in 2019, for the first time in many years, see special events below. The 7¼ inch gauge Woodland Miniature Railway will be relaunched with an extension in 2019, as will the model railway which now has a second coach with displays. There is a nature trail and two signal boxes which house historical information on the EKR. There are various other attractions in the area, with Canterbury, Sandwich and the Kent Coast all nearby.

Special Events during 2019

Steam trains will return in 2019, operating on 7 April, 6 May, 27 May, 30 June & 28 July.
19–22 April: £2 a Trip.
5–6 May: Charities Weekend.
26–27 May: Craft Weekend.
24–26 August: Beer Festival.
5 May, 30 June & 7 July: Cream Tea Trains (book online).
27 May, 23 June, 28 July & 29 September: Fish and Chip Supper Train (book online).

Fawley Hill

Introduction and History

Fawley Hill is the home of Lady McAlpine and was built in 1960 by Sir William McAlpine. In 1961, Hudswell Clarke 0-6-0ST number 31 was bought for scrap value by Sir William and became the first of many railway items that were brought to Fawley Hill. A railway with a length of approximately one mile has been built; this operates on selected dates and is also available for private hire. Some of the larger items which have been brought to the site include Somersham station from Cambridgeshire, a Midland Railway signal box and a footbridge from the Isle of Wight's Ryde–Shanklin line. There is a museum with a large collection of exhibits, which began as a home for Sir William's traction engines and car collection.

Contact Details

Website: www.fawleyhill.co.uk
Tel: 01491 574873
Email: events@fawleyhill.com
Address: Fawley Hill, Fawley, Henley-on-Thamas, Bucks, RG9 6JA.

Transport Links

By Rail: The nearest station is Henley-on-Thames, which is three miles away.
By Road: There is on-site parking for visitors.

▲ **Fawley Hill:** During the 16 May 2010 open day at the private Fawley Hill railway – set in part of the late Sir William McAlpine's estate in Buckinghamshire – Hudswell Clarke 0-6-0ST No. 31 climbs the 1 in 13 gradient towards Somersham station. Previously located at Blackfriars Bridge, the London Chatham & Dover Railway crest in the background is one of a number of architectural features at the site. **Ian Beardsley**

▼ **Isle of Wight Steam Railway:** Class 03 No D2059 leads a short rake of four-wheeled coaching stock away from Ashey on the Isle of Wight Steam Railway on 1 October 2016. **Tony Christie**

Opening Times
Fawley Hill is a private estate, which only opens to the public a few days each year (see special events). Entrance at other times is by arrangement for private functions or by invitation.

Line Mileage and Journey Time
The railway is nearly one mile long and the journey time is relatively short.

Stock List

Type	Number	Builder	Details
Steam	31	Hudswell Clarke	0-6-0ST
Diesel	D2120	British Railways	Class 03

Attractions
Fawley Hill has the steepest standard gauge railway in the world, with a gradient of 1 in 13 at its steepest point. The site and museum have a large collection of railway artefacts and some of the larger exhibits include the Great Eastern Railway Chairman's private wooden saloon and two Royal Train carriages; Her Majesty's private carriage and the nursery coach for Prince Charles and Princess Anne. There are two 'O' gauge railways and Iron Henge, which is a large circle of supports from the undercroft of St Pancras station. Fawley Hill has an animal sanctuary with over 20 different animal types, which have been transferred from a number of zoos and animal sanctuaries. Animal feeding trips are available by advance arrangement. The museum, Victorian railway station and waiting room can all be used as a venue for weddings and events.

Special Events during 2019
31 May–2 June: Three-day antiques fair, which is open to the public. Trains will be operating on Saturday 1st and Sunday 2nd June.

Finmere Railway Station

Introduction and History
Finmere is a railway station in Oxfordshire on the route of the Great Central Railway, which opened in 1899 and closed in 1963 when passenger services ended. The line closed in 1966 when it was severed south of Rugby; see the Great Central Railway listing on page 99 for more information. The station platform remains in place and there is a short stretch of operational railway track. The site is owned by Coulsdon Old Vehicle & Engineering Society (COVES) and is also home to The Network SouthEast Railway Society. COVES has acquired electro-diesel locomotive 73130, which was used for the first time on the site in 2016 to haul passengers during an open day. Finmere station is a privately owned site and access is only possible on selected dates when it opens to the public, or by advance arrangement.

Transport Links
By Rail: The nearest station is Bicester North, which is eight miles away.
By Road: The site is located to the south-west of Finmere village.

Opening Times
The site only opens to the public occasionally for special events.

Line Mileage and Journey Time
The railway is just under 300 m long and the journey time is relatively short.

Stock List

Type	Number	Builder	Details
Electro-Diesel	73130	English Electric	Class 73
EMU	10400	Southern Railway	Class 405
EMU	65302, 65304, 65379 & 65382	British Railways	Class 416
EMU	62043, 70721, 76048 & 76102	British Railways	Class 421
EMU	69339	BREL	Class 422
EMU	61183 & 75186	British Railways	Class 501

Isle of Wight Steam Railway

Introduction and History

The railway from Ryde to Newport opened in 1875 and was one of a number of lines on the Isle of Wight, which have generally used older rolling stock than those on the mainland. In 1966 the final steam trains ran and the railway from Ryde to Newport and Cowes closed. In 1967 a group of enthusiasts formed the Wight Locomotive Society and purchased steam locomotive 24 "Calbourne", which remains at the railway today. In 1971 the Isle of Wight Railway Company formed with the aim of acquiring the railway between Wooton and Havenstreet. This was successful and the first trains in preservation ran in 1971. The railway was extended to Smallbrook Junction, where it connects with the Ryde–Shanklin line, in 1991. There are aspirations to extend the railway both west towards Newport and further north towards Ryde. As the future of the Ryde–Shanklin route is unclear, it is possible that heritage trains could again work into Ryde St John's Road station.

Contact Details

Website: www.iwsteamrailway.co.uk
Tel: 01983 882204
Email: info@iwsteamrailway.co.uk
Address: The Railway Station, Havenstreet, Near Ryde, Isle of Wight, PO33 4DS.

Transport Links

By Rail: Change at Smallbrook Junction on the Ryde–Shanklin route (Island Line). Note, there is no road or footpath access at Smallbrook Junction.
By Road: Free car parking is available at Havenstreet (PO33 4DS) and Wooton (PO33 4RG) stations.

Opening Times

During 2019 trains will operate from 24 March to 31 October on these dates:
March: 24, 27, 28 & 31.
April: 3, 4, 7–25, 28 & 30.
May: Every Sunday, Tuesday, Wednesday & Thursday and every day from 25 May.
June: 1–6 and daily Sundays–Thursdays.
The railway then opens daily from 22 June to 3 October, then on Sundays, Wednesdays and Thursdays for the rest of October, finishing with 23–31 October.

Line Mileage and Journey Time

0.00	Smallbrook Junction
1.75	Ashey
3.25	Havenstreet
4.75	Wooton

A return journey takes about one hour.

Stock List

Type	*Number*	*Builder*	*Details*
Steam	INVINCIBLE	Hawthorn Leslie	0-4-0ST
Steam	24	LSWR	0-4-4T
Steam	192	Hunslet	0-6-0ST
Steam	198	Hunslet	0-6-0ST
Steam	3850	Hunslet	0-6-0ST
Steam	38 AJAX	Andrew Barclay	0-6-0T
Steam	W11 (BR No. 32640)	LBSCR	0-6-0T
Steam	2 NEWPORT	LBSCR	0-6-0T
Steam	8 (BR No. 32646)	LBSCR	0-6-0T
Steam	41298	British Railways	2-6-2T
Steam	41313	British Railways	2-6-2T
Diesel	235	Andrew Barclay	0-4-0
Diesel	D2059	British Railways	Class 03
Diesel	D2554	Hunslet	Class 05

Attractions
There is plenty to explore at the railway's Havenstreet base, including the Train Story Discovery Centre, Haven Bird of Prey Centre, a small museum, a railway gift and model shop, the carriage & wagon workshop, a picnic & children's play area and a woodland walkway. Attractions in the area include Appley Park, Dinosaur Isle, Butterfly & Fountain World and there are hundreds of miles of walking and cycling routes on the island.

Special Events during 2019
19–21 April: Easter Weekend.
4–6 May: Isle of Wight Real Ale Festival.
19 May: Festival of Transport.
25–27 May: Steam Gala.
6–7 July: 1940s Experience.
20 July: Real Ale Train Evening.
28–31 July: The Railway Folk.
23–26 August: Island Steam Show.
21–22 September: Cider & Cheese Event.
12–13 October: Beer & Buses.
28–31 October: Wizard Week.
December: Santa Specials.

Kent & East Sussex Railway

Introduction and History
The first section of the Kent & East Sussex Light Railway opened in 1900 between Robertsbridge and Rolvenden. It was extended to Tenterden Town in 1903 and to Headcorn in 1905, when it met the main line from Tonbridge to Ashford. After declining use, the Tenterden–Headcorn section closed in 1954 and the track was lifted soon afterwards. The branch from Robertsbridge to Tenterden continued to see freight and occasional charter trains until 1961 when it was closed. During the 1960s a preservation group worked towards the railway being reinstated; however, the Robertsbridge–Bodiam section had to be abandoned due to the number of roads crossing the line. The heritage railway between Tenterden and Rolvenden reopened in 1974 and was extended to Wittersham Road in 1977, Northiam in 1990 and to Bodiam in 2000. Plans are under way to extend and reconnect the railway to the main line under the auspices of the Rother Valley Railway (see page 185).

Contact Details
Website: www.kesr.org.uk
Tel: 01580 765155
Email: enquiry@kesr.org.uk
Address: Tenterden Town Station, Station Road, Tenterden, Kent, TN30 6HE.

Transport Links
By Rail: Robertsbridge station is five miles from Bodiam and the nearest stations to Tenterden are Ham Street (eight miles) and Headcorn (nine miles).
By Road: Free parking is available at Tenterden Town (TN30 6HE) and Northiam (TN31 6QT).

Opening Times
Trains operate 10.30–17.30 on Saturdays, Sundays and most weekdays from April to September and on selected other dates.

Line Mileage and Journey Time
0.00	Tenterden Town
1.50	Rolvenden
4.75	Wittersham Road
6.50	Northiam
10.25	Bodiam

A return journey from Tenterden takes about 1 hour 50 minutes.

Stock List

Type	Number	Builder	Details
Steam	12 (1631)	Peckett	0-4-0T
Steam	1	Dodman & Co	0-4-2WT
Steam	1638	British Railways	0-6-0PT
Steam	23 (3791)	Hunslet	0-6-0ST
Steam	25 (3797)	Hunslet	0-6-0ST
Steam	14 (1955)	Manning Wardle	0-6-0ST
Steam	32670	LBSCR	0-6-0T
Steam	32678	LBSCR	0-6-0T
Steam	5753	SECR	0-6-0T
Steam	65	Vulcan Iron Works	0-6-0T
Steam	300	Vulcan Iron Works	0-6-0T
Steam	5668	GWR	0-6-2T
Steam	6619	GWR	0-6-2T
Steam	376	Norwegian State Railways	2-6-0
Steam	4253	GWR	2-8-0T
Diesel	41	Ruston & Hornsby	0-4-0
Diesel	D2023	British Railways	Class 03
Diesel	D2024	British Railways	Class 03
Diesel	3174	British Railways	Class 08
Diesel	D4118	British Railways	Class 08
Diesel	D9504	British Railways	Class 14
Diesel	7594	British Railways	Class 25
Diesel	D6570	BRCW	Class 33
Electro-Diesel	40	British Thomson Houston	Bo-Bo
DMU	20	GWR	Railcar
DMU	50971 & 51571	British Railways	Class 108

Attractions
The Colonel Stephens Railway Museum, the carriage workshop and a souvenir and gift shop can all be found at the railway's Tenterden base. There are walks from each of the stations along the railway and its website has maps and instructions for these. Attractions in the area include Lashenden Air Warfare Museum, Bodiam Castle, Camber Sands, Rye Castle and Rye Harbour Nature Reserve.

Special Events during 2019
31 March: Mother's Day Event.
18–19 May: 1940s Weekend.
14–15 June: Real Ale & Cider Festival.
12 & 22 June, 24 & 31 July & 21 August: Fish & Chip Supper Trains.
18 August: Bus Rally.
7–8 September: Hop Fest.
25 October: Fright Night Express.
1, 7–8, 14–15, 21–24 December: Santa Specials.

The Lavender Line

Introduction and History
The railway between Uckfield and Lewes opened in 1858, providing an alternative route between London and Brighton. Closure of the line was suggested in Dr Beeching's 1963 report; however, due to considerable opposition, it did not close until 1969 and the track was lifted in 1970. Isfield station was purchased privately in 1983 after which the owner renovated the station, signal box and rebuilt the waiting room (the original building had been moved to the Bluebell Railway's nearby Sheffield Park site). A stretch of track was laid and the first steam locomotive subsequently arrived at Isfield. In 1991 ownership of the station and railway was transferred to the Lavender Line Preservation Society, the name being taken from Lavender & Sons, a local firm previously based at Isfield station. In recent years there has been a campaign for the Uckfield–Lewes line to reopen as a commercial railway, connecting to the main line network. The Lavender Line aims to extend; however, this would be subject to the main line project not proceeding.

▲ **The Lavender Line:** Class 309 EMU, formerly 309624 (vehicles 75965, 61928 & 75972) but now numbered 960102 and carrying the name "New Dalby", is pictured next to Class 205 DEMU 1133 at Isfield on the Lavender Line on 11 March 2018. **Tony Christie**

▼ **Mid Hants Railway:** Class 20 No. 8001 crosses Class 47 No. 47579 "James Nightall G.C." at Alresford on 1 June 2018, during a diesel gala on the Mid Hants Railway. Class 03 No. 03197 and Class 26 No. 26043 can be seen in the siding to the right. **Tony Christie**

Contact Details

Website: www.lavender-line.co.uk
Tel: 01825 750515
Email: Written enquiries can be made from the website.
Address: The Lavender Line, Isfield Station, Near Uckfield, East Sussex, TN22 5XB.

Transport Links

By Rail: The nearest stations are Uckfield (three miles) and Lewes to the south (six miles).
By Road: Free parking is available at Isfield (TN22 5XB).

Opening Times

The railway operates every Sunday and Bank Holiday (except Good Friday, Christmas Day, Boxing Day and 29 December) and on selected other dates for special events. Trains depart from Isfield approximately every half hour between 11.00 and 16.30.

Line Mileage and Journey Time

The railway is just over three quarters of a mile long and a return journey takes about 20 minutes.

Stock List

Type	*Number*	*Builder*	*Details*
Steam	2945	Cockerill	0-4-0VBT
Diesel	354	Andrew Barclay	0-4-0
Diesel	830	Drewry	0-4-0
Diesel	15	Hibberd	0-4-0
Diesel	422	Ruston & Hornsby	0-6-0
Diesel	D4113	British Railways	Class 09
DMU	56279	British Railways	Class 108
DMU	999507	Wickham	Railbus
DEMU	60117, 60122, 60151, 60820, 60828 & 60832	British Railways	Class 205
EMU	61928, 75965 & 75972	British Railways	Class 309
EMU	69333	BREL	Class 422

Attractions

Regular brake van rides are available on the demonstration freight train. Isfield station has a Grade II listed signal box, a gift shop, station buffet, picnic area and children's play area. There is a five inch gauge miniature railway which operates on selected Sundays and the proceeds from this are given to charity. Children's parties can be hosted in a decorated static carriage. The Bluebell Railway's southern terminus at Sheffield Park is eight miles from Isfield. Other attractions in the area include Wilderness Wood, the market town of Lewes and the South Coast.

Special Events during 2019

21–22 April: Miniature Traction Engine Rally.
5–6 October: Miniature Steam and Car Rally.

Mid Hants Railway

Introduction and History

The railway between Alton and Winchester via Alresford opened in 1865 and became known as the Watercress Line, due to the large volumes of the locally produced crop which were carried. The line from London to Alton was electrified in 1937, which brought an end to regular through trains and when the London–Southampton line was electrified in 1967, the line through Alresford became an isolated diesel section. The route survived the mass rural line closures of the 1960s, but only until 1973 when it was closed by British Rail between Alton and Winchester Junction. The Alresford–Alton section was purchased from BR in 1975 and the first heritage trains worked between Alresford and Ropley in 1977. The railway was extended to Medstead in 1983 and to Alton in 1985 where the line is now connected to the national network.

Contact Details

Website: www.watercressline.co.uk
Tel: 01962 733810
Email: Written enquiries can be made from the website.
Address: Mid Hants Railway Ltd, New Alresford, Hampshire, SO24 9JG.

Transport Links

By Rail: There is a rail connection at Alton; cross to the Mid Hants Railway platform.
By Road: Car parking is available at Alresford (SO24 9JG) and Alton (GU34 2PZ). Both are chargeable and note there are no heritage trains to and from Alton until August 2019 (see below).

Opening Times

Trains operate on Saturdays, Sundays, Bank Holidays and selected weekdays from February until October (including most weekdays April–August). The section between Alton and Medstead is closed until the end of July 2019, while a major infrastructure project is carried out, including the replacement of Whitedown Lane Bridge. A free bus between Alton and Medstead is operating during this time.

Line Mileage and Journey Time

0.00	Alton
4.50	Medstead and Four Marks
7.25	Ropley
10.25	Alresford

A return journey takes just over one hour between Medstead and Alresford and one hour 40 minutes between Alton and Alresford.

Stock List

Type	*Number*	*Builder*	*Details*
Steam	1 (3781)	Hunslet	0-6-0T
Steam	76017	British Railways	2-6-0
Steam	41312	British Railways	2-6-2T
Steam	80150	British Railways	2-6-4T
Steam	92212	British Railways	2-10-0
Steam	925	Southern Railway	4-4-0
Steam	73096	British Railways	4-6-0
Steam	75079	British Railways	4-6-0
Steam	30499	LSWR	4-6-0
Steam	30506	LSWR	4-6-0
Steam	30828	Southern Railway	4-6-0
Steam	850	Southern Railway	4-6-0
Steam	34007	Southern Railway	4-6-2
Steam	34058	Southern Railway	4-6-2
Steam	34105	British Railways	4-6-2
Diesel	03197	British Railways	Class 03
Diesel	08032	British Railways	Class 08
Diesel	08377	British Railways	Class 08
Diesel	D3358	British Railways	Class 08
Diesel	12049	British Railways	Class 11
Diesel	47579	Brush Traction	Class 47
Diesel	50027	English Electric	Class 50
DEMU	60124 & 60824	British Railways	Class 205

Attractions

Free behind the scenes tours of the engineering hub are available to fare paying passengers on selected dates at Ropley, where there is also a miniature railway. There is a Goods Shed Exhibition and Photo Exhibition at Medstead & Four Marks and a gift shop and model railway at Alton. The railway operates a number of dining trains, real ale trains and gin trains. The Curtis Museum in Alton town centre is nearby and Jane Austen's house in Chawton village is a few miles away. There are a number of themed walks in the area including the Jane Austen Trail linking Alton with her home in Chawton, the one mile Alresford Millennium Trail exploring Alresford and the Watercress Way which continues along the route of the former railway west of Alresford.

Special Events during 2019

13–22 April: Day Out with Thomas.
19 May: Watercress Festival.
15–16 June: War on the Line.
21 July: Alton Bus Rally.
3–11 August: Day Out with Thomas.
14–15 September: Heritage Open Days.
18–20 October: Autumn Steam Gala.
26–27 October: Wizard Weekend.

Spa Valley Railway

Introduction and History

The railway from East Grinstead to Groombridge and Tunbridge Wells West opened in 1866 and the Groombridge to Eridge, Uckfield and Lewes section opened in 1868. After declining use and with costly upgrade work being necessary, British Rail announced its intention to close the line between Tunbridge Wells and Eridge in 1983. Objections were overridden and the line was closed in 1985. In the same year, the Tunbridge Wells and Eridge Railway Preservation Society formed with the aim of reopening the railway. The Tunbridge Wells site was reduced in size after planning permission was given for a supermarket to be built on the rail yard; however, this was subject to the company covering the cost of a new station platform. In 1996 the group acquired the railway line as far as Birchden Junction near Eridge and operated its first trains from Tunbridge Wells West for about half a mile. The operational section was extended to Groombridge in 1997, Birchden Junction in 2005 and to Eridge in 2011, where the railway now connects with main line trains.

Contact Details

Website: www.spavalleyrailway.co.uk
Tel: 01892 537715
Email: Written enquiries can be made from the website.
Address: Spa Valley Railway, West Station, Royal Tunbridge Wells, TN2 5QY.

Transport Links

By Rail: The railway shares Eridge station with main line services which continue to Uckfield and London; through rail tickets are available. Both railways use single track working and are linked by the station footbridge. Alternatively Tunbridge Wells West is less than one mile from Tunbridge Wells main line station.
By Road: Free parking is available at High Rocks (TN3 9JJ) and pay and display parking is available near to Eridge (TN3 9LE) and Tunbridge Wells West (TN2 5QY) stations.

Opening Times

The railway opens every Saturday, Sunday and Bank Holiday and on selected weekdays from February until October. Departures are between approximately 10.30 and 16.30, depending on which timetable is in operation.

Line Mileage and Journey Time

0.00	Tunbridge Wells West
1.25	High Rocks
3.00	Groombridge
5.00	Eridge

A return journey takes about one hour 20 minutes.

Stock List

Type	*Number*	*Builder*	*Details*
Steam	3 (2315)	Andrew Barclay	0-4-0ST
Steam	68077	Andrew Barclay	0-6-0ST
Steam	2193	Bagnall	0-6-0ST
Steam	1589	Hunslet	0-6-0ST
Steam	57 (7668)	Robert Stephenson & Hawthorns	0-6-0ST
Steam	62 (7673)	Robert Stephenson & Hawthorns	0-6-0ST

Steam	32650	LBSCR	0-6-0T
Steam	47493	Vulcan Foundry	0-6-0T
Diesel	SOUTHERHAM (2591)	Drewry	0-4-0
Diesel	09026	British Railways	Class 09
Diesel	D3489	British Railways	Class 10
Diesel	15224	British Railways	Class 12
Diesel	31430	Brush Traction	Class 31
Diesel	33063	BRCW	Class 33
Diesel	33065	BRCW	Class 33
Diesel	33201	BRCW	Class 33
Electro-Diesel	73140	English Electric	Class 73
DMU	56408	Metropolitan Cammell	Class 101
DMU	51669 & 51849	British Railways	Class 115
DEMU	60142, 60616 & 60916	British Railways	Class 207
EMU	62402, 76764 & 76835	BREL	Class 421
EMU	69306	British Railways	Class 422
EMU	61277	British Railways	Class 489

Attractions

The Spa Valley line runs through High Weald, which is an Area of Outstanding Natural Beauty. At the railway's Tunbridge Wells West base, the 1886 engine shed can be visited and a buffet is housed within a multiple unit. Steam and diesel locomotive driving experiences are available. Nearby heritage railways include the Bluebell Railway (13 miles, see page 133), the Lavender Line (14 miles, see page 148), the Rother Valley Railway (17 miles, see page 185) and the Kent & East Sussex Railway (24 miles, see page 147). Groombridge Place and Enchanted Forest are a 15–20 minute walk from Groombridge station and combined tickets with the Spa Valley Railway can be purchased. Other attractions in the area include Ashdown Forest, Dunorlan Park and Tunbridge Wells, home of the Pantiles and Chalybeate Spring.

Special Events during 2019

11–12 May: Transport Film Festival.
2–4 August: Summer Diesel Gala.
28–29 December: Winter Steam Up & Kids for a Quid.

▲ **Spa Valley Railway:** Network SouthEast-liveried Class 73 No. 73140 hauls Class 207 DEMU vehicles 60916 and 60142 during a diesel gala at the Spa Valley Railway on 3 August 2018. Multiple unit vehicles are sometimes used as hauled coaching stock on heritage railways. **Nigel Gibbs**

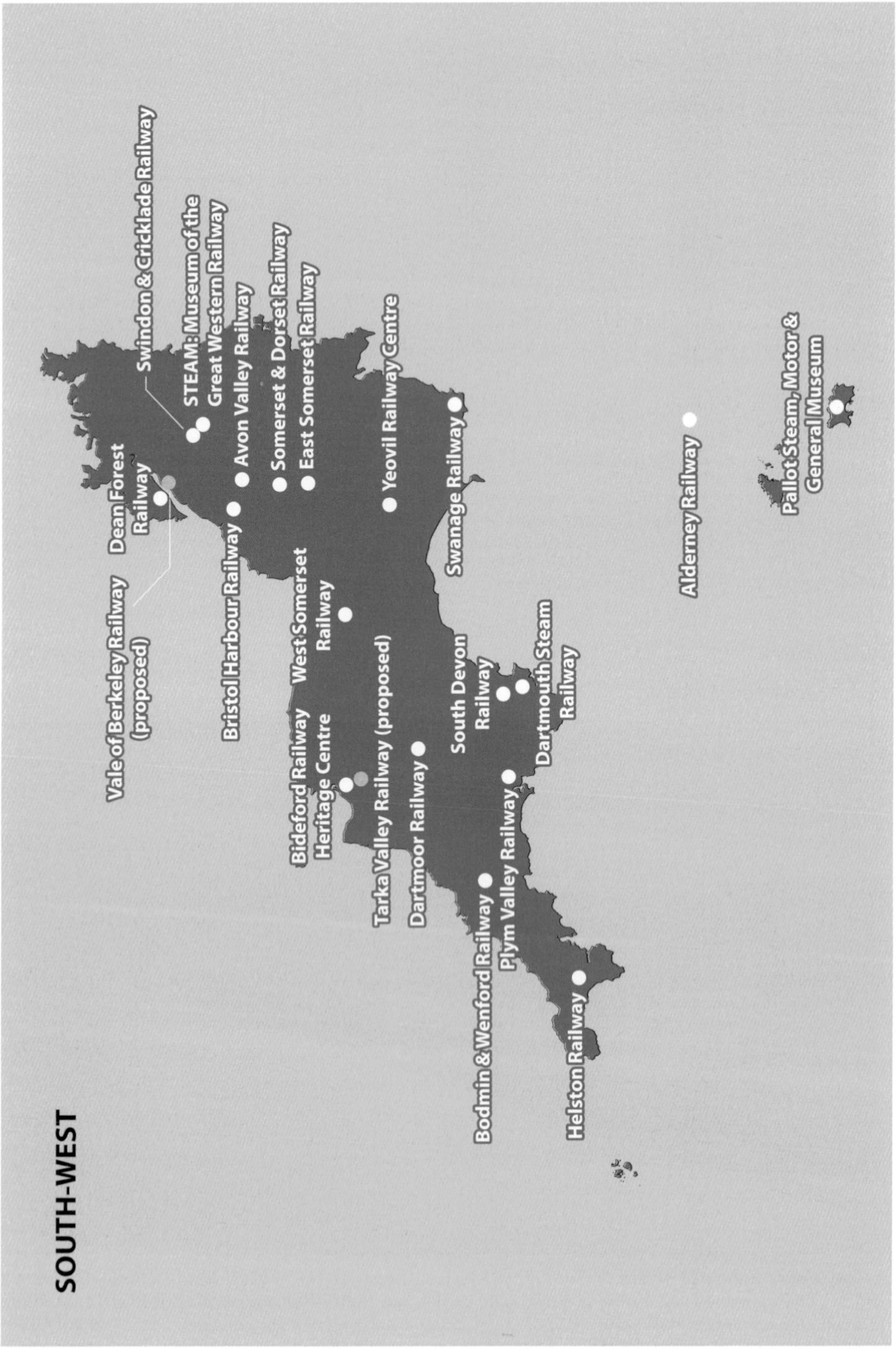

SOUTH-WEST

Vale of Berkeley Railway (proposed)
Dean Forest Railway
Swindon & Cricklade Railway
STEAM: Museum of the Great Western Railway
Bristol Harbour Railway
Avon Valley Railway
Somerset & Dorset Railway
East Somerset Railway
Bideford Railway Heritage Centre
West Somerset Railway
Tarka Valley Railway (proposed)
Yeovil Railway Centre
Dartmoor Railway
South Devon Railway
Swanage Railway
Bodmin & Wenford Railway
Plym Valley Railway
Dartmouth Steam Railway
Helston Railway
Alderney Railway
Pallot Steam, Motor & General Museum

Region 8 – South-West

Alderney Railway

Introduction and History
The Alderney Railway was constructed by the British Government to carry stone from the east of the island to build the breakwater and Victorian forts. It opened in 1847 and the first official passengers to be carried were Queen Victoria and Prince Albert in 1854. Stone quarrying stopped for a number of years from 1940 during the German occupation of Alderney, when part of the railway was replaced with a 60 cm gauge system. After the war, the standard gauge railway was reinstated and the British Home Office took it over. It was converted to a passenger line and services began in 1980. Today the railway follows a coastal route from Braye Road to Mannez Quarry and Lighthouse, using a diesel shunter to haul two 1959 former London Underground coaches, giving a unique view of Alderney.

Contact Details
Website: www.alderneyrailway.com
Tel: 07911 739572
Email: alderneyrailway@suremail.gg
Address: 7 Rue de Beaumont, St Anne, Guernsey.

Transport Links
By Rail: There are no other railways on Alderney.
By Road: Car parking is available at Braye Road station.
By Air: There are direct flights to Alderney from Southampton, Guernsey and Jersey.
By Sea: Ferries to Alderney sail from Guernsey and Cherbourg, France.

Opening Times
Trains operate every Sunday from 21 April to the end of September. During July and August trains also operate on Saturdays. Trains make two return trips, departing at 14.30 and 15.30 from Braye Road station.

Line Mileage and Journey Time
0.00	Braye Road
1.75	Mannez Quarry

A return journey takes about 45 minutes.

Stock List
Type	*Number*	*Builder*	*Details*
Diesel	D100	English Electric	0-4-0
Diesel	2	Ruston & Hornsby	0-4-0

Attractions
At Mannez Quarry visitors can ride the quarter mile long 7¼ inch gauge railway and go inside the rail shed to see the Wickham cars and the diesel locomotive which isn't currently in service. Mannez Quarry station is close to the coast, lighthouse and forts at the northern end of the island. Braye Road station is adjacent to the beach, harbour, breakwater and is a short walk from the centre of St Anne.

Special Events during 2019
21 April: An Easter Bunny will give an Easter egg to children.

Trains can be chartered for weddings and private functions.

Avon Valley Railway

Introduction and History
The railway was part of the Midland Railway's Mangotsfield and Bath branch line which opened in 1869 as a through route from the Midlands to the south coast. It connected with the Somerset & Dorset Railway. After being earmarked for closure in Dr Beeching's Reshaping Britain's Railways report, the final trains ran in 1966. A preservation group formed in 1972, initially leasing Bitton station; the first heritage trains operated on a short stretch of track in 1974. The line has since been extended to a length of three miles and there is potential for the railway to extend further south towards Bath.

Contact Details
Website: www.avonvalleyrailway.org
Tel: 0117 932 5538
Email: Written enquiries can be made from the AVR website.
Address: Bitton Station, Bath Road, Bristol, South Gloucestershire, BS30 6HD.

Transport Links
By Rail: Keynsham is the nearest railway station and is one and a half miles away.
By Road: There is free parking at Bitton station (BS30 6HD), which is on the A431 between Bristol and Bath.
By Bike: Bitton station has a cycle parking area and can be reached on the Bristol and Bath Railway Path (Route 4 of the National Cycling Network).

Opening Times
The Bitton site is open every day of the year except Christmas Day and trains operate on selected days through the year, including most weekends and school holidays, with one of three different timetables operating.

Line Mileage and Journey Time
0.00 Oldland Common
1.00 Bitton
2.50 Avon Riverside

A round trip from Bitton to Oldland Common and Avon Riverside takes about one hour.

Stock List

Type	Number	Builder	Details
Steam	7492	Sentinel	0-4-0
Steam	44123	LMS	0-6-0
Steam	1798 EDWIN HULSE	Avonside	0-6-0ST
Steam	132	Hunslet	0-6-0ST
Steam	5	Manning Wardle	0-6-0ST
Steam	4015	Fablok	0-6-0T
Steam	7151	Robert Stephenson & Hawthorns	0-6-0T
Diesel	446	Andrew Barclay	0-4-0
Diesel	70031	Ministry of Defence	0-4-0
Diesel	429	Ruston & Hornsby	0-6-0
Diesel	610	Sentinel	0-8-0
Diesel	D2994	Ruston & Hornsby	Class 07
Diesel	08202	British Railways	Class 08
Diesel	31101	Brush Traction	Class 31
Diesel	31130	Brush Traction	Class 31
DMU	52006 & 52025	British Railways	Class 107

Attractions
The railway is based at the beautifully restored Bitton station, which is part way along the 13 mile Bristol and Bath Railway Path, which connects the two cities and runs alongside the railway. There is a small museum and a buffet at Bitton which opens every day of the year except Christmas Day. The Avon Valley Adventure and Wildlife Park is very close and the nearby cities of Bath and Bristol have many attractions, including the Roman Baths and Bristol Zoo.

Special Events during 2019

16 March: Industrial Mixed Traffic Gala.
13–14 April: Fire and Water.
19–22 April: Chocolate Train.
31 May–1 June: Beer Festival.
21 June: Midsummer Wine Festival.
29–30 June & 14–15 September: Teddy Bear Weekend; children with a bear travel free.
3–4 August: 150th Anniversary Gala.
21 August: Open Air Theatre "Cranford".
21–22 September: 1940s Weekend.
December (various dates): Santa Specials.

▲ **Bodmin & Wenford Railway:** Two residents of the Bodmin & Wenford Railway, Class 50 No. 50042 "Triumph" and Class 37 No. 37142 are seen working top-and-tail on a service near Bodmin General on 5 May 2018. **Tony Christie**

Bideford Railway Heritage Centre

Introduction and History

The broad gauge railway from Barnstaple first reached Instow and Bideford in 1855 and was extended south to Torrington in 1872. It was converted to standard gauge in 1877 and closed to passenger traffic in 1965. Milk traffic continued until 1978 and ball clay and charter trains continued to use the route to Torrington until 1982. The track was lifted in 1985, which was when the first preservation group formed. Devon County Council purchased the trackbed from British Rail to create a coastal walkway and assisted the group's preservation efforts. These included redeveloping both the Bideford and Instow sites and laying a short stretch of railway track on part of the former route, along which trains have operated since 2004.

Contact Details

Website: www.bidefordrailway.co.uk
Tel: 07854 590503
Email: Written enquiries can be made from the website.
Address: Bideford Railway Heritage Centre, 4 Station Hill, Bideford EX39 4BB.

Transport Links

By Rail: Instow is six miles from Barnstaple station and the Bideford site is nine miles from both Barnstaple and Chapelton stations.
By Road: There are car parks a short walk from both Bideford station (EX39 4BB) and Instow signal box (EX39 4HW).
By Bike: Both sites are conveniently located on the traffic-free Tarka Trail and bicycles can be hired from various outlets along the trail, including at Bideford.

Opening Times

Bideford Station is open 10.00–16.00 on Saturdays and Sundays from Easter until the end of October, with additional opening days during the summer season. Instow signal box is open less frequently; please telephone or check the website for the latest opening times. Both sites are accessible and can be seen from the outside on dates when they are not open.

Line Mileage and Journey Time

The track is nearly a quarter of a mile long and the journey time is relatively short. At the start of 2019 the diesel locomotive was out of service but it is hoped that this will be repaired soon.

Stock List

Type	*Number*	*Builder*	*Details*
Diesel	3832	Hibberd	0-4-0

Attractions

At the Bideford site there is a visitor centre, model railway, a rebuilt signal box with working lever frame and a railway parcel van and carriage which between them house a museum and refreshments. Instow signal box is preserved as it was when train services ended; visitors can pull the levers and turn the level crossing gate wheel. Bideford is also home of the medieval Long Bridge, a museum, gallery and various other attractions. Bideford station and Instow signal box are on the Tarka Trail, which is one of the country's longest traffic-free walking and cycling trails and forms part of the Devon Coast to Coast cycle route. The former Torrington Station, the base of the Tarka Valley Railway (see page 186) is five miles to the south on the Tarka Trail.

Special Events during 2019

27 May: Opening of the new museum and Gala Day.
8 September: 30th Anniversary Celebration of Bideford Railway Heritage Centre.

Bodmin & Wenford Railway

Introduction and History

The broad gauge railway between Plymouth and Truro opened in 1859, with a station at Bodmin Road, which is now known as Bodmin Parkway. The standard gauge branch from Bodmin Road to Bodmin General opened 1887, extending to Boscarne in 1888 making a connection with the existing Bodmin & Wadebridge Railway which had opened as early as 1834. Passenger services from Padstow to Bodmin ceased in 1967, with freight continuing to Wadebridge until 1978 and china clay traffic to Wenfordbridge (via Bodmin General) surviving until 1983 when the line closed. Shortly after closure, in 1984 the Bodmin Railway Preservation Society formed and the trackbed from Bodmin Parkway to Boscarne Junction was subsequently purchased from British Rail. The first shunting operations were carried out at Bodmin General station in 1986 and the first heritage passenger trains ran from Bodmin General to Bodmin Parkway in 1990, with services extending to Boscarne Junction in 1996. The railway plans to extend to the outskirts of Wadebride in a number of stages, sharing the route with the Camel Trail.

Contact Details

Website: www.bodminrailway.co.uk
Tel: 01208 73555
Email: enquiries@bodminrailway.co.uk
Address: Bodmin & Wenford Railway, General Station, Bodmin, Cornwall, PL31 1AQ.

Transport Links

By Rail: There is a main line rail connection at Bodmin Parkway; simply cross to Platform 3.
By Road: Free parking is available at Bodmin General station only (PL31 1AG).
By Bike or on Foot: The traffic-free Camel Trail runs from Padstow and Wadebridge, directly to Boscarne Junction station. There are a number of locations on the route where bikes can be hired.

Opening Times

Trains operate on selected dates from mid-February until the end of October and every day from mid-May until early October, plus Santa Specials in December. The times vary, depending on which timetable is in operation, with trains operating 11.00–16.00, or longer.

Line Mileage and Journey Time

0.00	Bodmin Parkway
1.25	Colesloggett Halt
3.50	Bodmin General
6.25	Boscarne Junction

A return journey takes around two hours, depending on the starting station.

Stock List

Type	Number	Builder	Details
Steam	2962	Bagnall	0-4-0ST
Steam	2572 JUDY	Bagnall	0-4-0ST
Steam	3058 ALFRED	Bagnall	0-4-0ST
Steam	4612	GWR	0-6-0PT
Steam	6435	GWR	0-6-0PT
Steam	75178	Bagnall	0-6-0ST
Steam	30587	LSWR	2-4-0WT
Steam	5552	GWR	2-6-2T
Steam	4247	GWR	2-8-0T
Diesel	22928	Fowler	0-4-0
Diesel	443642	Ruston & Hornsby	0-4-0
Diesel	P403D	Sentinel	0-4-0
Diesel	08444	British Railways	Class 08
Diesel	D3452	British Railways	Class 10
Diesel	33110	BRCW	Class 33
Diesel	37142	English Electric	Class 37
Diesel	47306	Brush Traction	Class 47
Diesel	50042	English Electric	Class 50

DMU	51947	British Railways	Class 108
DMU	55020	Pressed Steel	Class 121

Attractions
The branch line from Bodmin travels through rural Cornwall. Luxury dining trains and footplate driving experiences are available on the railway. The traffic-free Camel Trail from Wadebridge to Padstow follows the route of the current and former railway and the River Camel. There are many other attractions in the region, including Bodmin Moor and many Cornish coastal walks and beaches, which can be reached from the railway and the Camel Trail.

Special Events during 2019
31 March: Mother's Day Cream Tea Train.
7–22 April: Easter at the Railway.
26–27 October: Half Price Travel & Kids Go Free.
December: Santa Specials.

Bristol Harbour Railway

Introduction and History
When it opened in 1872, the Bristol Harbour Railway was a commercial railway operating within Bristol Harbour. A preserved railway was established in 1978 as part of Bristol Museum (now known as M Shed) which ran on the section connecting the site with the SS Great Britain. When the last commercial rail traffic ceased in 1987, the museum railway expanded to include the line which runs alongside the River Avon. However, this section recently experienced subsidence when works on a new bus system started and has been cut back to Vauxhall Bridge. At the start of 2019 only the line to SS Great Britain is operating. It is hoped that repairs will be completed on the southern section during 2019, enabling trains to continue to the new Ashton Gate site, near Vauxhall Bridge.

Contact Details
Website: www.bristolmuseums.org.uk/m-shed
Tel: Written enquiries can be made from the M Shed website.
Email: 0117 352 6600
Address: M Shed, Princes Wharf, Wapping Road, Bristol, BS1 4RN.

Transport Links
By Rail: Bristol Temple Meads station is just under one mile from M Shed.
By Road: Chargeable car parking is available nearby at The Grove (BS1 4RB) and Wapping Wharf (BS1 4RH).

Opening Times
M Shed is open 10.00–17.00 Tuesday to Sunday. Train services operate at selected times, subject to availability.

Line Mileage and Journey Time
The operational section from M Shed to SS Great Britain is approximately half a mile and a return journey takes about 15 minutes.

Stock List

Type	*Number*	*Builder*	*Details*
Steam	1764	Avonside	0-6-0ST
Steam	242	Fox Walker	0-6-0ST
Steam	1940 HENBURY	Peckett	0-6-0ST
Diesel	418792	Ruston & Hornsby	0-4-0

Attractions
As well as an operational railway, M Shed has a 1950s working dockside with electric cranes, boats, train transit and quayside operations. The site also has a café and shop. M Shed is located within Bristol Harbour, a short walk from SS Great Britain and close to the city centre, Bristol Museum & Art Gallery and Bristol Zoo.

Special Events during 2019

16 March–16 June 2019: British Tattoo Art Exhibition.
18 May: Introduction to Aerial Archaeology.
6 July–29 September: On set with Aardman: Making Early Man.

Dartmoor Railway

Introduction and History

The railway from Exeter to Plymouth via Okehampton opened in stages. From Exeter, it reached North Tawton in 1865, Sampford Courtenay in 1867, Okehampton in 1871, Lydford in 1874 and it opened as through route in 1876. The line was closed west of Meldon Quarry in 1968 and passenger services between Exeter and Okehampton ended in 1972. The section from Coleford Junction to Meldon Quarry was later sold to Aggregate Industries, which collaborated with other local organisations and returned trains to Meldon Quarry from 1997. The railway was acquired by British American Railway Services in 2008 (see Weardale Railway on page 59) and is leased to the Dartmoor Railway. Stone trains continued to Meldon Quarry until it was mothballed in 2011 and in recent years passenger trains have operated between Exeter and Okehampton on summer Sundays. The Dartmoor Railway operates heritage trains to Sampford Courtenay and the Network Rail boundary during some special events and hopes to return regular services to Yeoford, where they could connect with trains on the Exeter–Barnstaple line.

Contact Details

Website: www.dartmoorrailway.com
Tel: 01837 52762 or for ticket sales 0800 0232 383.
Email: dartmoorrailwayenquiries@britamrail.com
Address: Dartmoor Railway, Okehampton Station, Station Road, Okehampton, Devon, EX20 1EJ.

Transport Links

By Rail: On Sundays from mid-May to mid-September, Great Western Railway operates trains from Exeter to Okehampton, giving a main line connection. At other times, the nearest stations are Copplestone, Morchard Road and Lapford, all of which are 14 miles from Okehampton.
By Road: Free parking is available at Okehampton (EX20 1EJ).
By Bike: Travel on the Granite Way or Devon Coast to Coast Path, arriving via Meldon Viaduct.

Opening Times

Trains operate approximately 10.45–16.45 on Saturdays, Sundays and Bank Holidays from April to September.

Line Mileage and Journey Time

0.00	Meldon Quarry
2.00	Okehampton
5.75	Sampford Courtenay
16.50	Yeoford
27.00	Exeter St Davids

A return journey from Okehampton to Meldon Quarry takes about 45 minutes.

Stock List

Type	*Number*	*Builder*	*Details*
Diesel	D4167	British Railways	Class 08
Diesel	31452	Brush Traction	Class 31
DMU	59520	Pressed Steel	Class 117
DEMU	60146, 60150, 60673, 60677, 60827 & 60831	British Railways	Class 205
EMU	61742, 61743 & 70273	British Railways	Class 411
EMU	76747, 69310 & 69332	British Railways	Class 421
EMU	76277	British Railways	Class 491

▲ **Dartmoor Railway:** Class 08 No. 08937 is seen at Okehampton on the Dartmoor Railway on 20 May 2018. The railway's heritage signage is in stark contrast to the modern signs at the end of each platform ahead of the Network Rail boundary. **Tony Christie**

▼ **Dartmouth Steam Railway:** BR Standard Class 4MT 4-6-0 No. 75014 "Braveheart" stands at Churston on the Dartmouth Steam Railway on 30 April 2018. **Tony Christie**

Attractions

The Old Station Tea Room at Okehampton opens every day. The Castle and Museum of Dartmoor Life are both less than one mile from Okehampton station. Many walks can be taken from the area, such as reaching the summit of nearby Yes Tor. The traffic-free Granite Way runs from Meldon Quarry station, crossing Meldon Viaduct and continues along the railway trackbed to Lydford and beyond. The route is also part of the Devon Coast to Coast Path. There are many other attractions in Devon, including the narrow gauge Lynton & Barnstaple Railway, Dartmouth Steam Railway (see below) and South Devon Railway (see page 173).

Dartmouth Steam Railway

Introduction and History

The broad gauge railway reached Torre in 1848 and this was extended to Paignton in 1859 and Kingswear in 1864. The line was converted to a standard gauge railway in 1892. The Dart Valley Railway was a commercial venture established in 1962 to operate the line from Totnes to Buckfastleigh, after the route was closed by British Rail in 1962 (see South Devon Railway on page 173). The line from Paignton to Kingswear was first threatened with closure in 1968. In 1972 the Dart Valley Railway acquired the route and started operating trains from the start of 1973. In 2010 the Dart Valley Railway acquired two passenger carrying boats and its two heritage railways became separate organisations. The route from Paignton to Kingswear and connecting river cruises is now known as the Dartmouth Steam Railway & River Boat Company.

Contact Details

Website: www.dartmouthrailriver.co.uk
Tel: 01803 555872
Email: Written enquiries can be made from the website.
Address: Dartmouth Steam Railway, Queens Park Station, Torbay Road, Paignton, TQ4 6AF.

Transport Links

By Rail: The railway connects with the main line network at Paignton.
By Road: Churston (TQ5 0LL) is the only station with free parking, which is very limited. There are chargeable car parks near to Paignton (TQ4 6AF), Goodrington (TQ4 6LN) and Kingswear stations (TQ6 0AA), which can be very busy during the peak season.
By Boat: River crossings from Dartmouth to Kingswear carry foot passengers. As the River Dart is tidal, the crossing times vary.

Opening Times

Trains operate approximately 10.30–17.00 every day of the year, except for a number of weekdays between November and March inclusive.

Line Mileage and Journey Time

0.00	Paignton
0.75	Goodrington Sands
3.00	Churston
4.00	Greenway Halt
6.75	Kingswear

A return journey takes one hour 15 minutes.

Stock List

Type	*Number*	*Builder*	*Details*
Steam	4555	GWR	2-6-2T
Steam	4277	GWR	2-8-0T
Steam	7827	British Railways	4-6-0
Steam	75014	British Railways	4-6-0
Diesel	03371	British Railways	Class 03
Diesel	D2192	British Railways	Class 03
Diesel	D3014	British Railways	Class 08
Diesel	6975	English Electric	Class 37
DMU	59719	British Railways	Class 115

DMU	59003 & 59004	British Railways	Class 116
DMU	59488, 59494, 59503, 59507, 59513 & 59517	Pressed Steel	Class 117

Attractions

The railway offers a number of round trips, with different combinations of rail, river cruise, paddle steamer and bus tours available. Trains offer views of the English Channel and River Dart and there are various walks which can be taken from or between the railway's stations. The visitor centre situated in a railway carriage at Kingswear is free to enter and the railway offers steam locomotive footplate experiences. Greenway House and Garden are a short walk (or shuttle bus ride) from Greenway Halt. The area and the towns of Brixham, Torquay, Totnes and Dartmouth are popular holiday destinations and there are plenty of coastlines, beaches and attractions within reach from the railway.

Special Events during 2019

30–31 August: Dartmouth Regatta, during which additional trains usually operate.
December: Santa Express and Train of Lights.

▲ **Dean Forest Railway:** GWR 4500 Class 2-6-2T No. 5541 arrives at Parkend, the western terminus of the Dean Forest Railway, on 16 May 2018. **Tony Christie**

Dean Forest Railway

Introduction and History

A three foot six inch gauge horse-drawn plateway from Lydney to Parkend opened in 1810. This was used to carry minerals from the Dean Forest to the River Severn for onward transit and became part of a larger network of tramways. When the broad gauge main line from Gloucester to Chepstow opened in 1851, an interchange station was built at Lydney, allowing the minerals to be carried further by rail. The railway's owners purchased five three foot six inch gauge steam locomotives in the 1860s. However, the line was converted to Brunel's seven foot broad gauge in 1872 and was further converted to standard gauge within 20 years. Traffic on the route increased as passenger services from Lydney to Parkend and beyond commenced in 1875 and when the Severn Bridge opened 1879, it connected the railway with Sharpness Docks (see Vale of Berkeley Railway, page 187). Passenger services ended in 1929 and freight on the line declined through the 20th Century. Traffic across the Severn Bridge ended when it was damaged beyond repair in 1960 and by 1967 there was just one daily goods train from Lydney Junction to Parkend. A preservation group formed in 1970 and held its first event in 1971. The trackbed was purchased from British Rail in 1985 and the railway has been extended in stages, reaching Norchard, then Lydney Junction in 1995 and Parkend in 2005. There are plans to extend the line north, initially to Speech House Road and it is hoped that it can be further extended to Cinderford.

Contact Details

Website: www.deanforestrailway.co.uk
Tel: 01594 845840
Email: infodfr@btconnect.com
Address: Dean Forest Railway, Forest Road, Lydney, Gloucestershire, GL15 4ET.

Transport Links

By Rail: The nearest station is Lydney, which is a five minute walk to Lydney Junction.
By Road: Free parking is available at Norchard station (GL15 4ET). There is no parking at the other stations.

Opening Times

The railway operates 10.30–16.30 every Wednesday, Saturday, Sunday, most Bank Holidays and on selected other weekdays from mid-March to early November. Santa Specials also operate during December.

Line Mileage and Journey Time

0.00	Lydney Junction
0.75	Lydney Town
1.50	Norchard Low Level & High Level
3.00	Whitecroft Halt
4.25	Parkend

A return journey takes about one hour 45 minutes, depending where the journey starts from.

Stock List

Type	*Number*	*Builder*	*Details*
Steam	2221	Andrew Barclay	0-4-0ST
Steam	USKMOUTH 1 (2147)	Peckett	0-4-0ST
Steam	9681	British Railways	0-6-0PT
Steam	65	Hunslet	0-6-0ST
Steam	2411	Hunslet	0-6-0ST
Steam	2413	Hunslet	0-6-0ST
Steam	WARRIOR (3823)	Hunslet	0-6-0ST
Steam	WILBERT (3806)	Hunslet	0-6-0ST
Steam	152	Robert Stephenson & Hawthorns	0-6-0ST
Steam	5541	GWR	2-6-2T
Diesel	4210127	Fowler	0-4-0
Diesel	3947	Hibberd	0-4-0
Diesel	6688	Hunslet	0-4-0
Diesel	DON CORBETT (5622)	Hunslet	0-4-0

Diesel	08238	British Railways	Class 08
Diesel	08473	British Railways	Class 08
Diesel	08769	British Railways	Class 08
Diesel	D9521	British Railways	Class 14
Diesel	D9555	British Railways	Class 14
Diesel	D7633	Beyer Peacock	Class 25
Diesel	31210	Brush Traction	Class 31
Diesel	31235	Brush Traction	Class 31
Diesel	31466	Brush Traction	Class 31
Diesel	37308	English Electric	Class 37
Electro-Diesel	73001	British Railways	Class 73
Electro-Diesel	73002	British Railways	Class 73
DMU	50619, 51566, 51914, 56492 & 59387	British Railways	Class 108

Attractions

There is a railway museum at Norchard, which has a large number of exhibits. The site also has a locomotive restoration shed (guides are usually available to show visitors around), a shop and café. The railway operates regular 'Cream Tea & Steam Trains' and footplate experiences. There are a number walks in the area, with routes from each of the railway's stations, including a one mile walk from Lydney Junction along the trackbed to Lydney Harbour, which has views of the River Severn and Sharpness. Parkend station is less than half a mile from route 42 of the National Cycle Network, some of which continues along the railway trackbed. Other attractions in the area include Clearwell Caves and the Dean Forest, with its sculpture trail.

Special Events during 2019

6 April: Murder Mystery.
28 April: Vintage Vehicles.
10 May: Day Out With Thomas.
18–19 May: 1940s Weekend.
7–9 June: Royal Forest of Steam Gala 2019.
26 August: Parkend Carnival.
13–15 September: Diesel Gala.
27–29 September: Day Out With Thomas.
5 October: Murder Mystery.
10 November: Remembrance Day.
7–8, 14–15 & 21–24 December: Santa Specials.
28–29, 31 December & 1 January 2020: Mince Pie Specials.

East Somerset Railway

Introduction and History

The railway from Witham (between the extant Frome and Bruton stations) to Shepton Mallet opened in 1858 and was later extended to Wells where it continued to Yatton. It carried locally quarried rock as well as passengers, originally as a broad gauge railway until it was converted to standard gauge in 1874. The line closed to passenger traffic in 1963 and freight traffic ceased the following year. In the early 1970s, the late artist, David Shepherd, was looking for a home for two steam locomotives he had acquired and he purchased and developed the Cranmore site. This became the East Somerset Heritage Railway, which first opened in 1974. It remains connected to the main line network via the nearby Torr Works Quarry. It is hoped the railway can extend in the future, with the potential to extend in either direction, however there are no immediate plans to proceed with this.

Contact Details

Website: www.eastsomersetrailway.com
Tel: 01749 880417
Email: info@eastsomersetrailway.com
Address: Cranmore Railway Station, Cranmore, Shepton Mallet, Somerset, BA4 4QP.

Transport Links
By Rail: The nearest railway stations are Frome (nine miles) and Bruton (eight miles).
By Road: There is a large, free car park, a short walk from Cranmore Station (BA4 4QP).

Opening Times
Trains operate on Saturdays, Sundays and some weekdays from mid-March until late October, plus Santa Specials in December. The times vary across operating days and are usually 11.00–15.30.

Line Mileage and Journey Time
0.00	Cranmore
0.50	Cranmore West
1.00	Merryfield Lane
2.00	Mendip Vale

Average time taken for a return journey is 40 minutes.

Stock List
Type	*Number*	*Builder*	*Details*
Steam	1719	Andrew Barclay	0-4-0ST
Steam	5637	GWR	0-6-2T
Steam	46447	British Railways	2-6-0
Steam	5239	GWR	2-8-0T
Diesel	10165	Sentinel	0-4-0
Diesel	10175	Sentinel	0-4-0
Diesel	10199	Sentinel	0-4-0
Diesel	10218	Sentinel	0-6-0
Diesel	10221	Sentinel	0-6-0
DMU	51909 & 56271	British Railways	Class 108

Attractions
Visitors can explore the engine shed and workshop, the small museum, signal box, miniature railway, children's play area, café and shop. The new second platform at Cranmore station and the David Shepherd Discovery Centre are both due to open during 2019. The railway offers footplate experiences, 'Driver for a Tenner' days and heritage diesel (DMU) operating dates from 22 April. There is an independent model shop adjacent to the car park, which includes model railway items. Nearby attractions include Nunney Castle, Shepton Mallet, Glastonbury and Wells. The Strawberry Line Trail is further west on the former railway; a mainly traffic-free route from Yatton to Cheddar.

Special Events during 2019
23–24 March: Steam Gala.
19–22 April: Easter Fun.
24 April: Peter Rabbit Visits.
5 May: Animals Day.
27 May: Gruffalo Visits.
29 May: Superheroes Event.
29 June: Dinosaurs Event.
24–26 August: The Way We Were.
December: Santa Specials.

Helston Railway

Introduction and History

The branch line from Gwinear Road, between Hayle and Camborne, to Helston opened in 1887, creating the most southerly railway and station in mainland Britain. Despite much opposition to the threatened closure, the final passenger train left Helston behind Class 22, D6312 in 1962. Freight services continued until 1964 and the track was lifted in 1965. The first preservation group formed in 2005, established a base at Trevarno Halt and began clearing vegetation from the trackbed. One mile of track was relaid and the first trains ran from Truthall Halt to Prospidnick in 2011. The railway plans to extend to Nancegollan and Water-Ma-Trout on the outskirts of Helston, increasing the line to a length of around three miles.

Contact Details

Website: www.helstonrailway.co.uk
Tel: 07901 977 597
Email: info@helstonrailway.co.uk
Address: Trevarno Farm, Prospidnick, Helston, Cornwall, TR13 0RY.

Transport Links

By Rail: The nearest railway station is Camborne, which is seven miles away.
By Road: Free car parking is available at Prospidnick Halt (TR13 0RY).

Opening Times

The railway operates on Sundays, Thursdays and selected other weekdays from mid-March to early November, with trains usually operating 10.30–16.00.

Line Mileage and Journey Time

0.00	Truthall Halt
1.00	Prospidnick Halt

A return journey takes about 30 minutes from Prospidnick.

Stock List

Type	*Number*	*Builder*	*Details*
Steam	KILMERSDON (1788)	Peckett	0-4-0ST
Steam	WILLIAM MURDOCH	Peckett	0-4-0ST
Diesel	97649	Ruston & Hornsby	0-4-0
Diesel	395305	Ruston & Hornsby	0-4-0
DMU	50413 & 56169	Park Royal	Class 103
DMU	59521	Pressed Steel	Class 117

Attractions

At the Prospidnick base there is a buffet in a restored railway carriage and a gift shop with railway books, gifts and souvenirs. Truthall Halt has been rebuilt as an exact replica of the original building and the quality of the rebuild was recognised in early 2019 with a Heritage Railways Association award. There are many other attractions in western Cornwall, including the National Seal Sanctuary, Poldark Mine, Lizard Peninsula and the South West Coastal Path.

Special Events during 2019

19–22 April: Easter Family Fun & Easter Egg Trail.
26–27 May: Return to the 1940s.
14–15 September: Heritage Weekend.
27 October: Kids for a Quid.
7–8, 14–15, 20–23 December: Santa Specials.

Pallot Steam, Motor & General Museum, Jersey

Introduction and History
The museum is one of the few sites within this book which is not located on the site of a former railway. Don Pallot (1910–1996) was an engineer and inventor, who after collecting various mechanical items including steam engines, created a museum to house these; this first opened in 1990. The collection includes locomotives brought from mainland Britain, Belgium and Alderney. In 1996 the engine shed, railway line and station were opened and the engine shed was extended in 2002.

Contact Details
Website: www.pallotmuseum.co.uk
Tel: 01534 865307
Email: info@pallotmuseum.co.uk
Address: The Pallot Steam, Motor & General Museum, Rue de Bechet, Trinity, Jersey, Channel Islands, JE3 5BE.

Transport Links
By Rail: There is no rail service on Jersey.
By Road: There is ample free car parking at the museum (JE3 5BE).

Opening Times
During 2019 the museum opens 10.00–17.00 Mondays–Saturdays from 1 April to 31 October. Steam trains depart on the hour 11.00–16.00 on Thursdays and during the event on 7 September.

Line Mileage and Journey Time
Trains operate on an oval shaped circuit, for a length of just over a quarter of a mile and the journey time is relatively short.

Stock List

Type	*Number*	*Builder*	*Details*
Steam	2085	Peckett	0-4-0ST
Steam	J T DALY	Bagnall	0-4-0ST
Steam	2129 Kestrel	Peckett	0-4-0ST
Steam	LA MEUSE	Belgian	0-6-0T
Diesel	27734	North British	0-4-0

Attractions
The museum's exhibits include a 1912 steam roller, steam locomotives, tractors, classic and vintage motor vehicles, toys, a church pipe organ, a Compton theatre organ and details of Jersey's history. The museum is close to Jersey Zoo (two miles), St Helier (three and a half miles), the island's coast and various other attractions.

Special Events during 2019
9 May: Liberation Day Steam & Motor Fayre.
7 September: Steam Threshing & Motor.

Plym Valley Railway

Introduction and History

The original broad gauge railway from Devonport Junction (to the east of Plymouth) to Tavistock South and Lydford opened in 1859. This was extended to Launceston in 1865 and the line was converted to standard gauge in 1892. Passenger services ended in 1962 and it closed as a through route when freight trains ceased in 1964. The Plym Valley Railway group formed in 1981 and began working towards creating a heritage railway. The first section of track was laid in 2001 and the heritage railway opened in 2008, travelling north along the original route from Marsh Mills. This was extended to a new station at Plym Bridge in 2012, which opened exactly 50 years after the final passenger train ran in 1962. There are long-term aims to extend the railway further; however, resources are currently being used to improve the Marsh Mills area.

Contact Details

Website: www.plymrail.co.uk
Tel: 07580 689380
Email: plymrail@yahoo.co.uk
Address: Plym Valley Railway, Coypool Road, Plympton, Plymouth, PL7 4NW.

Transport Links

By Rail: The nearest station is Plymouth, which is four miles from Marsh Mills.
By Road: There are car parks at Coypool Park and Ride (PL7 4TB) and Plymbridge Road (PL7 4SR), which are very close to Marsh Mills and Plym Bridge stations respectively.
By Bike: Route 27 of the National Cycle Network follows the course of the present and former railway.

Opening Times

The railway operates 11.00–16.30 on Sundays from March to November and on selected other dates.

Line Mileage and Journey Time

0.00	Marsh Mills
1.25	Plym Bridge

A return journey takes about half an hour.

Stock List

Type	*Number*	*Builder*	*Details*
Steam	705	Andrew Barclay	0-4-0ST
Steam	ALBERT (2248)	Andrew Barclay	0-4-0ST
Steam	BYFIELD (2655)	Bagnall	0-6-0ST
Steam	TKH49 (5374)	Fablok	0-6-0T
Diesel	10077	Sentinel	0-4-0
Diesel	125V	Thomas Hill	0-4-0
Diesel	D2046	British Railways	Class 03
Diesel	13002	British Railways	Class 08
Diesel	51365 & 51407	Pressed Steel	Class 117

Attractions

There is a heritage railway centre at Marsh Mills where steam and diesel locomotives and other rolling stock are being restored, as well as a café and shop. Diesel-hauled brake van rides travel to Lee Moor Crossing and operate subject to demand. The Devon Coast to Coast cycle route (route 27 of the National Cycle Network) passes the railway on its journey from Plymouth to Barnstaple in north Devon. Saltram House is near to Marsh Mills and Plymbridge Woods is adjacent to Plym Bridge station (both National Trust). Further nearby attractions include Plymouth Ski Centre, Crownhill Fort, the National Marine Aquarium and Merchant's House Museum.

Special Events during 2019

21–22 April: Easter Event.
25–26 May: Teddy Bears' Picnic.
13–14 July: Transport Festival.
30 August–1 September: Rails & Ales.

▲ **East Somerset Railway:** GWR 5600 Class 0-6-2T No. 5637 climbs away from Mendip Vale on the East Somerset Railway with a demonstration goods train on 30 April 2017. **Glen Batten**

▼ **South Devon Railway:** On 18 February 2017, GWR 2251 Class 0-6-0 No. 3205 heads along Stretchford straight on the South Devon Railway with the 13.35 Totnes Riverside–Buckfastleigh combined milk and passenger service. **David Hunt**

27–28 October: Witches & Wizards Weekend.
Weekends in December: North Pole Express Trains.

Evening dining and cream tea trains also operate on a number of dates.

Somerset & Dorset Railway, Midsomer Norton

Introduction and History

Midsomer Norton South station opened in 1874, when a single-track extension of the Somerset & Dorset Railway (S&D) to Bath was completed. The track was doubled in 1886, but after declining use, Midsomer Norton station and the S&D route closed in 1966. The Somerset & Dorset Railway Heritage Trust acquired the Midsomer Norton site in 1995 and has since restored the station building, signal box and goods shed. A stretch of operational track has been laid from the station and this is being extended south towards Chilcompton Tunnel. After this new section has been brought to an operational standard it is hoped that the railway can be extended further south, which would first require the infilled cutting to be cleared.

Contact Details

Website: www.sdjr.co.uk
Tel: 01761 411 221
Address: Somerset & Dorset Railway, Midsomer Norton Station, Silver Street, Midsomer Norton, BA3 2EY.

Transport Links

By Rail: The nearest stations are Frome (11 miles), Bath (11 miles) or Trowbridge (14 miles).
By Road: There is limited parking outside Midsomer Norton South station (BA3 2EY) and free parking at Norton Hill School (BA3 4AD) at weekends and during school holidays, or on Charlton Road opposite the station.
By Bike: The Five Arches Cycle & Walkway from Radstock to Midsomer Norton is a spur off the Colliers Way, which is route 24 of the National Cycle Network.

Opening Times

Trains operate 11.00–16.00 on selected Saturdays and Sundays. The station, shop and museum also open every Sunday and Monday throughout the year.

Line Mileage and Journey Time

When the extension is completed (due early 2019), the railway will be nearly one mile long and a return journey will take about 20 minutes.

Stock List

Type	*Number*	*Builder*	*Details*
Steam	7109	Sentinel	4wVBT
Diesel	D1120	English Electric	0-6-0
Diesel	D4095	British Railways	Class 08
DMU	59664	British Railways	Class 115

Attractions

The Midsomer Norton base is home to the restored Victorian station buildings, a museum devoted to the S&D, a small pillar box war museum, a gift shop and a second-hand bookshop. The East Somerset Railway (see page 166) and Avon Valley Railway (see page 156) are eight and 13 miles away respectively. Nearby attractions include Radstock Museum, The Colliers Way cycle route, the city of Bath and the Mendip Hills.

Special Events during 2019

9–10 March: Spring Diesel Gala.
21–22 April: Easter Egg Hunt.
18 May: Real Ale Trains.
15–16 June: Midsummer at Midsomer.
11 August: Family Fun Day.
7–8 September: Autumn Steam Gala.
26 October: Real Ale Trains.
27 October: Pumpkins on the Platform.
1, 8 & 15 December: Santa Specials.

South Devon Railway

Introduction and History

The broad gauge branch line from Totnes to Ashburton opened in 1872 and was converted to standard gauge over a single weekend in 1892. After usage declined, it was closed to passengers in 1958 and to freight in 1962. The Dart Valley Light Railway formed in 1962 to operate the route as a commercial tourist railway; the first locomotives arrived in 1965 and the railway was formally opened by Dr Richard Beeching in 1969. The line from Buckfastleigh to Ashburton was severed in 1971 when improvements were made to the A38. The venture became uneconomical and was threatened with closure in 1989, until an existing charity based at the railway took it over and renamed the charity the South Devon Railway Association. The first trains to officially operate in preservation ran in 1991 and in the years since the railway has continued to grow in popularity and success. Ashburton station building survives; plans to redevelop the site have been successfully fought off, with the hope that it can again be connected to the South Devon Railway in future.

Contact Details

Website: www.southdevonrailway.co.uk
Tel: 01364 644370
Email: trains@southdevonrailway.org
Address: South Devon Railway, Dartbridge Road, Buckfastleigh, Devon, TQ11 0DZ.

Transport Links

By Rail: Totnes railway station is less than half a mile away and the journey involves crossing a footbridge over the River Dart.
By Road: Ample car parking is available at Buckfastleigh (TQ11 0DZ). There are a number of car parks near Totnes Riverside station, the nearest of which is about half a mile away.

Opening Times

The railway operates every day from mid-March until early November and during December for Santa Specials and Mince Pie Specials.

Line Mileage and Journey Time

0.00	Buckfastleigh
3.00	Staverton
6.75	Totnes Riverside

A return journey takes about 1 hour 15 minutes.

Stock List

Type	Number	Builder	Details
Steam	151 TINY	Sara & Co	0-4-0 Broad Gauge
Steam	1690	Peckett	0-4-0T
Steam	2031	Peckett	0-4-0T
Steam	1420	GWR	0-4-2T
Steam	3205	GWR	0-6-0
Steam	L92 (5786)	GWR	0-6-0PT
Steam	1369	GWR	0-6-0PT
Steam	6412	GWR	0-6-0PT
Steam	5474	Kitson	0-6-0ST
Steam	GLENDOWER	Hunslet	0-6-0ST
Steam	5526	GWR	2-6-2T
Steam	5542	GWR	2-6-2T
Steam	2873	GWR	2-8-0
Steam	3803	GWR	2-8-0
Steam	4920	GWR	4-6-0
Diesel	MFP4	Fowler	0-4-0
Diesel	2745	Yorkshire Engine Co.	0-6-0
Diesel	D2271	Robert Stephenson & Hawthorns	Class 04
Diesel	D2246	Robert Stephenson & Hawthorns	Class 04
Diesel	D3721	British Railways	Class 09
Diesel	D7535	British Railways	Class 25

Diesel	D7541	British Railways	Class 25
Diesel	D7612	British Railways	Class 25
Diesel	D6501	BRCW	Class 33
Diesel	6737	English Electric	Class 37
Diesel	D402	English Electric	Class 50
DMU	59740	British Railways	Class 115
DMU	59493	Pressed Steel	Class 117
DMU	55000	GRCW	Class 122

Attractions
The railway travels along a secluded route following the River Dart and has a museum at Buckfastleigh which tells the story of the route and houses the UK's only surviving original broad gauge locomotive. Footplate driving experiences are available and nearby attractions include Totnes Rare Breeds Farm, Dartmoor Otters & Buckfast Butterflies, Buckfast Abbey and Totnes town centre and market.

Special Events during 2019
6–14 April: 50th Anniversary Gala.
4–6 May: Days Out with Thomas.
24–27 May: Spring Beer Festival.
14–16 June: Ticket to Ride (1960s Event).
6–7 July: South Devon 1940s Festival.
19–21 July: Summer Diesel Gala.
23–26 August: Rails & Ales.
7–8 September: Heritage Open Days & Behind the Scenes.
28–29 September: Models & Miniatures.
19–21 October: Days Out with Thomas.
2–3 November: Buy One Get One Free Weekend.
7–8, 14–15 & 18–24 December: Santa Specials.
12–13 December: Carols Down the Line.
27 December–1 January 2020: Mince Pie Specials.

STEAM: Museum of the Great Western Railway

Introduction and History
The museum is located within a remnant of Swindon Works, which was one of the largest railway engineering sites in the world. The works opened in 1843 and operated as a locomotive building and railway maintenance workshop for the Great Western Railway and British Railways for almost 150 years. At its height Swindon Works employed over 14 000 people and it is the main reason that Swindon has grown to the size it is today. The works closed in 1986. The building which houses the museum is Grade II listed and preserves some important architectural, industrial and railway heritage. There is no operational railway at the site but it has been included in the listings due to the significance of its history and the railway exhibits it contains. The locomotives displayed move to and from other sites from time to time.

Contact Details
Website: www.steam-museum.org.uk
Tel: 01793 466646
Email: steammuseum@swindon.gov.uk
Address: Fire Fly Avenue, Swindon, SN2 2EY.

Transport Links
By Rail: Swindon railway station is just over one mile away.
By Road: Free parking is available with a standard admission ticket at either of the Swindon Designer Outlet car parks (SN2 2DY).

Opening Times
The museum is open 10.00–17.00 (11.00–16.00 on Sundays & Bank Holidays) every day of the year except 24–26 December. Last admission is one hour before closing time.

Stock List

Type	Number	Builder	Details
Steam	2516	GWR	0-6-0
Steam	9400	GWR	0-6-0PT
Steam	NORTH STAR (replica)	GWR	2-2-2 Broad Gauge
Steam	2818	GWR	2-8-0
Steam	4248	GWR	2-8-0T
Steam	3717	GWR	4-4-0
Steam	4073	GWR	4-6-0
Steam	6000	GWR	4-6-0

Attractions

"Meet the Railway Workers" takes place on selected Saturdays, when volunteers allow visitors to board locomotives 4073 'Caerphilly Castle', 3717 'City of Truro' and 6000 'King George V' and share anecdotes of their time working on the railway. The museum has many exhibits to explore; an on-site café and can be hired as meeting or function venue. It is located at the site of Swindon Designer Outlet, which has more than 100 stores. Other attractions nearby include the Museum of Computing, Stanton Park & Nature Reserve, Lydiard Park and the Swindon & Cricklade Railway (see page 177), which is less than five miles away.

Special Events during 2019

14 January–31 December: Time on Trial Exhibition; detailing the speed trials which took place between the GWR and other railway companies between 1910 and 1948.
6 April–11 May: World's Fastest; exhibition on GWR's speed racing, marking 115 years since 3717 'City of Truro' achieved a record speed of 100mph.
26 July–1 January 2020: Spark of Genius; a look at some of the GWRs most influential designers, engineers and inventors.
7–8 September: Swindon Railway Festival.
5–6 October: Great Western Brick Show.
30 November–1 December: Christmas at STEAM.

▲ **STEAM: Museum of the Great Western Railway:** GWR broad gauge 2-2-2 locomotive "North Star" is seen on display in Steam, the Museum of the Great Western Railway at Swindon on 25 September 2010. Although classed as a replica, this locomotive was built by the Great Western Railway in 1925, using parts from the 1837 original. **Robert Pritchard**

Swanage Railway

Introduction and History

The branch line from Wareham to Swanage opened in 1885 and remained in use until it was closed by British Rail in early 1972, after which the track was promptly lifted. The Swanage Railway Society formed in 1972 and successfully thwarted a number of attempts to demolish Swanage station. Trains first worked on a short section of track in 1979 and the line was lengthened in a number of stages, reaching Norden in 1992 and reconnecting to the main line at Wareham in 2017. On summer Saturdays in 2018 through services from Salisbury to Wareham returned for the first time in many years.

Contact Details

Website: www.swanagerailway.co.uk
Tel: 01929 425800
Email: info@swanagerailway.co.uk
Address: Swanage Railway, Station House, Swanage, Dorset, BH19 1HB.

Transport Links

By Rail: There is a main line rail connection at Wareham. However, the railway only operates through trains to Wareham seasonally.
By Road: Norden station has a 350 space car and coach park just off the A351 and charges apply (BH20 5DW). There is no car parking at Corfe Castle station or Herston Halt. Harmans Cross has a small car park where charges apply (BH19 3EB) and there is a paid car park a five minute-walk from Swanage station (BH20 1PW).
By Boat: From April to October cruises from Poole Quay to Swanage operate and take one hour each way.

Opening Times

Trains operate throughout the year, with services every day from late March to mid-October and on selected dates at other times.

Line Mileage and Journey Time

0.00	Swanage
0.50	Herston Halt
3.00	Harmans Cross
5.00	Corfe Castle
5.50	Norden
11.00	Wareham

A return journey takes slightly more than one hour.

Stock List

Type	*Number*	*Builder*	*Details*
Steam	30053	LSWR	0-4-4T
Steam	31625	Southern Railway	2-6-0
Steam	31806	Southern Railway	2-6-0
Steam	31874	Southern Railway	2-6-0
Steam	80104	British Railways	2-6-4T
Steam	30120	LSWR	4-4-0
Steam	34072	British Railways	4-6-2
Steam	34010	Southern Railway	4-6-2
Steam	34028	Southern Railway	4-6-2
Steam	34053	Southern Railway	4-6-2
Steam	34070	Southern Railway	4-6-2
Diesel	4210132	Fowler	0-4-0
Diesel	BERYL	Hibberd	0-4-0
Diesel	08436	British Railways	Class 08
Diesel	D3591	British Railways	Class 08
Diesel	33111	BRCW	Class 33
Diesel	D6515	BRCW	Class 33
DMU	51356, 51388, 59486	Pressed Steel	Class 117
DMU	55028	Pressed Steel	Class 121
EMU	76275	British Railways	Class 491

Attractions
There is a small railway museum at Corfe Castle station and Purbeck Mineral & Mining Museum can be found at Norden station. Corfe Castle is visible from the railway and can be reached by way of an uphill walk from its namesake station. There is plenty to see in the busy town of Swanage, the surrounding Isle of Purbeck and other well-known sites nearby, including Lulworth Cove, Durdle Door, Poole and the Jurassic Coast.

Special Events during 2019
29–31 March: Spring Steam Up.
9–12 May: Diesel Gala & Beer Festival.
27 July–3 August: Swanage Regatta, Carnival & Fireworks.
6–8 September: Classic Transport Rally.
11–13 October: Autumn Steam Gala.
10, 17 & 24 November: Autumn Diesel Service.
30 November–24 December: Santa Specials.
28 December: Winter Warm Up.

Swindon & Cricklade Railway

Introduction and History
The railway from Swindon Town to Cirencester Watermoor opened in 1883. Cricklade and Blunsdon were intermediate stations on the route and opened in 1883 and 1895 respectively. Blunsdon closed to passengers in 1924 and all passenger services were withdrawn in 1961. After this trains occasionally ran to Moredon Power Station, which was near the site of the present-day Taw Valley Halt, until 1969. The Swindon & Cricklade Railway Preservation Society formed in 1978 and took over the empty trackbed. Track laying began in 1980 and the first heritage steam trains used the route in 1984. In 2000 the line reached Hayes Knoll and it has been extended in a number of stages since. The railway is being further extended in both directions; to the south a new larger station at Moulsdon Country Park is being constructed and work is progressing to extend north to the village of Cricklade.

Contact Details
Website: www.swindon-cricklade-railway.org
Tel: 01793 771615
Email: scr@gmx.co.uk
Address: Swindon & Cricklade Railway, Blunsdon Station, Tadpole Lane, Swindon, SN25 2DA.

Transport Links
By Rail: Swindon railway station is five miles from Blunsdon.
By Road: Free car parking is available at Blunsdon station (SN25 2DA). At Mouldon Hill car park, which is a short walk from Taw Valley Halt (SN25 1WH) free parking is provided by Swindon Borough Council. There is no road access at Hayes Knoll station.

Opening Times
During 2019 the railway operates every Sunday from 3 February to 22 December, every Saturday from 6 April to 5 October, every Wednesday in July and August and on selected other weekdays. Trains operate either 11.00–16.00 or 10.30–16.30, depending on which timetable is in operation.

Line Mileage and Journey Time
0.00	Taw Valley Halt
1.25	Blunsdon
1.75	Hayes Knoll

A return journey takes about one hour.

Stock List

Type	Number	Builder	Details
Steam	2354	Andrew Barclay	0-4-0ST
Steam	1555	Peckett	0-4-0ST
Steam	2138	Andrew Barclay	0-6-0ST
Steam	2411	Hunslet	0-6-0ST
Steam	2413	Hunslet	0-6-0ST
Steam	3135	Fablok	0-6-0T
Steam	1464	Hudswell Clarke	0-6-0T
Steam	6984	British Railways	4-6-0
Diesel	7342	Fowler	0-4-0
Diesel	4220031	Fowler	0-4-0
Diesel	21442 WOODBINE	Fowler	0-4-0
Diesel	D2022	British Railways	Class 03
Diesel	D2152	British Railways	Class 03
Diesel	D3261	British Railways	Class 08
Diesel	09004	British Railways	Class 09
Diesel	97651	Ruston & Hornsby	Class 97
Electro-Diesel	E6003	British Railways	Class 73
DMU	59514	Pressed Steel	Class 117
DMU	51074 & 51104	GRCW	Class 119
DEMU	60669 & 60822	British Railways	Class 205
DEMU	60127	British Railways	Class 207

Attractions

There are two museums at Blunsdon. One displays railway memorabilia and has an emphasis on the line in British Rail times. The other is a wartime museum which is run in connection with a re-enactment group and has various exhibits including an air raid shelter. The railway's restoration and maintenance centre and a restored signal box are at Hayes Knoll. Train driver experience days are available. The Cotswold Water Park is nearby and is home of the largest amount of redundant gravel pits in the country. These have been converted for social uses including an inland beach resort, power boating and sailing.

Special Events during 2019

31 March: Mother's Day (mothers go free with paying children).
11–12 May: Diesel Gala.
18–19 May: Behind the Scenes weekend.
25–27 May: Real Ale & Cider Festival.
22–23 June: Mixed Traffic Gala.
13–15 September: Steam Gala.
10–11 August: Vintage Weekend.
7–8 September: Military Weekend.
From 30 November: Santa Specials.

There are also various events aimed at children and Murder Mystery evenings through the year.

West Somerset Railway

Introduction and History

The broad gauge branch line from Taunton to Watchet opened in 1862 and was extended to Minehead in 1874. It was converted to a standard gauge railway in 1882. By the 1960s it was only profitable during the summer months, when larger volumes of seasonal passengers were carried. British Rail closed the line in 1971 but unlike many other closed railways, the track was left in place. In 1975 vegetation was cleared to allow Class 25 25059 to make a trip to Minehead to collect LMS 6229 'Duchess of Hamilton' by rail from the Butlins holiday camp. The first heritage trains operated between Minehead and Blue Anchor in 1976 and they were extended to Bishops Lydeard in 1979. When British Rail upgraded signalling in the Taunton area in 1981, the rail connection to Bishops Lydeard was removed. The structure of the railway changed during the 1980s, utilitising more volunteers which, along with support from Somerset County Council, triggered a growth in passenger revenues and investment in the infrastructure. The main line connection at Taunton has since been reinstated and is used by occasional through charter trains. The railway aims to return regular services to Taunton station.

Contact Details

Website: www.west-somerset-railway.co.uk
Tel: 01643 704996
Email: info@wsrail.net
Address: West Somerset Railway, The Railway Station, Minehead, Somerset, TA24 5BG.

Transport Links

By Rail: The nearest station is Taunton, which is five miles from Bishops Lydeard station.
By Road: There is a large free car park at Bishops Lydeard (TA4 3RU), limited parking at Williton (TA4 4RQ) and a pay & display car park adjacent to Minehead station (TA24 5BG).

Opening Times

The railway operates every day from 30 March to 2 November, except 1, 5, 8, 12, 23, 26 & 29 April, 3, 10 & 24 May, 27 & 30 September, 7, 11, 14, 18, 21 & 25 October and 1 November.

Line Mileage and Journey Time

0.00	Bishops Lydeard
4.00	Crowcombe Heathfield
6.50	Stogumber
9.75	Williton
10.75	Doniford
11.50	Watchet
14.00	Washford
16.25	Blue Anchor
18.00	Dunster
19.50	Minehead

0.00	Bishops Lydeard
2.25	Norton Fitzwarren
5.00	Taunton

A return journey takes about 3 hours.

Stock List

Type	*Number*	*Builder*	*Details*
Steam	CALEDONIA WORKS (1219)	Andrew Barclay	0-4-0ST
Steam	44422	LMS	0-6-0
Steam	6695	Armstrong Whitworth	0-6-2T
Steam	9351	GWR	2-6-0
Steam	4110	GWR	2-6-2T
Steam	4561	GWR	2-6-2T
Steam	53808	Robert Stephenson & Co	2-8-0
Steam	7822	British Railways	4-6-0
Steam	7828	British Railways	4-6-0
Steam	4936	GWR	4-6-0
Steam	6024	GWR	4-6-0
Steam	6960	GWR	4-6-0
Steam	7027	British Railways	4-6-0
Diesel	DH16	Sentinel	0-4-0
Diesel	1 (578)	Andrew Barclay	0-6-0
Diesel	2 (579)	Andrew Barclay	0-6-0
Diesel	D2133	British Railways	Class 03
Diesel	D4107	British Railways	Class 09
Diesel	D9518	British Railways	Class 14
Diesel	D9526	British Railways	Class 14
Diesel	D6566	BRCW	Class 33
Diesel	D6575	BRCW	Class 33
Diesel	D7017	Beyer Peacock	Class 35
Diesel	D7018	Beyer Peacock	Class 35
Diesel	D1661	British Railways	Class 47
Diesel	D1010	British Railways	Class 52
DMU	51859, 51880, 51887 & 59678	British Railways	Class 115

Attractions

The WSR is one of the longest heritage railways in Britain and one of the most popular attractions in the South-West. There are a number of museums on the railway; the Gauge Museum at Bishops Lydeard has exhibits of local and railway interest. The Great Western Railway Museum at Blue Anchor opens Sundays & Bank Holidays, from Easter to September and during galas. The Somerset and Dorset Railway Trust have a museum at Washford. The Diesel & Electric Preservation Group's depot at Williton is open during weekends. There is a model railway at Bishops Lydeard and a bookshop and café at Minehead. Steam and diesel engineman courses are available on selected dates. On some dates there is a bus link from Dunster station to Dunster Castle (National Trust). Bishops Lydeard is situated at the foot of the Quantock Hills and the station at Minehead is adjacent to the beach and town centre, which has a number of visitor attractions.

Special Events during 2019

19–20 April: Children's Character Event.
2 June: Classic Car Run.
8–9 June: Mixed Traction Event celebrating the 40th Anniversary of the WSR reopening.
20–23 June: Diesel Gala (Mixed Traction Day on 23 June).
26 July: Children's Character Day.
3–4 August: WSR Association Steam Rally.
14–15 September: 1940s Weekend.
3–6 October: Autumn Steam Gala.
30 November–24 December: Santa Services.
6–7 December: Dunster By Candlelight Services.
9–10 December: Carol Trains.
29–30 December: Winter Steam Festival.

Yeovil Railway Centre

Introduction and History

The railway centre occupies railway sidings which were previously part of Yeovil Junction station. The station opened in 1860 and the site which the centre occupies included a transfer shed, which was used to transfer goods from broad gauge to standard gauge railway wagons. Closure of Yeovil Junction station was proposed in 1964 and whilst local opposition prevented this, much of the freight traffic was lost and the railway was downgraded to single track in the 1960s. The first heritage railway group formed in 1994 and a lease for the site was agreed. A new engine shed was constructed, opening in 1999 and since then various steam and diesel locomotives have visited or been renovated at the centre.

Contact Details

Website: www.yeovilrailway.freeservers.com
Tel: 01935 410420
Email: yeovilrailway@hotmail.com
Address: Yeovil Railway Centre, Yeovil Junction Station, Stoford, Yeovil, BA22 9UU.

Transport Links

By Rail: The Railway Centre is adjacent to Yeovil Junction station.
By Road: There is free parking on-site, turn right under the railway bridge when approaching Yeovil Junction station (BA22 9UU).

Opening Times

The centre is open from 10.30 on railway operating dates, which for 2019 are 17 March, 7 & 21–22 April, 5 & 19 May, 9 & 23 June, 28 & 30 July, 6, 13, 18, 20 & 27 August, 1, 15 & 29 September and 29 December. Trains are due to be steam-hauled, except on the Tuesdays during August.

Line Mileage and Journey Time

The railway line is one third of a mile long and the journey time is relatively short.

Stock List

Type	*Number*	*Builder*	*Details*
Steam	1398 LORD FISHER	Andrew Barclay	0-4-0ST
Steam	1579 PECTIN	Peckett	0-4-0ST
Diesel	44	Fowler	0-4-0
Diesel	22900 SAM	Fowler	0-4-0
Diesel	DS1174	Ruston & Hornsby	0-4-0
DMU	59515	Pressed Steel	Class 117

Attractions

The Centre has a 70 foot operational turntable, which is used when main line steam locomotives are serviced, as well as model and miniature railways which are in use when the standard gauge railway operates. Steam locomotive driver experience courses are available. The visitor centre has various railway themed exhibits and serves light refreshments. Nearby attractions include Yeovil Country Park, a number of National Trust sites and various rural locations across Somerset and nearby Dorset.

Special Events during 2019

27–28 April: Model Railway Weekend.
13–14 July: 25th Anniversary Weekend.
4 August: Tractor Day.
26 & 31 October: Halloween Event.
1, 8, 14–15 & 22–23 December: Santa Specials.

▲ **Swanage Railway:** With the driver about to return the token for the single-track section from Norden to station staff, 1962-built Class 45 No. 45041 arrives into Corfe Castle station, which is roughly half way along the Swanage Railway, at the head of the 1020 Norden–Swanage service, during the railway's annual diesel gala on 11 May 2018. **Andy Chard**

Proposed Heritage Railways

The railways in the preceding regional listings operate trains and open to the public on specified dates. There are a number of railway preservation groups working towards running heritage passenger trains and some are closer to that point than others. Where such projects are at a more advanced stage, they are listed in this section, the criteria for which is most or all of the following:

- The organisation has been granted access to the railway line or trackbed. In most cases, this consists of an agreement with Network Rail or the land owner to lease or access the railway line.
- They are in possession of rolling stock for operating passenger carrying trains. This could be minimal, such as a brake van and small shunting locomotive or a DMU which requires renovation.
- The group have an online presence, with details of their activities, aims and any events which are open to the public.

The proposed heritage railway listings follow a similar format to their established counterparts. Any readers considering visiting or volunteering with these organisations are encouraged to do so, making advance arrangements as necessary. There are other proposed heritage railways and preservation groups which are at earlier stages in their journey than those below. As these progress, it is hoped that they can be included in future editions of this book.

Garw Valley Railway, Wales Region

Background

The railway from Tondu to Nantymoel opened in 1865 and the steeply graded branch from Brynmenyn Junction near Tondu to Blaengarw opened in 1876. The area's small population grew substantially after the railway opened, enabling the Garw Valley's rich coal resources to be exported via the ports of South Wales. Blaengarw lost its passenger services in 1953 although coal trains continued on the route until 1986, ending shortly after the closure of Ocean Colliery. The nearby line to Tondu and Maesteg was reopened to passenger trains in 1992 and trains briefly returned to Pontycymer during the 1990s to remove spoil tips. The northern-most section of the line between Pontycymer and Blaengarw was demolished in the 1990s but the majority of the route from Tondu to Pontycymer has remained in situ since.

Heritage Railway Progress and Future Plans

The first preservation group formed in 1988 with the aim of creating a museum and heritage railway centre at Brynmenyn. Since then a base and locomotive shed has been established at Pontycymer and the four and three quarter mile railway to Brynmenyn has been leased from Network Rail. In 2016, the first section of a new station at Pontycymer was built and 200 m of track was laid. It is hoped that by 2020 trains can operate on a section of a few hundred metres from the new Pontycymer station and in following years the operational section will be extended to approximately one and a quarter miles. Work towards the creation of the heritage centre at Pontycymer also continues and the long-term aim is to extend the railway south to Tondu, where it would reach the line from Bridgend to Maesteg.

Contact Details

Website: www.garwvalleyrailway.co.uk
Email: enquiries@garwvalleyrailway.co.uk
Address: Garw Valley Railway, Pontycymer Locomotive Works, Old Station Yard, Pontycymer, Bridgend, CF32 8AZ.

Opening Times & Transport Links

The locomotive shed at Pontycymer is open 09.30–15.30 most Wednesdays and Saturdays. Please check the website before travelling, as it will say when the shed is closed. There will be open days during the Bank Holiday weekends in late May and August, which will be advertised beforehand.

By Rail: The nearest railway station is Tondu, which is six miles away.
By Road: There is free parking, which is shared with the leisure centre (CF32 8AZ).

Stock List

Type	*Number*	*Builder*	*Details*
Steam	7705	Robert Stephenson & Hawthorns	0-4-0ST
Steam	3840 PAMELA	Hunslet	0-6-0ST
Diesel	3890	Hibberd	0-4-0
Diesel	4006	Hibberd	0-4-0
DMU	51919 & 52048	British Railways	Class 108

Local Attractions

Attractions in the area include Bryngarw Country Park, South Wales Miners Museum, Parc Slip Nature Reserve and Bridgend Miniature Railway.

Leiston Works Railway, Eastern Region

Background

Richard Garrett & Sons was established in 1778 and manufactured steam engines, traction engines and a variety of agricultural machinery across two sites in Leiston, Suffolk which were known as The Works. Initially horse-drawn transport was used and when the railway from Saxmundham to Leiston opened in 1859 it connected to The Works, allowing products to be transported within and away from the two sites. In 1860 the railway was extended to Aldeburgh. By the early 20th Century, there was a comprehensive track network within Leiston linking the two sites and at its height the company employed over 3500 people. The industry was declining by the 1950s as road transport and motor vehicles were increasingly replacing steam traction. Passenger services on the railway from Saxmundham to Aldeburgh were withdrawn in 1966 and the line to The Works closed soon afterwards in 1968. After further decline both sites of The Works closed in 1981. Much of the two sites were demolished and used for property development; however, some parts have been preserved and these can be seen in The Long Shop Museum. The railway track was lifted between Aldeburgh and Sizewell after passenger services ended, leaving a single line for nuclear fuel traffic from Saxmundham to Sizewell. This remains in the possession of Network Rail and sees intermittent use today.

Heritage Railway Progress and Future Plans

In 2011 a group of railway enthusiasts formed the Leiston Works Railway Trust with the aim of opening a section of The Works railway and returning trains to the town. Since then, they have purchased and cleared much of the former trackbed and are about to start relaying a short section of track from the Long Shop Museum, using track panels acquired from the former Ipswich Docks line. The group have restored steam locomotive "Sirapite", which worked on the site until 1962, and are restoring a number of vintage carriages and a brake van which will be used to carry passengers. There will be a number of events during 2019 to mark the 160th anniversary of the railway reaching Leiston Works, most notably on 1 and 2 June when there are plans to operate the first heritage steam trains. Leiston Works Railway would then become Britain's newest heritage railway.

A second phase will involve extending the heritage railway north to Buller Road, which is less than 100 m from the Network Rail line to Sizewell Power Station, giving around 200 m of operational track. Longer-term aims include reconnecting the railway to the former Garrett Works site at the Long Shop Museum and it is hoped that it may be possible to reconnect to the Sizewell branch line, giving a much longer heritage railway.

Contact Details

Website: www.lwr.org.uk
Tel: 07774 640708
Email: theleistonworksrailway@gmail.com
Address: Access is by prior arrangement. Please contact the railway.

Opening Times & Transport Links

Working parties for members meet each Friday 14.00–17.00 and 18.30–21.30 at the workshop. Membership is £6 per year; please contact the railway if you are interested in joining.

Events planned for 2019 include a music concert on 18 May and the 160th anniversary celebrations on 1 and 2 June, which are due to see the first preserved steam trains in operation. Details of further events will be announced when they have been confirmed.

By Rail: Saxmundham is the nearest railway station and is four miles away.
By Road: Free car parking is available for Long Shop Museum visitors (IP16 4ES).

Stock List

Type	Number	Builder	Details
Steam	SIRAPITE	Aveling & Porter	0-4-0WT

Local Attractions

The Long Shop Museum in the former works at Leiston showcases the town's industrial history. Other nearby attractions include RSPB Minsmere, Orford Ness National Nature Reserve and various coastal and rural sites across Suffolk.

Poulton & Wyre Railway, Northern England Region

Background

The railway from Poulton-le-Fylde to Fleetwood opened in 1840 and was one of the first railways in the world to regularly carry holidaymakers. It also served the busy port at Fleetwood; intermediate stations at Thornton-Cleveleys and Burn Naze were opened subsequently. In 1966 Fleetwood station closed and the line was cut back to a new terminus at Fleetwood Wyre Dock. Passenger services to Fleetwood ended in 1970 and the line was singled in 1973. Freight trains continued to use the route until 1999, when the final train to the chemical plant at Burn Naze ran. The track from Poulton-le-Fylde to Fleetwood remains in place; however, the main line connection at Poulton was severed in 2018 when the Preston to Blackpool North line was electrified and resignalled.

Heritage Railway Progress and Future Plans

The Poulton & Wyre Railway Society (PWRS) formed in 2006 and Network Rail provided the group with a license giving access to the track, Thornton-Cleveleys and Burn Naze stations. The Society then began clearing vegetation, restoring the railway and the two stations. In 2010 a Fowler shunter was acquired, followed by a Class 108 DMU in 2016, which is being renovated at Midland Railway-Butterley. This should be ready to be transferred to the railway by about spring 2019. It was hoped that the heritage railway could connect with the main line at Poulton-le-Fylde, but this became much less likely after Network Rail developed the line to Blackpool North and removed the junction at Poulton. The railway hopes to operate trains along a short section of track soon; the long-term plan is for regular trains to operate between Poulton and a newly constructed Fleetwood South station.

Contact Details

Website: www.pwrs.org
Tel: 01253 975757
Email: crawford-brian@sky.com
Address: Poulton & Wyre Railway Society, c/o The Print Room, Hillhouse Business Park, Thornton, Lancashire, FY5 4QD.

Opening Times & Transport Links

Volunteer working sessions take place 09.30–12.30 on most Saturdays and Wednesdays at Thornton or Burn Naze. Membership of the PWRS is required to take part in these.

By Rail: Poulton-le-Fylde station is approximately two miles from Thornton.
By Road: Free parking is available near to Thornton station. There is no parking at Burn Naze station.

Stock List

Type	Number	Builder	Details
Diesel	4210108	Fowler	0-4-0
DMU	51937 & 56484	British Railways	Class 108

Local Attractions
The Wyre Way is a walking route which runs from Fleetwood, where it crosses the railway, along the Wyre estuary and continues to the Forest of Bowland in north east Lancashire. Nearby attractions include Farmer Parr's Animal World and the coastal resorts of Fleetwood and Blackpool, which are home to many museums, theme parks and other attractions.

Rother Valley Railway, South East Region

Background
The railway between Robertsbridge on the Tonbridge–Hastings main line and Rolvenden opened in 1900. Details of the background and history of this route are given in the listing for the Kent & East Sussex Railway (K&ESR) on page 147.

Heritage Railway Progress and Future Plans
The Rother Valley Railway (RVR) formed in 1991, with the intention of acquiring the trackbed and reinstating the disused railway between Robertsbridge and Bodiam, which is the western terminus of the K&ESR. Sections of trackbed at each end of the two and a half mile Rother Valley route were acquired and, starting in 2009, the railway relaid approximately three quarters of a mile of track near Bodiam. The first heritage trains operated in 2011. A further half mile of track was subsequently relaid at Robertsbridge and trains first used this in 2013. The RVR is in the process of acquiring the remainder of the route, which has been met with some local opposition. In 2017 Rother District Council issued planning permission for the line to be reinstated and the railway is currently waiting for the Transport & Works Act Order to be approved, after which the remaining track can be relaid. Once the two sections have been joined, it is planned for the RVR to be absorbed into the K&ESR, which could then operate through trains from Tenterden to Robertsbridge.

Contact Details
Website: www.rvr.org.uk
Tel: 01580 881833
Email: reception@rvr.org.uk
Address: Rother Valley Railway, Robertsbridge Junction Station, Station Road, Robertsbridge, East Sussex, TN32 5DG.

Opening Times & Transport Links
There is a small shop and visitor centre at Robertsbridge, which is open 10.00–16.00 each Sunday. Gala events are occasionally held on the railway and details will be announced when they have been finalised.

By Rail: The railway has a main line connection at Robertsbridge.
By Road: There is a pay & display car park at Robertsbridge station.

Line Mileage and Journey Time
There is currently half a mile of track, which runs north-east from Robertsbridge station.

Stock List

Type	*Number*	*Builder*	*Details*
Steam	CHARWELTON (1955)	Manning Wardle	0-6-0ST
Diesel	D77	Vulcan Foundry	0-4-0
Diesel	Titan (D140)	Vulcan Foundry	0-4-0
Diesel	D2112	British Railways	Class 03

Local Attractions
As well as the visitor centre at Robertsbridge, there is also a small collection of railway vehicles. The Kent & East Sussex Railway is nearby and details of other attractions in the area are given in the K&ESR listing.

Tarka Valley Railway, South West Region

Background

The broad gauge railway from Barnstaple reached Bideford in 1855 and was extended to Torrington in 1872, where it was initially a terminus. The line was converted to standard gauge in 1877. In 1880 the three foot gauge Torrington & Marland Railway opened, travelling south from Torrington. This was converted to standard gauge in 1925 and extended south to Halwill, where it connected with the railway to Bude, creating a through route from Barnstaple to Bude. This closed to passenger traffic in 1965; however, milk traffic continued until 1978 and ball clay and charter trains ran from Barnstaple to Torrington until 1982. The track was lifted in 1985 and Devon County Council purchased the trackbed from British Rail in order to create a coastal walkway.

Heritage Railway Progress and Future Plans

The Tarka Valley Railway Group formed in 2008 to preserve the remaining traces of the railway at Torrington station and investigate the possibility of reinstating a railway line towards Bideford. A short length of track was laid alongside the platform of the former Torrington station in 2008 and in 2013 the group gained planning approval to extend this for about 300m to the first overbridge. Devon County Council granted a lease in 2018, enabling work to start on laying the first 300m of track and a further 100m for two sidings alongside the old coal loading bay.

During 2018 the Tarka Trail pathway was realigned slightly to create space for the railway to run alongside; a dividing fence was erected and the first 60 foot track panel was laid. When the 300m of track and sidings have been laid, brake van rides using the Ruston or Fowler shunters can begin. This could be as soon as 2020; however, progress is subject to levels of funding and the number of available volunteers.

There are plans to rebuild the signal box, platelayers' hut and trolley shed at the Torrington site. The long-term aim is for the railway to operate from Torrington to Bideford, between which are three small river bridges, a tunnel and a viaduct. Works will need to be completed at the sites of each of these to enable both the railway and the Tarka Trail to travel through each location together.

Contact Details

Website: www.tarkavalleyrailway.co.uk
Email: tarkavalleyrailway@gmail.com
Address: TVR Membership Secretary, Puffing Billy, Torrington Station, Station Hill, Great Torrington, Devon, EX38 8JD.

Opening Times & Transport Links

The site and sales & information centre in the carriage are open every Thursday (whatever the weather!) except at Christmas. There will be an open weekend on 13–14 July and details of this will be announced on the TVR website.

By Rail: The nearest railway station is Barnstaple, which is 11 miles away.
By Road: Car parking is available at the Torrington site (EX38 8JD).
By Bike: By way of the traffic-free Tarka Trail.

Stock List

Type	*Number*	*Builder*	*Details*
Diesel	PROGRESS	Fowler	0-4-0
Diesel	TORRINGTON CAVALIER	Ruston & Hornsby	0-4-0

Local Attractions

The Puffing Billy is a public house within the former Torrington station building, located directly on the Tarka Trail and is open 09.00–17.00 every day of the week. Bicycle hire is available at the station site, which the traffic-free Tarka Trail runs directly through. Bideford Railway Heritage Centre (see pag 158) is five miles to the north and can be reached by road, on foot or by cycling along the trail.

Vale of Berkeley Railway, South West Region

Background

The four mile branch line from Berkeley Road (between Bristol and Cheltenham) to Sharpness opened to freight in 1875 and to passengers in 1876. In 1879 it became a through route when the Severn Railway Bridge opened, connecting Sharpness to Lydney Town, which is now part of the Dean Forest Railway (see page 165). The bridge was damaged beyond repair in 1960 and Sharpness was relegated back to terminus status until passenger services ended in 1964. Shortly after this Sharpness and Berkeley station buildings were demolished. Network Rail own the line from Berkeley Junction to Sharpness Docks and freight trains operated by Direct Rail Services use it infrequently to reach the sidings on the site of the former Berkeley station. This is half way along the branch and is where spent nuclear fuel from the decommissioned Berkeley and Oldbury power stations is loaded onto trains. As there is no run-round facility at the sidings, trains have to proceed further along the branch to Oldminster Sidings on the outskirts of Sharpness Docks in order for the locomotives to run round. Consequently, almost the full length of the line remains in commercial use.

Heritage Railway Progress and Future Plans

The preservation group formed in 2013 and since 2015 it has leased the old engine shed at Sharpness Docks as a base. This is being used to restore various locomotives and other rolling stock. Discussions are in progress with the various stakeholders regarding the creation of a run-round loop at the Berkeley loading site, which would alleviate the need for nuclear fuel trains to travel to the run-round loop at Oldminster Sidings, Sharpness. The western half of the branch would then be freed up for heritage use and stations could then be built at the Berkeley and Oldminster sites. After receiving a license from Network Rail, the group cleared the vegetation at Oldminster in 2018, in preparation for it to be used as an operational base. Negotiations with Network Rail for the terms of leasing the branch line are continuing and it is hoped that heritage trains can start operating in 2020 or 2021. A second phase of works would involve rebuilding Sharpness station, where the original platform remains. The long-term aim is for a heritage railway to operate from Sharpness to Berkeley Junction, where it would connect to the main line but this may only be possible after spent nuclear fuel trains cease to use the branch line.

Contact Details

Website: www.valeofberkeleyrailway.co.uk
Email: valeofberkeleyrailway@gmail.com
Address: Vale of Berkeley Railway, The Old Engine House, The Docks, Sharpness, Gloucestershire, GL13 9UD.

Opening Times & Transport Links

The Engine Shed is open 10.00–16.00 on Tuesdays, Wednesdays, Fridays and Saturdays. During these times visitors are welcome to look around the shed and meet volunteers who are working.

By Rail: The nearest railway station is Cam and Dursley which is nine miles away.
By Road: Parking is available at The Old Engine House site (GL13 9UD).

Stock List

Type	*Number*	*Builder*	*Details*
Steam	4027	LMS	0-6-0
Steam	15	Andrew Barclay	0-6-0ST
Steam	44901	LMS	4-6-0
Diesel	British Gypsum No. 2	Thomas Hill	0-4-0
Diesel	7069	LMS	0-6-0
Diesel	D2069	British Railways	Class 03
Diesel	D9553	British Railways	Class 14

Local Attractions

There are a number of locomotives, items of rolling stock, signalling and railway equipment to be seen at the Old Engine House site in Sharpness. Attractions in the area include Wildfowl & Wetlands Trust Slimbridge Wetland Centre, Cattle Country Adventure Park, Dr Jenner's House and Berkeley Castle.

▲ **West Somerset Railway:** At first glance, only the single track gives a clue that this photo is not a GWR express train of yesteryear! 6959 Class 4-6-0 No. 6960 "Raveningham Hall" approaches Blue Anchor on the West Somerset Railway on 23 September 2017. **Tony Christie**

▼ **West Somerset Railway:** BRCW Class 33 No. D6566 is seen near Williton, home of the Diesel & Electric Preservation Group's depot, on 10 June 2018. **Tony Christie**

Appendix I: Locomotive and Multiple Unit Builders

Builder name used in listings	Builder's Full Name
82045 Steam Locomotive Trust	82045 Steam Locomotive Trust
AC Cars	AC Cars Ltd
AEG, Berlin	Allgemeine Elektricitäts-Gesellschaft, Berlin
Alan Keef	Alan Keef Ltd
American Locomotive Co.	American Locomotive Company
Andrew Barclay	Andrew Barclay Sons & Co.
Armstrong Whitworth	Armstrong Whitworth & Co
Aveling & Porter	Aveling & Porter
Avonside	Avonside Engine Company
B17 SLT	B17 Steam Locomotive Trust
Baby Deltic Project	Baby Deltic Project
Bagnall	W. G. Bagnall
Baguley	E. E. Baguley Ltd
Baldwin Locomotive Works	Baldwin Locomotive Works, USA
Beyer Peacock	Beyer, Peacock & Company
Black Hawthorn	Black, Hawthorn & Co.
Bluebell Railway SC2P	Bluebell Railway Standard Class 2 Project
Borrows	E Borrows & Sons
BRCW	Birmingham Railway Carriage & Wagon Co.
BREL	British Rail Engineering Limited
British Railways	British Railways
British Thomson Houston	British Thomson Houston
Brown Boveri	Brown, Boveri & Cie, Switzerland
Brush Traction	Brush Traction
Bury Curtis & Kennedy	Bury, Curtis & Kennedy
Caledonian Railway	Caledonian Railway
Clayton	Clayton Equipment Company
Cockerill	John Cockerill Company
Consett	Consett Iron Company
Cravens	Cravens
Danske Statsbaner	Danske Statsbaner, Denmark
DB, Germany	Deutsche Bahn, Germany
Dodman & Co	Dodman & Co.
Drewry	Drewry Car Co.
Dübs & Company	Dübs & Company
English Electric	English Electric
Fablok	Fablok, Poland
Fairfield Shipbuilding & Engine Co.	Fairfield Shipbuilding & Engine Co.
Fire Fly Trust	The Fire Fly Trust
Fletcher Jennings	Fletcher, Jennings & Co.
Foster Rastrick	Foster Rastrick & Co
Fowler	John Folwer & Co.
Fox Walker	Fox, Walker & Company
Friends of MOSI	Friends of the Museum of Science and Industry
GEC Traction Ltd	GEC Traction Ltd
George England	George England & Co.
George Stephenson	George Stephenson
GER	Great Eastern Railway
GNR	Great Northern Railway
Grant Richie	Grant Richie & Company
GRCW	Gloucester Railway Carriage & Wagon Co. Ltd
Great Central Railway	Great Central Railway
Great Western Society	The Great Western Society
Greenwood & Batley	Greenwood & Batley Ltd
GWR	Great Western Railway
Hagglund and Soner	Hagglund and Soner, Sweden
Hartmann	Richard Hartmann, Germany
Hawthorn Leslie	Hawthorn Leslie & Company
Haydock	Haydock Foundry
Head Wrightson	Head Wrightson

Hibberd	F. C. Hibberd & Co.
Howard	J & F Howard
Hudswell Clarke	Hudswell Clarke
Hunslet	Hunslet Engine Company
Kerr Stuart	Kerr, Stuart and Company
Kitson	Kitson and Company
Lancashire & Yorkshire	Lancashire and Yorkshire Railway
LBSCR	London, Brighton and South Coast Railway
Lima Locomotive Co	Lima Locomotive Corporation
Lister Blackstone	Lister Blackstone
LMS	London, Midland and Scottish Railway
LMS-Patriot Project	LMS-Patriot Project
LNER	London and North Eastern Railway
LNWR	London and North Western Railway
Locomotion Enterprises	Locomotion Enterprises
LSWR	London and South Western Railway
LT&SR	London, Tilbury and Southend Railway
Manning Wardle	Manning Wardle
Markham & Co	Markham & Co Ltd
Metropolitan Cammell	Metropolitan Cammell
Metropolitan Vickers	Metropolitan Vickers
Midland Railway	Midland Railway
Ministry of Defence	Ministry of Defence
Motala Verkstad	Motala Verkstad, Sweden
Nasmyth Wilson	Nasmyth, Wilson & Co.
Neilson & Co.	Neilson & Co.
Neilson Reid	Neilson, Reid & Co.
NER	North Eastern Railway
North British	North British Locomotive Company
North London Railway	North London Railway
North Staffordshire Railway	North Staffordshire Railway
Norwegian State Railways	Norwegian State Railways (NSB)
Park Royal	Park Royal Vehicles Limited
Peckett	Peckett and Sons
Pressed Steel	Pressed Steel Company
R & W Hawthorn	R & W Hawthorn
Resco Railways	Resco (Railways) Ltd
Robert Heath	Robert Heath and Sons Ltd
Robert Stephenson & Co	Robert Stephenson & Company
Robert Stephenson & Hawthorns	Robert Stephenson & Hawthorns
Rolls Royce Sentinel	Rolls Royce Sentinel
Ruston & Hornsby	Ruston & Hornsby
Sara & Co	Sara & Co
SECR	South Eastern and Chatham Railway
Sentinel	Sentinel Waggon Works
Sharp Stewart	Sharp Stewart and Company
Siemans Harton	Siemans Harton
Simplex	Simplex (Motor Rail)
South Durham Steel & Iron	South Durham Steel & Iron Co
Southern Railway	Southern Railway
Stephen Lewin	Stephen Lewin
Thomas Hill	Thomas Hill (Rotherham) Ltd
Timothy Hackworth	Timothy Hackworth
Trevithick 200	Trevithick 200
Vulcan Foundry	Vulcan Foundry
Vulcan Iron Works	Vulcan Iron Works, USA
Waggon und Maschinenbau	Waggon & Maschinenbau, Germany
Wickham	D. Wickham and Company
Yorkshire Engine Co.	Yorkshire Engine Company

Appendix II: Abbreviations

Steam Locomotives Suffixes

T	Side Tank.
CT	Crane Tank.
PT	Pannier Tank.
ST	Saddle Tank.
WT	Well Tank.
VBT	Vertical Boiler Tank.
VBGT	Vertical Boiler Geared Tank.
F	Fireless.

Other Abbreviations Used

DMU	Diesel Multiple Unit.
EMU	Electric Multiple Unit.
DEMU	Diesel-Electric Multiple Unit.
BR	British Railways; later British Rail.

Appendix III: Index of Heritage Railways